STUDENT ENGAGEMENT AND QUALITY ASSURANCE IN HIGHER EDUCATION

Using a range of international examples to compare the reality, purpose and effect of student engagement in universities across the globe, *Student Engagement and Quality Assurance in Higher Education* argues that teachers and students need to collaborate to improve the quality of university education and student learning.

The growing trend of assessing and assuring quality in Higher Education is incredibly complex, as there are so many variables affecting both experiences and measures. With case studies from ten countries, covering a variety of cultural and environmental settings, this book focusses on ways of working with students to produce applicable, implementable strategies for universities the world over. Internationally applicable, this book presents ideas from a range of cultures, that can be adapted to be implemented in a variety of cultures. The reader is provided with a range of approaches where both the advantages and disadvantages are clearly presented. The ten case studies consider the macro, meso and micro levels of each approach, allowing for an exploration of the growing area of research and practice that is student–staff partnerships, showcasing ways of working with students to enhance engagement and quality, that are vital for a long-term approach.

Focussing on one of the main reform topics for universities, *Student Engagement and Quality Assurance in Higher Education* is essential reading for educational researchers, institutional leaders and all concerned with the implementation and progression of student engagement and quality assurance in higher education.

Masahiro Tanaka is an Associate Professor at the Research Centre for University Studies, the University of Tsukuba, Japan.

STUDENT ENGAGEMENT AND QUALITY ASSURANCE IN HIGHER EDUCATION

International Collaborations for the Enhancement of Learning

Edited by Masahiro Tanaka

Routledge
Taylor & Francis Group

LONDON AND NEW YORK

First published 2019
by Routledge
2 Park Square, Milton Park, Abingdon, Oxon OX14 4RN

and by Routledge
52 Vanderbilt Avenue, New York, NY 10017

Routledge is an imprint of the Taylor & Francis Group, an informa business

British Library Cataloguing in Publication Data
A catalogue record for this book is available from the British Library

Library of Congress Cataloging-in-Publication Data
Names: Tanaka, Masahiro, editor.
Title: Student engagement and quality assurance in higher education : international collaborations for the enhancement of learning / editor, Masahiro Tanaka.
Description: Abingdon, Oxon : New York, NY : Routledge, 2019. | Series: Higher education | Includes bibliographical references.
Identifiers: LCCN 2018043102| ISBN 9780367132828 (hbk) | ISBN 9780367132835 (pbk) | ISBN 9780429025648 (ebk)
Subjects: LCSH: Education, Higher--Evaluation--Case studies. | Education, Higher--Aims and objectives--Case studies. | Student participation in administration--Case studies.
Classification: LCC LB2331.62 .S78 2019 | DDC 378--dc23
LC record available at https://lccn.loc.gov/2018043102

ISBN: 978-0-367-13282-8 (hbk)
ISBN: 978-0-367-13283-5 (pbk)
ISBN: 978-0-429-02564-8 (ebk)

Typeset in Bembo
by Taylor & Francis Books

CONTENTS

List of illustrations   vii
List of contributors   ix
Acknowledgements   xiv
Foreword by Alison Cook-Sather   xv

1 The international diversity of student engagement   1
   Masahiro Tanaka

2 Students as partners in Swedish higher education: A driver for
   quality   9
   Åsa Kettis

3 Student engagement in Finnish higher education: Conflicting
   realities?   24
   Jani Ursin

4 Student engagement in quality in UK higher education: More
   than assurance?   35
   Stuart Brand and Luke Millard

5 Student engagement in the United States: From customers to
   partners?   46
   Peter Felten

6 Old technologies, new opportunities: Rethinking traditional
   approaches to student engagement in Australia   57
   Ryan Naylor

7 Student engagement in Brazilian higher education and its
sociopolitical dimension 73
Bernardo Sfredo Miorando

8 The relevance of student engagement in African higher
education: The Mozambican case 90
Nelson Casimiro Zavale and Patrício V. Langa

9 Student engagement in quality assurance of higher education in
Kazakhstan: Ambiguous forms and invisible procedures 109
Kuanysh Tastanbekova

10 Student engagement in Chinese higher education institutions
for the improvement of educational quality 124
Tong Yang

11 Student engagement for the improvement of teaching: The
peculiar form of student faculty development in Japan 136
Masahiro Tanaka

12 Transformation toward pro-learning outcomes in Japanese
higher education institutions: The role and challenges of
assessment for student engagement 149
Reiko Yamada

13 The future of student engagement 162
*Masahiro Tanaka, Ryan Naylor, Jani Ursin and
Nelson Casimiro Zavale*

Index 170

ILLUSTRATIONS

Figures

1.1	Views of students and positioning of responsibility for student engagement	3
3.1	ePortfolio process of the University of Jyväskylä	29
3.2	The elements of student engagement	31
6.1	Factors contributing to success for two individuals	67
9.1	Expenditure on education in Kazakhstan (1991–2016)	111
9.2	Number of higher education institutions and students enrolled (1991–2017)	112
10.1	Distribution of different types of students in HEIs	130
11.1	The implementation of student mutual support system such as peer support (by university type)	139
11.2	Areas of support in universities	140
12.1	The relationship of precollege, college environment, and learning outcome	155
12.2	Integration model of direct and indirect assessments	157
13.1	Views of students and positioning of responsibility for student engagement	163

Tables

5.1 High-impact educational practices   48
6.1 Importance of different factors to having a successful
     university experience   66
7.1 Undergraduate students' study hours per week   79
7.2 Micro level student engagement according to Enade   80

Box

2.1 Uppsala University in brief   14

CONTRIBUTORS

Stuart Brand is Emeritus Professor and Consultant at Birmingham City University. He was the University's Director of Learning and Teaching (2007–11) then Director of Learning Experience (2011–16). Partnership with Birmingham City Students' Union has been central in this work and was recognised with a Times Higher Education Award in 2010. He was awarded a National Teaching Fellowship in 2012. He led the development of a Student Academic Partners scheme through which students are employed to work in partnership with staff on enhancement projects. He is currently leading a project across four UK universities on measurement of Learning Gain. His publications include: 'Students as partners: a three-layered approach for enhancement', in *The Student Engagement Handbook: Practice in Higher Education* (Emerald, 2013).

Peter Felten is professor of history, assistant provost for teaching and learning, and executive director of the Center for Engaged Learning at Elon University in the United States. His books include the co-authored volumes: *The Undergraduate Experience: Focusing Institutions on What Matters Most* (Jossey-Bass, 2016); *Transforming Students: Fulfilling the Promise of Higher Education* (Johns Hopkins University Press, 2014); and, *Engaging Students as Partners in Learning and Teaching* (Jossey-Bass, 2014). He has served as president of the International Society for the Scholarship of Teaching and Learning (2016–17) and also of the POD Network (2010–2011), the U.S. professional society for educational developers. He is co-editor of the International Journal for Academic Development and a fellow of the John N. Gardner Institute for Excellence in Undergraduate Education.

Åsa Kettis is director of the division for Quality Enhancement at Uppsala University, Sweden. She is also an associate professor in Social Pharmacy, and has experience from being a senior lecturer, director of studies and research leader. She works with policy issues with regard to QA and QE at Uppsala University, and at the national level. She has served as a member of the Swedish Association of Higher Education's Experts Committee on Quality, and is a member of the Swedish Higher Education Authority's Advisory Board on the national system for QA of higher education. She has been appointed as reviewer in agency-led institutional reviews in Denmark and Norway, and is an international reviewer for the Enhancement-led Institutional Review (ELIR), which is run by the Quality Assurance Agency for Higher Education (QAA), Scotland.

Patrício V. Langa is a Sociologist and Associate Professor of Higher Education at the Faculty of Education of Eduardo Mondlane University (Maputo, Mozambique) and at the Institute for Post-School Studies at the University of the Western Cape (Cape Town, South Africa). Prof Langa advises the Rector of UEM on strategic planning and is a visiting professor in various universities and research centers in the US and Europe. He served as the first Executive Director for External Evaluation in the National Council on Higher Education Quality Assurance and Accreditation in Mozambique (CNAQ) and currently serves on the board of Non-Executive Directors. Prof Langa founded and served as Director of the Centre for Higher Education Studies and Development (CESD), in Mozambique. He is also the founding member and current president of the Mozambican Sociological Association (AMS). Prof Langa's research interest is located at the intersection of sociology and higher education studies in Africa. He has published in both sociology and higher education journals.

Luke Millard is Director of the Education Development Service at Birmingham City University which supports academic staff practice, student academic development and employability. He is a Principal Fellow of the HEA and has research interest in student transitions and the first year experience and student employability. One of his most recent publications was 'Addressing potential challenges in co-creating learning and teaching: overcoming resistance, navigating institutional norms and ensuring inclusivity in student–staff partnerships – Bovill, Felten, Cook Sather and Millard – *Studies in Higher Education* (37) 2015.

Bernardo Sfredo Miorando is a doctoral candidate in Education sponsored by a Capes grant at Universidade Federal do Grande do Sul (UFRGS), Brazil. As a member of Research Group Innovation and Evaluation in University, he focuses on internationalization of postgraduate education. He was a visiting researcher at the Finnish Institute for Educational Research at the University of Jyväskylä, with a scholarship by the Finnish National Agency of Education. He currently serves a postgraduate student representative in UFRGS's Institutional Evaluation Commission. His recent publications include Leite, D. B. C. & Sfredo Miorando, B. (2015) "The Bologna Process from a Brazilian perspective: Reports from the Other side of the Atlantic", *Journal of the European Higher Education Area*, issue 1.

Ryan Naylor is a nationally recognised scholar in the fields of student equity and the student experience, and has also collaborated widely across many areas in higher education research. He is currently leading research projects examining structural inequality in the Australian higher education sector, student mental health and wellbeing, and the similarities and differences between university students and staff in their expectations of the student role. Ryan's research has informed policy and practice at a national level, particularly through his work on national frameworks for equity initiatives, evaluation, and refugee participation, and several projects funded by the Office of Learning and Teaching. Ryan is currently Core First Year Coordinator (Health Sciences) at La Trobe University.

Masahiro Tanaka is currently an associate professor of the Research Centre for University Studies, the University of Tsukuba in Japan. He holds a PhD degree in Education from the Institute of Education, the University of London in the UK. His doctoral thesis is now available as a book entitled *The Cross-Cultural Transfer of Educational Concepts and Practices: A Comparative Study* (Oxford, Symposium Books). One of his recent referred papers written in English is 'The Mobility of Universities', *Comparative Education*, Vol.45, No.3, pp.405–418.

Kuanysh Tastanbekova is an assistant professor at the Faculty of Human Sciences of the University of Tsukuba in Japan. She holds a PhD in Education from the same university. Her research interests include language education policy, policy borrowing and lending process, legacies of Soviet education, teacher training system reformation, gender equality, citizenship education and development of education for sustainable development in Russia and Central Asia. Her recent publication is "Post-Soviet Legacies in Girls' Education in Kazakhstan and Uzbekistan" in the Routledge Global Gender Series edited by Yulia Gradskova and Ildiko Asztalos Morell "Gendering Postsocialism: Old Legacies and New Hierarchies" (2018, pp.172–192).

Jani Ursin is senior researcher at the Finnish Institute for Educational Research of the University of Jyväskylä, Finland. His research has focussed on quality assurance in higher education, mergers of Finnish universities, implementation of the Bologna Process, academic work as well as learning outcomes in higher education. He is the former president of the Consortium of Higher Education Researchers in Finland (CHERIF). Ursin is national editor of Scandinavian Journal of Educational Research and editorial board member of several scientific journals. His latest publications include 'Finnish adult students' perspectives on short-cycle study programmes: Motives and evaluations', *Higher Education Research & Development* (together with Helena Aittola) and 'How to measure students' innovation competences in higher education: Evaluation of an assessment tool in authentic learning environments', *Studies in Educational Evaluation* (together with Meiju Keinänen and Kari Nissinen).

Reiko Yamada is Dean and Professor of the Faculty of Social Studies and Director of the Center for Higher Education and Student Research at Doshisha University, Kyoto, Japan. She was the inaugural President of the Japanese Association of the First-year Experience. She received a PhD from UCLA. She will co-edit the new book *New Directions of Stem Research and Learning in the World Ranking Movement: A Comparative Perspective* (Eds. By J. N. Hawkins, A. Yamada., R. Yamada., J.W. Jacob) (Palgrave Macmillan, 2018). Her recent publications include *Measuring Quality of Undergraduate Education in Japan* (Springer, 2014), "Comparison of Student Experiences in the Era of Massification: Analysis of Student Data from Japan, Korea and the USA" in *Managing International Connectivity, Diversity of Learning and Changing Labour Markets: East Asian Perspectives* (Springer, 2016, pp.169–187), "Comparative Study of Student Learning and Experiences of Japanese and South Korean Students" in *Assessment of Learning Outcomes in Higher Education: Cross-National Comparisons and Perspectives* (Springer, 2018, pp.285–308).

Tong Yang is currently a lecturer at School of Languages, Southeast University in China. She graduated from Shanghai International Studies University in China with a BA in literature, and completed her MA and PhD in Education at the University of Tokyo in Japan. Her research has focused on higher education practices and policies especially in Japan and China. Her research interests include education quality, learning outcomes, general education, liberal education, higher education curriculum, as well as comparative education on these issues among East Asian countries. Her most recent publication written in English is: 'A Comparison of General Education Policies or Institutions of Higher Education in Japan and China since the 1990s', *The International Journal of Comparative Education and Development*, 17(2), 36–53 (The Comparative Education Society of Hong Kong, 2015).

Nelson Casimiro Zavale is Associate Professor of Sociology of Education and Higher Education Studies and Director of the Quality Assurance Office at Eduardo Mondlane University (UEM), Mozambique. He is (2018–2021) Humboldt Research Fellow at the International Centre for Higher Education Research (INCHER), University of Kassel, in Germany, and he was a Swiss government excellence post-doctoral fellow at University of Basel in Switzerland. Some of his recent publications include: "University-industry linkages in Sub-Saharan Africa: systematic literature review and bibliometric account", *Scientometrics* (Springer, 2018); "Branding and the Search for Competitive advantage in the Field of Mozambican Higher Education through the use of Websites" (Palgrave MacMillan, Springer, 2018); "Expansion versus contribution of higher education in Africa: university-industry linkages in Mozambique from firms' perspective", *Science and Public Policy* (Oxford University Press, 2017); "Decision-making in African Universities demands rigorous data: evidence from graduation rates at UEM in Mozambique" (2017) *International Journal of Educational Development* (Elsevier); "How and what knowledge do universities and academics transfer to industry in

African low-income countries? Evidence from the stage of university-industry linkages in Mozambique" (2016) *International Journal of Educational Development* (Elsevier); Main features and challenges of implementing an Internal Quality Assurance in African higher education institution: the case of UEM, in Mozambique", *International Journal of African Higher Education* (Boston College–CIHE, 2015).

ACKNOWLEDGEMENTS

As an editor of this book, I wish to express my deep gratitude to the authors of the book for their unfailing support during the completion of this comparative study. I would also like to thank Ms Sarah Tuckwell, an editor at Routledge, for her professional advice. This study was financially supported by the JSPS Grants-in-Aid for Scientific Research, Grant Number 26285171.

FOREWORD

Alison Cook-Sather

BRYN MAWR COLLEGE

As many scholars have argued, and as the authors of the chapters in this volume further illuminate, student engagement is a complex phenomenon. It encompasses student involvement, excitement, and persistence (Ahlfeldt et al. 2005); layered and meaningful participation in, and commitment to, learning (Kuh & Ewell 2010); and emotional as well as intellectual investment (Bovill et al. 2016). Rooted in concerns about the time and effort students invest in learning (Astin 1984), student engagement has evolved to focus on what inspires students to seek and stick with educationally purposeful activities that, in turn, lead to their more general persistence and thriving in higher education (Wolf-Wendel et al. 2009). Because of the deepening recognition of the importance of student engagement, it is more and more frequently evoked to drive decisions in policy and practice in higher education and to frame possible new visions for education (Matthews et al. 2018).

If we understand student engagement as what can result at the intersection of what students do and what institutions do (Felten, Chapter 5, this volume; Kuh, 2001; Tanaka, Chapter 11, this volume), then any exploration of student engagement needs to consider that intersection at multiple levels. Citing Kahu (2013), Ursin (Chapter 3, this volume) reminds us that it is essential to keep in mind as well "the critical influence of the socio-cultural context; that is, successful student engagement is a combination of the student, the teacher, the institution and the government." The authors featured in this volume throw into relief how different that combination, or intersection, can be in different international contexts and what it might take to foster a "culture of engagement" (Williams et al. 2013, p. 54). Poole and Simmons (2013) suggest that culture changes are most likely to happen when efforts are undertaken simultaneously at the microsocial level (individual instructors), the mesosocial level (instructors working collaboratively), and macrosocial level (senior administrators governing the entire institution) (cited in Williams et al. 2013, p. 54).

The chapters in this volume analyze student engagement in the improvement of educational quality at the micro, meso, and macro levels as Tanaka (Chapter 11, this volume) defines those: Micro: student engagement in their own learning and that of other students; Meso: engagement in quality assurance and enhancement processes; and Macro: engagement in strategy development. In relation to each of the three levels, and cutting across all of them, students, faculty, researchers, and institutions must attend to the ways that students experience engagement (inward-facing attention) and contribute to engagement (outward-facing attention), both of which affect the quality of the education. This "meta-intersection," for lack of a better term, of levels of social and institutional interaction and direction of attention yields new insights into what we mean by engagement in the improvement of educational quality and how we might foster it. It is essential to keep in mind, though, as Miorando (Chapter 7, this volume) reminds us, that concepts, such as student engagement, "are not equally available across national contexts." Each chapter in this volume offers us insight from one perspective on a national context but does not claim to represent fully every institution with that context.

The multilayered analysis (micro, meso, and macro level) offered in each chapter throws into relief the perspective achievable from each ring of the concentric circles of policy and practice that constitute institutions of higher education. And, as the authors point out, there can be contrasts and even conflicts between and among those levels and perspectives. Writing about the Finnish context, Ursin (Chapter 3, this volume) suggests:

> It seems that the reality of student engagement is very different from the government's point of view and the students' point of view. These two realities often collide in the everyday practices of higher education institutions, which have to deal with the pressure coming from the government and wishes stemming from the students.

Likewise, Tanaka (Chapter 11, this volume) describes the difference between a student perspective on the organization of the curriculum in a Japanese university (disorganized) and the perspective of an accrediting body ("high evaluation of the curriculum being systematically organized"). Perspectives based in different levels need not lead to collisions of realities, conflicts of perspective, or either/or prioritizing, however. Writing in Australia, Naylor (Chapter 6, this volume) suggests that,

> As well as being valuable to universities, student representation and other forms of organised citizenship and participation could be valuable to students as learning experiences. That is, participation can serve universities at the meso and macro level, while students benefit from the same process at the micro level.

These "both/and" possibilities are among the most compelling in this collection of chapters.

At the same time, these chapters do not shy away from naming the challenges of student engagement in the improvement of educational quality or the ways in which such engagement may happen at some levels but not others. These challenges may be linked to the difficulty of balancing expansion of higher education with attention to student experience (Zavale & Langa, Chapter 8, this volume), to the lack of concepts, structures, and beliefs about the potential of student engagement (Yang, Chapter 10, this volume), or to "tectonic transformations after a systemic collapse" (Tastanbekova, Chapter 9, this volume). For example, Zavale and Langa (Chapter 8, this volume) offer a case study of Mozambican higher education as it illuminates what they argue should be Africa's focus on not only expanding access to higher education but also expanding effective access to learning and knowledge. Yang (Chapter 10, this volume) suggests that lack of democratic management concepts as well as trust and attention to students among institutional leaders; lack of guarantee and incentive system within universities for student engagement; lack of clear rules and regulations on the issues in which students have the right to be involved and should be involved; and students' sense that they lack relevant knowledge, capacity, and confidence make student engagement in the improvement of educational quality challenging in China. Finally, Tastanbekova (Chapter 9, this volume) indicates that selected students in higher education in Kazakhstan participate in the process of university accreditation (at the macro level) and complete questionnaires related to a particular teacher and subject's quality as part of a university's internal quality monitoring and assessment processes (meso level), but that there is little evidence of student engagement at the micro level, and that all of these situations are reflective of an ongoing reformation process.

While the analysis at the micro, meso, and macro levels offered in these chapters is explicit, less explicit is the way the inward- and outward-facing attention students do or can experience through engagement intersects with these levels. I highlight just a few examples from the chapters to make this aspect of the discussions more explicit. Two approaches developed by the University of Jyväskylä in Finland, ePortfolios and Goodies well-being advisors, explained by Ursin (Chapter 3, this volume), are two examples of approaches that promote both inward-facing attention (reflection, meta-cognitive analysis) and outward-facing attention (seeking connections with others, striving to care for oneself through relationship) as ways of promoting engagement. The five things Felten (Chapter 5, this volume) suggests that students in the United States need to *do* to be engaged—spend time focused on educationally purposeful activities; put forth considerable effort in these activities; receive and respond constructively to feedback; practice applying and using what they are learning in different contexts; and reflect on both what and how they have learned—and the three things they need to *think*— "I belong here"; "I can learn this"; and "I find this meaningful"—highlight the interaction of inward- and outward-facing attention. Acknowledgement of this two-way dynamic is important because it suggests a different way of thinking about what students do and what institutions do—not only a "both/and" set of possibilities but also a set of approaches that allow greater collaboration across the levels and in the assessment of the extent to which the approach fosters engagement in the improvement of educational quality.

Pedagogical partnership in relation to student engagement takes this different way of thinking to its logical conclusion. Naylor (Chapter 6, this volume) argues that "universities must do more to interact with students on an individual level and allow them to shape their own curricular and co-curricular experiences as co-creators rather than subjects (or even objects) of university activities." Similarly, Brand and Millard (Chapter 4, this volume) write:

> it can be argued that those interested in a constructive role, that goes further than merely a customer survey approach, have had to recast the position of students into partners and co-creators to engage them effectively in quality assurance and enhancement processes.

Kettis (Chapter 2, this volume) asserts: "For the partnership idea to become an integral part of the culture, it has to be supported by the academic leadership at all levels, including collegial bodies, heads of departments, deans and the university management." Writing in the context of Brazil, Miorando (Chapter 7, this volume) argues for the efficacy of a movement "from activism to partnership to effect change." Finally, Felten (Chapter 5, this volume) argues that:

> partnership offers the possibility of re-orienting engagement towards preparing students – and their faculty and staff partners – to not only develop 'a craft or skill or a way of being in the world that frees us to act with greater knowledge or power. But [also to] remind us of obligations we have to use our knowledge and power responsibly ... exercising our freedom in such a way as to make a difference in the world for more than just ourselves' (Cronon, 1998, p. 79).

These assertions are in keeping with the argument Matthews (2016) has made for redefining engagement as partnership.

The chapters in this volume offer insight into how student engagement in the improvement of educational quality can be promoted at the micro, meso, and macro levels in diverse locales: Australia, Brazil, China, Finland, Japan, Kazakhstan, Mozambique, Sweden, the United Kingdom, and United States. I recommend reading the chapters with an eye not only to the different perspectives—to what is perceivable—within and from each of the micro, meso, and macro levels but also to the ways in which engagement invites inward- and outward-facing attention. The challenge of conceptualizing, inspiring, and supporting student engagement in the improvement of educational quality can be understood as part of a culture change, described by a growing number as a movement toward a culture of collaboration and partnership among all stakeholders. The multilevel, multidirectional, cross-context analysis of engagement that this collection offers has the potential to expand both what we perceive and what we do to maximize student engagement in the improvement of educational quality—for the students themselves, for those they work with, for the institutions in which they work, and for the contexts in which all this work unfolds. In so doing, it actually redefines what "the improvement of educational quality" might mean.

References

Ahlfeldt, S., Mehta, S., & Sellnow, T. (2005). Measurement and analysis of student engagement in university classes where varying levels of PBL methods of instruction are in use. *Higher Education Research & Development* 24(1), 5–20. doi:10.1080/0729436052000318541

Astin, A. W. (1984). Student involvement: a developmental theory for higher education. *Journal of College Student Personnel* 25(4), 297–308. Retrieved 6 August 2018 from www.middlesex.mass.edu/ace/downloads/astininv.pdf

Bovill, C., Cook-Sather, A., Felten, P., Millard, L., & Moore-Cherry, N. (2016). Addressing potential challenges in co-creating learning and teaching: overcoming resistance, navigating institutional norms and ensuring inclusivity in student–staff partnerships. *Higher Education* 71(2), 195–208. doi:10.1007/s10734-015-9896-4

Cronon, W. (1998). Only connect…: the goals of a liberal education. *American Scholar*, 67 (4), 73–80.

Kahu, E. R. (2013). Framing student engagement in higher education . *Studies in Higher Education* 38(5), 758–773.

Kuh, G. D. (2001). Assessing what really matters to student learning. *Change* 33(3), 10–17.

Kuh, G. D., & Ewell, P. T. (2010). The state of learning outcomes assessment in the United States. *Higher Education Management and Policy* 22(1), 1–20. doi:10.1787/hemp-22-5ks5dlhqbfr1

Matthews, K. E. (2016). Students as partners as the future of student engagement. *Student Engagement in Higher Education Journal* 1(1), 1–5. Retrieved 6 August 2018 from https://journals.gre.ac.uk/index.php/raise/article/view/380

Matthews, K. E., Cook-Sather, A., Acai, A., Dvorakova, S. L., Felten, P., Marquis, E., & Mercer-Mapstone, L. (2018). Toward theories of partnership praxis: an analysis of interpretive framing in literature on students as partners in university teaching and learning. *Higher Education Research & Development*. doi:10.1080/07294360.2018.1530199

Poole, G., & Simmons, N. (2013). Contributions of the scholarship of teaching and learning to quality enhancement in Canada. In R. Land & G. Gordon (Eds.) *Enhancing Quality in Higher Education: International Perspectives*. London: Routledge.

Williams, A. L.Verwoord, R., Beery, T. A., Dalton, H., McKinnon, J., Strickland, K., Pace, J., & Poole, G., (2013). The power of social networks: a model for weaving the scholarship of teaching and learning into institutional culture. *Teaching and Learning Inquiry: The International Society for the Scholarship of Teaching and Learning Journal* 1(2): 49–62.

Wolf-Wendel, L., Ward, K., & Kinzie, J. (2009). A tangled web of terms: the overlap and unique contribution of involvement, engagement, and integration to understanding college student success. *Journal of College Student Development* 50(4), 407–428. doi:10.1353/csd.0.0077

1

THE INTERNATIONAL DIVERSITY OF STUDENT ENGAGEMENT

Masahiro Tanaka

UNIVERSITY OF TSUKUBA

Introduction

The term 'student engagement' has become commonplace in global writings on higher education (Millard et al., 2013). However, the meanings of this term are actually quite diverse. One of the reasons for this diversity is that the specific who, what, where, when, how (to implement), and why (in pursuit of what objectives) of student engagement differ significantly across countries. In Sweden and Finland, for example, importance is placed on the work of student representatives elected by the student council. The representatives coordinate with operational partners and teaching staff for the continuous improvement, evaluation, and support of education through participation in committees related to educational operations. In the United States, in contrast, emphasis is placed on regular student surveys to obtain an understanding of the degree of student participation in student life as a whole. Notwithstanding such clear differences, both types of engagement can be categorised as 'student engagement'.

At the same time, global similarities can be discerned in the motivations behind the promotion of student engagement. These similarities lie in the shared recognition of the need to draw on student perspectives in educational enhancement. The system or form of student engagement then differs according to whether the methods for gaining an accurate understanding of such perspectives are direct (personal exchange of perspectives between students and instructors) or indirect (aggregation of perspectives through questionnaire surveys). This book offers expert analyses of the methods of a variety of countries: Australia, Brazil, China, Finland, Japan, Kazakhstan, Mozambique, Sweden, the United Kingdom and the United States.

The experts who author the chapters in this volume are Stuart Brand and Luke Millard (Birmingham City University, UK), Peter Felten (Elon University, USA), Åsa Kettis (Uppsala University, Sweden), Kuanysh Tastanbekova (University of Tsukuba, Japan), Bernardo Sfredo Miorando (Federal University of Rio Grande do Sul, Brazil), Ryan Naylor (La Trobe University, Australia), Jani Ursin (University of Jyväskylä, Finland), Reiko Yamada (Doshisha University, Japan), Tong Yang (Southeast University, China), Nelson Casimiro Zavale and Patrício V. Langa (Eduardo Mondlane University, Mozambique) and the author of this chapter, Masahiro Tanaka (University of Tsukuba, Japan). While their analyses will form the contents of Chapter 2 onwards, this chapter will focus on presenting an overview of the existing literature on student engagement and drawing on the literature to develop a clearer definition of the concept.

Existing literature and the definition of student engagement

The research of George Kuh, who developed the National Survey of Student Engagement (NSSE), is well known throughout the world in the field of student engagement (Kuh, 2001). This study can be considered to be the defining text emerging from the college impact research conducted mainly in the United States since the 1960s. Kuh was strongly influenced by three research outputs.

The first research output that influenced Kuh was the analyses of Nevitt Sanford. Sanford's research showed that student growth is greatly influenced by the inclusion of extracurricular activities within the learning environment of the university (Sanford, 1962). On this basis, there are many questions in the NSSE that focus on the level of satisfaction with the learning environment. The second output that Kuh drew on was Alexander Astin's Student Development Theory (Astin, 1984), which states that the deeper students become involved in their learning, the better their learning outcomes will be. He later proposed the I-E-O (Input-Environment-Outcomes) model and demonstrated the utility of comprehensively investigating student engagement levels (Astin, 1991). Based on these studies, the NSSE questionnaire items cover a range of holistic topics. The third influential research output was Arthur Chickering and Zelda Gamson's seven principles for good practice in undergraduate education that they presented to university teaching staff (Chickering and Gamson, 1987). The NSSE was designed to measure the levels of adherence to these principles.

According to Kuh's definition of the development of the NSSE, 'Student engagement represents (1) the time and effort students devote to activities that are empirically linked to desired outcomes of college *and* (2) what institutions do to induce students to participate in these activities' (2009: 683, emphasis by Kuh, but numbers in parentheses are added by the author of this chapter). The interesting aspect of this definition is that (2) shows that it is the responsibility of the university to guarantee the amount and quality of (1). Conversely, there are no duties required of or responsibilities placed upon the student.

Should the practice of student engagement be the obligation of the student, the university, or both parties? This question may be very important in developing an understanding of student engagement. In this context, it can be proposed that the locus of responsibility for student engagement differs according to whether the student is positioned as disciple, customer, or partner, as shown in Figure 1.1.

The perspective that views students as disciples is one that has long been upheld in higher education institutions since the establishment of Humboldt University in Berlin. In universities that maintain the Humboldt philosophy, the right of instructors to freely impart the results of their own research (academic freedom) is guaranteed (Tanaka, 2005). In such an environment, instructors need not take an interest in the curriculum as a whole and some-times may not even question their own educational methods, while actions by students to improve educational methods are considered the height of rudeness. In such a situation, it is difficult to maintain the view that promotion of stu-dent engagement is the responsibility of the university. Furthermore, it is unli-kely that students will be given the right to participate in attempts to improve their education.

A perspective that views students as customers has been proposed in a number of countries, including the United States: in that case, the commercialisation of higher education has become highly advanced through the introduction of and increases in tuition fees due to decreases in public funding. According to Maringe:

> HE became a tradable service, based on demand and supply laws under which students became key consumers while universities and their staff were the providers. Consumerism is the central tenet of the free market in which busi-ness success depends almost entirely on satisfying customer needs and exceed-ing their expectations. (2011: 142)

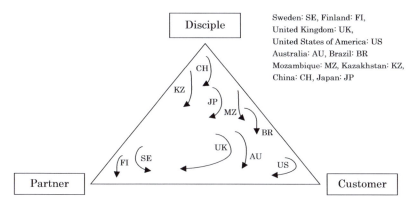

FIGURE 1.1 Views of students and positioning of responsibility for student engagement
Note: the arrows in Figure 1.1 describe positions of the ten countries examined in this book. These positions will be tested in the final chapter of the book through analysis of the countries.

In sum, universities that cannot provide education to the satisfaction of students will lose students and eventually go bankrupt in a competitive environment. Accordingly, it can be said that the promotion of student engagement for the purpose of gaining accurate knowledge of student demands and expectations is the obligation of the university, as its survival may depend upon it. Note, however, that the student has no duty to provide such information.

The perspective that positions students as partners took root relatively early in countries such as those of Northern Europe: here, the law establishes the principle of tripartite governance, comprising teachers, administrators, and students. At present, this viewpoint has gained political support, primarily in European countries, with the advocacy of steps such as the inclusion of students in the Bologna Process (Levy et al., 2011). When students are positioned as partners of the instructors, they acquire the right to participate in the decision-making processes of the university but at the same time become duty bound to cooperate in the support, evaluation, and enhancement of education and to shoulder a collective responsibility with respect to the outcomes of such processes. Regarding this responsibility, Cook-Sather et al. comment:

> student-faculty partnerships rooted in the principles of respect, reciprocity, and responsibility are most powerful and efficacious. Each of these principles is foundational to genuine relationships of any kind, and each is particularly important in working within and, in some cases, against the traditional roles students and faculty are expected to assume in higher education. All three of them require and inspire trust, attention, and responsiveness. (2014: 2)

As noted by Cook-Sather et al., instructor respect (and, implicitly, trust) for students is essential for building a mutually beneficial relationship in the context of educational enhancement. Students should, however, be treated as adults in the midst of a process of growth, meaning that there are some limits to the degree to which they can be trusted to deal with operational tasks. This book utilises multiple country-level analyses to discuss this aspect.

In addition to identifying the responsibility for student engagement, the investigation into the objectives of student engagement is also essential for developing a clearer understanding of the concept. This book will conduct this investigation by examining student engagement through the lens of the following three levels posited by Healey et al. (2010: 22):

- Micro: engagement in their own learning and that of other students
- Meso: engagement in quality assurance and enhancement processes
- Macro: engagement in strategy development

The core objective of micro-level student engagement is the improvement of learning experiences and outcomes for the individual student. In the words of Coates (2006: 26), 'learning is influenced by how an individual participates in educationally purposeful activities'. Furthermore, if activities that support the learning of fellow students (peer support) are included in micro-level student engagement, then the improvement of learning outcomes for others can also be considered to be a main objective.

Meso-level student engagement is the main theme of this book. The primary objective of student engagement in this level is the inclusion of the voice of the students in educational evaluation and enhancement. As noted above, there are direct (the personal exchange of perspectives between students and instructors) and indirect (aggregating perspectives through questionnaire surveys) ways to collect student experiences and perspectives. The results of the NSSE, which can be regarded as an indirect method, for example, can be used to clarify the current student situation and as evidence of educational enhancement. The reason for this, as pointed out by Pascarella et al. (2010: 21) is that 'the NSSE results regarding educational practices and student experiences are good proxy measures for growth in important educational outcomes such as critical thinking, moral reasoning, intercultural effectiveness, personal well-being, and a positive orientation toward literacy activities'.

In broad terms, there are two types of direct method – participation in external quality assurance and participation in internal quality assurance. The former refers to students carrying out some kind of evaluation activity as employees of a third-party evaluation organisation such as an accreditation body (for example, participation as a member of an evaluation group that visits an institution undergoing an accreditation audit). The latter can be assumed to refer to activities such as (1) the creation of 'student reports' to be submitted to external evaluation bodies, (2) participation in interviews with such bodies, and/or (3) participation by a student as an official member of an internal quality assurance organisation of the university.

It should be clarified that, in higher education, quality assurance (QA) is not the same as quality enhancement (QE), although these are seen as a continuum. According to Elassy (2015: 259):

> whereas QA focusses more on assessing the quality to determine the limitations and the strengths of HEIs, it could also be understood as a diagnostic process in an institution. QE is concerned more with improving the quality as a curing process of the limitations that might be found when the quality was assured, and at the same time, develop the strengths in HEI, if there is any.

The macro-level objective of student engagement lies in the reflection of university operations in benefits for students. Note, however, that in cases where the interests of students and the university are in conflict, dialogue between both parties is essential in order to elucidate common ground. Further, consideration must be given to benefits not only for students and the university but also to benefits for society as a whole. Moreover, the involvement of students in the management of the university can be regarded as having the effect of increasing the transparency of the university's decision-making process (Lizzio and Wilson, 2009).

In light of the above, the following considers the definitions of student engagement offered in the existing literature. Based on Kuh's definition discussed above, Trowler sets out his own definition as follows:

> Student engagement is concerned with the interaction between the time, effort and other relevant resources invested by both students and their institutions intended to optimise the student experience and enhance the learning outcomes and development of students and the performance, and reputation of the institutions. (2010: 2)

Trowler stressed that the collaboration of the student and the university (instructors) is not only for the sake of the student. It should also benefit the university. Considering the meso- and macro-level student engagement objectives, this aspect can be strongly agreed with.

In positing the following definition, Bryson refrains from specifying explicitly the objectives of student engagement in the way that Kuh and Trowler do:

> Student engagement is about what a student brings to Higher Education in terms of goals, aspirations, values and beliefs and how these are shaped and mediated by their experience whilst a student. SE is constructed and reconstructed through the lenses of the perceptions and identities held by students and the meaning and sense a student makes of their experiences and interactions. (2014: 17)

From the above definition, it can be seen that Bryson understands student engagement as not only the process of a student 'doing something' but also what occurs as a result of such an action. In summary, it can be said that there is no great contrast from the definitions of Kuh and Trowler because Bryson also emphasises the importance of participation in activities that have educational significance.

Harper and Quaye (2009: 2) simplify this definition further, expressing it as follows: 'Student engagement is simply characterized as participation in educationally effective practices, both inside and outside the classroom, which leads to a range of measurable outcomes'. Despite the fact that the word 'measurable' implies a focus on student surveys or other forms of evaluation, this definition can be viewed as similar to other definitions for the way it places importance on not only the process of participation but also its results.

As outlined above, the definitions in the existing literature show that student engagement is expected to benefit both the student and the university. In this context, the definition used in this book shall emphasise the accomplishment of objectives on the micro-, meso-, and macro-levels and be expressed as follows:

> Student engagement is where students provide their own efforts and information to the university in pursuit of any or all of the following objectives: (1)

maximising the learning outcomes of oneself or one's fellow students, (2) assuring/improving quality of university education, and (3) reflecting benefits for students, the university, and society in which the university operations.

To test whether this definition is applicable to countries of differing cultures, Chapter 2 and onwards of this book will, as discussed above, analyse the current state of and challenges for student engagement in the ten countries: Australia, Brazil, China, Finland, Japan, Kazakhstan, Mozambique, Sweden, the United Kingdom, and the United States.

References

Astin, A. (1984) 'Student Involvement: A Developmental Theory for Higher Education', *Journal of College Student Development*, 40(5), 518–529.

Astin, A. (1991) *Assessment for Excellence: The Philosophy and Practice of Assessment and Evaluation in Higher Education*, New York: McMillan Publishing.

Bryson, C. (2014) 'Clarifying the Concept of Student Engagement', Bryson, C. (Ed.) *Understanding and Developing Student Engagement*, Abingdon: Routledge, 1–22.

Chickering, A. and Gamson, Z. (1987) 'Seven Principles for Good Practice in Undergraduate Education', *AAHE Bulletin*, March, 3–7.

Coates, H. (2006) *Student Engagement in Campus-based and Online Education: University Connections*, London: Routledge.

Cook-Sather, A., Bovill, C., and Felten, P. (2014) *Engaging Students as Partners in Learning and Teaching: A Guide for Faculty*, San Francisco: Jossey Bass.

Elassy, N. (2015) 'The Concepts of Quality, Quality Assurance and Quality Enhancement', *Quality Assurance in Education*, 23(3), 250–261.

Harper, S. R. and Quaye, S. J. (2009) 'Beyond Sameness, with Engagement and Outcomes for All: An Introduction', Harper, S. R. and Quaye, S. J. (Eds.) *Student Engagement in Higher Education: Theoretical Perspectives and Practical Approaches for Diverse Populations*, Abingdon: Routledge, 1–15.

Healey, M., Mason-O'Connor, K., and Broadfoot, P., (2010) 'Reflections on Engaging Student in the Process and Product of Strategy Development for Learning, Teaching, and Assessment: An Institutional Case Study', *International Journal for Academic Development*, 15(1), 19–32.

Kuh, G. (2001) 'Assessing What Really Matters to Student Learning Inside The National Survey of Student Engagement', *Change: The Magazine of Higher Learning*, 33(3), 10–17.

Kuh, G. (2009) 'What Student Affairs Professionals Need to Know about Student Engagement', *Journal of College Student Development*, 50(6), 683–706.

Levy, P., Little, S., and Whelan, N. (2011) 'Perspectives on Staff-Student Partnership in Learning, Research and Educational Enhancement', Little, S. (Ed.), *Staff-Student Partnerships in Higher Education*, London: Continuum, 1–15.

Lizzio, A. and Wilson, K. (2009) 'Student Participation in University Governance: The Role Conceptions and Sense of Efficacy of Student Representatives on Departmental Committees', *Studies in Higher Education*, 34(1), 69–84.

Maringe, F. (2011) 'The Student as Consumer: Affordances and Constraints in a Transforming Higher Education Environment', Molesworth, M., Scullion, R., and Nixon, E. (Eds.), *The Marketisation of Higher Education and the Student as Consumer*, Oxford: Routledge, 142–154.

Millard, L., Bartholomew, P., Brand, S. and Nygaard, C. (2013) 'Why Student Engagement Matters', Nygaard, C., Brand, S., Bartholomew, P., and Millard, L. (Eds.) *Student Engagement: Identity, Motivation and Community*, Faringdon: Libri, 1–15.

Pascarella, E. T., Seifert, T. A.And Blaich, C. (2010) 'How Effective are the NSSE Benchmarks in Predicting Important Educational Outcomes?', *Change: The Magazine of Higher Learning*, 42(1), 16–22.

Sanford, N. (Ed.) (1962) *The American College: A Psychological and Social Interpretation of Higher Learning*, New York: Wiley.

Tanaka, M. (2005) *The Cross-Cultural Transfer of Educational Concepts and Practices: A Comparative Study*, Oxford: Symposium Books.

Trowler, V. (2010) *Student Engagement Literature Review*, York: Higher Education Academy, www.heacademy.ac.uk/resources/detail/evidencenet/Student_engagement_literature_ review (accessed 26 July 2017).

2

STUDENTS AS PARTNERS IN SWEDISH HIGHER EDUCATION

A driver for quality

Åsa Kettis

UPPSALA UNIVERSITY

Introduction

Student influence, student consultation, student empowerment, student democracy, student power, student voice, student engagement, student participation, student involvement and student activity … *A beloved child has many names* is a Swedish saying, meaning that the more loved one is, the more names one has. And yes, students partaking in higher education is increasingly embraced in Sweden as in many other parts of the world, and it takes many forms, which is reflected in the partially overlapping and partially diverging terms used to describe it. *Student democracy* first and foremost brings student union lobbying to mind, while *student consultation* can be exemplified by students providing feedback via course evaluations. *Student engagement* brings the mind to students as active learners inside and outside the classroom, while students taking part in comprehensive decision-making on boards and committees at higher education institutions (HEIs) rhymes well with *student participation*. The NUS/HEA student engagement toolkit, and Bovill's and Bulley's (2011) ladder of student participation in curriculum design, also illustrate that there are degrees of student participation, where partnership in teaching and learning falls far to one end of the ladder (Healey, 2014).

The terms listed above all have the *student* as the common denominator, while the teacher is absent. The emphasis on the student can be understood as a reaction to the prevailing teacher-centred tradition in HEIs, where the active role of students has long been underemphasized. Now the two are being brought together, as the interdependent partnership dimension of learning and teaching is becoming increasingly acknowledged. Teachers and students increasingly join forces to make the most out of higher education, and it seems to work. According to research, the benefits of partnership in teaching and learning include increased student engagement, as well as enhanced motivation and learning. Further, the students' awareness of their own learning process strengthens; they develop their meta-cognitive awareness and a gain stronger sense of identity. Finally, the quality of teaching and the classroom experience improves (Cook-Sather, Bovill, & Felten, 2014). The student is an obvious winner, but according to Cook-Sather and colleagues, so are faculty. Faculty's thinking about and practice of teaching are transformed, as is their understanding as they experience different perspectives, and they tend to reconceptualize learning and teaching as a collaborative process.

Partnership can both be seen as approach and ethos, and can be framed in different ways. Healey et al.'s conceptual model for partnership in learning and teaching identifies four areas in which students can act as partners: 1) learning, teaching and assessment; 2) subject-based research and inquiry; 3) scholarship of teaching – and learning; and 4) curriculum design and pedagogic consultancy. These can be further divided into two partially overlapping areas: partners in learning and partners in development and change. Additionally, students can be partners in institutional governance, quality assurance activities, extra-curricular activities etc. (Healey et al., 2014). The partnership idea is given more and more attention as reflected by an increasing number of conferences and journals that are dedicated to this theme.

In the following, students participation in Sweden will be discussed in its broadest sense: on the micro, meso and macro levels (as described in the beginning of this book), and including all steps on the ladder of participation – from the teacher being in control at the lowest level to true partnership, and students being in control at the highest. The focus, however, will primarily be on how student engagement influences *quality of education*, i.e. on students as partners in development and change and in pedagogic consultancy. In the following, *student engagement* will be used as a comprehensive term, covering all facets of active student participation, unless referring to initiatives where other terms are used.

The quality of education is primarily safeguarded by ensuring that teachers are highly qualified, i.e. that they have appropriate subject knowledge and teaching skills. It also rests on the leadership (collegial bodies, heads of department, directors of study, deans, vice rectors and the vice chancellor) providing good conditions for student learning – and student engagement. Nowadays, most HEIs have become more systematic in their striving for quality by introducing university-wide quality assurance (QA) policies, procedures for systematic monitoring and evaluation, and different means of supporting the further development of learning and teaching (Hénard, 2010). The results of the European University Association's Trends reports 2010–2015 confirm that there is a rapid development of both internal and external QA processes, shaping HEIs, and that these increasingly involve students (Sursock, 2015).

Uppsala University will be used as an example of in what ways student engagement permeates QA and quality enhancement (QE) at a Swedish university. Although Uppsala University is not representative to all Swedish HEIs, since they differ according to age, size, profile, tradition, culture and other factors, it is likely to reflect some signature features of student engagement in Sweden.

Before looking into student engagement at Uppsala University, the environment in which the university operates will be presented, i.e. the national, macro level of student engagement. What characterizes Swedish higher education, and the Swedish student experience? How is student engagement supported at the national level? What is the legal status of student engagement in Sweden? What role does the national QA agency play with regard to student engagement?

Swedish higher education

The Swedish system for higher education consists of 48 HEIs of which the majority are public authorities. Higher education is free of charge, and there are grants and favourable loans for living expenses for all Swedish citizens. Citizens in the EU/EES or Switzerland can also attend Swedish higher education for free, and given that some additional criteria are fulfilled, they are also entitled to economic support for living expenses. Since Swedish higher education is part of the integrated European Higher Education Area, it is also adjusted according to the Bologna Process. Sweden was quick to adopt the idea of learning outcomes, and in introducing the two-year master degree to harmonize with the rest of Europe. A distinctive feature of Swedish higher education is the relatively high proportion of freestanding courses that can be freely combined by students and result in a customized Bachelor's Degree or Master's Degree, if certain requirements are met. This feature of the system also supports lifelong learning, since adult, professionally active people can take freestanding courses as a part of their continuous professional development.

The Swedish student experience

What characterizes the Swedish student experience? Of course, the question has as many answers as there are students, but are there any defining features that stand out at the aggregated level?

The International Student Barometer (ISB) taps into the attitudes and experiences of international students around the world. In the 2016 round, 159,959 international students responded from 196 institutions in 17 countries. Judging from these results, international students in Sweden have a strong propensity to recommend that others apply to the Swedish HEI they attend. Four Swedish HEIs are found among top seven in this regard. There were a few student engagement oriented items in the ISB. Students were asked to think back over 'this academic year' and rate to what extent their course challenged them to: 1) analyse ideas or concepts in greater depth; 2) do their best work; and 3) use information, ideas or concepts from different topics to solve problems. Out of the international students, 63%, 59% and 65% said that this had happened often or very often, while 2–3% said that it never happened (Uppsala University did not differ from the Swedish average). Unfortunately, the ISB report did not tell if, and in what way, this differs from what international students in the rest of the ISB population experience.

However, in interviews of international students at Uppsala University, they often say that they find studying in Sweden different from their earlier experiences in that they are expected to be very independent in their studies. They describe it as challenging, but as one student put it: 'After having studied in Sweden, I know that I will manage doing just anything.' What these students have encountered is the Swedish tradition of independent learning, where students are given much 'freedom with responsibility'. This approach may support the development of empowered students, but students may also feel abandoned. It is a delicate balance to be kept between fostering independence and challenging students on one hand and providing sufficient support on the other hand. There was recently a heated debate in Sweden regarding students' own responsibility for their learning. The Swedish government has increased the pressure on the HEIs to make sure that *all* students succeed in their studies, and as a reaction some university teachers find that the government overlooks the students' own responsibility for their achievement.

Regulations and reviews at the national level – supporting and challenging student engagement

The legal framework

In Sweden, student engagement is protected by law. The Swedish Higher Education Act states that: *Quality assurance and quality enhancement are the shared concern of staff and students.* It further states that: *HEIs shall endeavour to enable students to play an active role in the continued development of courses and study programmes.*

The higher education ordinance acts says that: *Students are entitled to have at least three members in all decision-making bodies. The Student Unions appoint the student representatives.* It states further that: *Students have the right to express their views through course evaluations. The HEIs have to inform about their results and any actions prompted by them.*

Given that Sweden is part of the European Higher Education Area, the European Standards and Guidelines for Quality Assurance in the European Higher Education Area (ESG, 2015) is another important document. In the newly revised version, student-centred learning is emphasized: *Institutions should ensure that the programmes are delivered in a way that encourages students to take an active role in creating the learning process and the assessment of students reflect this approach (ESG 1.3).*

The student unions

Student unions have a strong standing in Sweden, partially because students' union membership used to be compulsory before it became optional in 2010. According to a recent investigative report from the UKÄ (Universitetskanslersämbetet, in English: The Swedish Higher Education Authority, hereafter referred to as 'the Authority'), today's system for student influence is well defined in terms of both rules and regulations and in day-to-day operations (UKÄ, 2017a). It works well from the perspective of both HEIs and the student unions, although HEIs are more satisfied than the student unions. Still, the voluntary union membership has proved to be a challenge. The Authority concludes that many unions became more economically dependent on their HEIs and other sponsors once student union membership became optional in 2010, and the number of members went down. Today less than half of the Swedish students belong to a student union, which is a democratic problem since only members are allowed to vote in union elections, and it is the student unions that appoint student representatives to decision-making bodies at HEIs. The Authority suggests the government to 1) increase funding to improve student influence, 2) encourage HEIs and student unions to develop ways of increasing student involvement in improving higher education, and 3) find ways to increase student unions' knowledge about the rules and regulations that underpin student influence.

The Swedish Higher Education Authority and student engagement

The Authority evaluates the quality of higher education, analyses developments, has responsibility for official statistics about higher education and monitors that universities and university colleges follow laws and regulations (Universitetskanslersämbetet, 2017b). The Authority has recently developed a new system for review of higher education that was in effect as of January 1, 2017. In the new system, HEIs are responsible for developing and controlling the quality of their study programmes/subjects, and the role of the Authority will mainly be to review the functionality of the HEIs' own QA systems. In the former system, Authority-led reviews of individual study programmes/subjects formed the major part of the national system, and although this component will remain, it will be much reduced. The intent is that the new system should be more closely aligned with the ESG, and one consequence is that the student perspective will be even more emphasized in the reviews. In the Authority's upcoming institutional audits, HEIs will have to prove that study programmes are designed, developed and implemented in a way that encourages students to take an active role in the learning process, and that this is reflected in student assessment as well. HEIs also have to show evidence that they work systematically to ensure students' right to exercise influence over their education and their situation. HEIs also have to demonstrate that they work systematically to monitor, evaluate and develop student influence, and that measures that are planned or implemented as a result of student influence are communicated to relevant stakeholders. Student engagement is also ensured in the review process itself. Students are expected to be involved in the HEIs' processes for writing up the self-evaluation that underpins the Authority's review. Additionally, the student unions will be invited to submit independent statements directly to the Authority, expressing their unrestricted views on the quality of learning and teaching at their HEI. Students are also part of the review process itself. The Authority's reviews are based on peer review by an independent external review panel that always includes student representatives nominated by the student unions. Representatives of Sveriges förenade studentkårer (in English: The Swedish National Union of Students) have also been deeply involved in the development of the new system. Another important change in the new national system is that the Authority is now tasked to review quality assurance of research as well. This will increase the possibilities to keep tight ties between research, teaching and research to the benefit of students.

Summing up student engagement at the upper macro level

There is strong support for student engagement at the national level. Student influence has a long tradition in Sweden, although it has been somewhat challenged by the abolishment of compulsory student union membership. Student engagement is embedded in the Swedish academic culture by long tradition, and the law stipulates that students are to co-govern at all levels of HEIs, and that they have the right to give their feedback on every course. Further, students have been serving as reviewers in the Authority's reviews for a long time. Student engagement is now further reinforced by the revised ESG, meaning that the new national system will be more oriented towards student centred learning than ever.

At the national level, it may seem as if Sweden is a student engagement heaven on earth, possibly in resemblance to the other Nordic countries. The results of the World Value Survey may contribute to the understanding of why student engagement has such a strong position in this part of the world (World Values Survey, 2017). In particular in Sweden, but also in Norway, Denmark and the Netherlands, secular-rational values and self-expression values are strong. There is low emphasis on authority, and a sense of individual agency, which increase the demands for participation in decision-making in all facets of life, including when being a student.

Uppsala University – an example of Swedish student engagement converted in practice

In trying to understand the features of student engagement at an individual institution, it is useful to have some basic knowledge about the institution. In Box 2.1, the reader will find a brief description of Uppsala University.

BOX 2.1 UPPSALA UNIVERSITY IN BRIEF

Uppsala University was the first university in Sweden – founded in 1477. Today, the University embraces three disciplinary domains: humanities and social sciences, medicine and pharmacy, and science and technology (Uppsala University, 2017b). In all, there are currently nine faculties, 60 departments, 45,000 students and 6,800 employees. The number of professors is 600 (30% women), and the number of PhD students 2,500 (50% women). The University has a broad range of courses from undergraduate level to doctoral level, including 140 degree programmes and 2,000 freestanding courses. There are some 40 international Master's programmes, and 800 freestanding courses that are taught in English. Uppsala University is found among the top 100 in major international university rankings (although rankings should be relied on with caution). Uppsala University's aspirations are shared with many other universities in the world. The University aims to gain and disseminate knowledge for the benefit of humankind and for a better world. This includes being a meeting place for knowledge, culture and critical dialogue, developing new areas of knowledge through cross-disciplinary collaboration, being an integrated education and research environment, being open to the outside world, contributing to sustainable solutions to the challenges facing society, having a working environment characterized by openness, responsibility and trust, and acting ethically and observing equal opportunities.

Uppsala University is research-intensive, which is reflected in budget share and in the mind-set. Further, the University has a strong culture of peer quality review, academic freedom and collegial decision-making. A firm belief in devolved leadership with a high degree of self-governance and associated local ownership is indicative of the culture. To a high degree, decision-making rests with the peer-elected faculty boards, deans, department boards and department heads, and academic staff is relatively autonomous.

Quality assurance and quality enhancement at Uppsala University

Uppsala University has a devolved model of governance, which applies to the University's approach to QA and QE as well, which is highly decentralized yet systematic. The University Board and the Vice Chancellor take decisions on overall aims and strategies, while the Disciplinary Domains and their Faculty Boards are in charge of matters pertaining to quality of education and research within their respective remit. The Quality Advisory Board advises the Vice Chancellor on QA and QE, and facilitates the coordination of activities and the exchange of experiences and good practice between faculties. The Board is led by a Vice Rector and is constituted by academic staff and students.

The University has institution–wide guidelines on QA and QE, providing direction and guidance for activities at all levels, while also allowing for adjustment to local contexts and needs. The Guidelines rest on a firm belief in the quality-promoting effects of academic values and procedures, with a heavy emphasis on peer review as a QA and QE tool, not only in research, but also in teaching, learning and administration. The importance of clear leadership promoting QA and QE is also emphasized, as is the importance of student involvement. According to the Guidelines, QA and QE activities are to be integrated into daily life at all levels of the University, relevant for action, cost-effective and (at least to some degree) documented to be available for enquiry.

QA and QE activities aim at sustaining, developing and strengthening the University's academically rooted quality culture, meet internal and external quality requirements and contribute to achieving the objectives defined in the University's Mission and Core Values document. The students are vital in achieving this. The University's goals and strategies state that: 'Together, teachers and students take shared responsibility for creating learning environments characterized by active student participation and engagement.'

Student engagement at Uppsala University

As mentioned earlier, student engagement is strongly supported at the national level, and visible in Uppsala University's (and the other Swedish HEIs') rhetoric, but what happens in practice? Does genuine student engagement permeate the University at the organization's macro, meso and micro levels?

In 2012, the University's capacity for development of learning and teaching was reviewed by an international panel within the framework of the self-initiated CrEd project, *Creative Educational Development at Uppsala University* (Uppsala University, 2013). The panel commended the level of student engagement at Uppsala University (although the two Swedish panel members stated that Uppsala University was no different from other Swedish universities in this regard):

> We were impressed by the students we met and their commitment to the University and their fellow students. The relationship that has been established with the University staff to engage together in building a high quality educational and learning experience for the students is commendable; noting the commitment to further develop the relationship and responsibilities of both. (Uppsala University, 2013)

It was in particular a student-led initiative within the CrEd project that caught the panel's eye. The project aimed at strengthening and broadening student engagement with an emphasis on peer-to-peer learning and peer mentoring. The students that were engaged in the project wrapped up the insights generated by the project in an anthology: *Students, the university's unspent resource. Revolutionising higher education through active student participation* (Gärdebo and Wiggberg, 2012), which became internationally recognized.

Although the panel praised the University and its students for their commitment to student engagement, the panel suggested that the University should not be complacent. Instead, it was encouraged to build further on this strength — i.e. the long tradition of student engagement and the recent student initiative — and create a forward-looking Uppsala model of student engagement.

Macro level: student engagement in strategy development

So what made the international panel praise student engagement at Uppsala University? In what way are students engaged at the strategy level?

In accordance with Swedish law, student representatives participate in all advisory boards and decision-making bodies at the University. This means that they contribute to whatever strategic agenda there is on all levels, from the university board to the department board. Most of the time students co-govern in a very responsible manner. When they get a place at the table, they become informed and come to understand the complexity of university governance. Sometimes the divide in perspective is rather between these co-governing students and the students that they are to represent, than between the student representatives on one hand, and academic leaders and teacher representatives on the other hand.

Students are also involved in designing and revising the University's Goals and Strategies and other policy documents. One such guiding document, *Teaching and Learning at Uppsala University. Visions for educational activity and development* (Uppsala University, 2018, hereafter referred to as the Guidelines), has been especially important for the further development of student engagement. The current Guidelines have been in effect since 2009, and were cautiously updated in 2018. They were developed through an elaborated bottom-up process with a high degree of ownership by academic staff and — importantly — students. For each aim in the Guidelines the respective role of *the University* and *the Student* in achieving the aim is defined. This way the mutuality in the partnership becomes explicit and visible. In developing the Guidelines, student representatives worked alongside teacher representatives in a university-wide working group, and the student role part of the guidelines was articulated by a sub-group of which the majority of the participants were student representatives. This way the students themselves had most say in stipulating what to expect from students. The kind of student role that emerges when reading the Guidelines is that of an active and responsible student who makes the most out of the opportunities that are offered and who provides constructive feedback to teachers about how they as students learn best.

All in all, the Guidelines gather faculty and students around a joint point of departure when discussing and improving the quality of learning and teaching, while still allowing for variation between faculties and subjects. The Guidelines are operationalized and put into practice by the disciplinary domains and their faculties.

The international CrEd panel commended the Guidelines as a useful means of providing structure and guidance in work with educational development, and in highlighting aspects of special importance. The panel especially appreciated that the responsibility of achieving various goals is delineated, and that the Guidelines cover the responsibility of students in their obtaining a good education. They also concluded that the Guidelines seem to be well known throughout the University. Nevertheless, the panel said that good Guidelines can be made even better. The role of students should be further developed, and the implementation of the Guidelines should be strengthened in some parts of the University. The panel's suggestions have been most useful in the recent revision of the Guidelines.

So what happened in response to the panel's suggestion to raise the ambitions for student engagement even further, beyond updating the Guidelines? When the CrED-project ended, a group of students, supported by some teachers, approached the Vice Chancellor and suggested that there should be a university-wide strategic initiative to take student engagement to the next level. The Vice Chancellor approved and provided resources to spur the further development of active student engagement both with regard to students as resources in each other's learning (peer-to-peer learning) and students as co-creators in the planning, implementation and evaluation of education. The project was given the name *Active Student Participation* (ASP) at Uppsala University. An ASP team consisting of three senior students and an academic developer was created to develop and start implementing a support function that would facilitate the advancement of student participation at the University (Barrineau et al., 2016). Based on their macro level mandate and endorsement, the ASP team was resourced to work inventively on the meso level for two years (see below).

Meso: engagement in quality assurance and enhancement processes

The degree to which students are truly involved in QA and QE processes at the University varies. Far too often, students are given a reactive, rather than a proactive role, e.g. students respond to surveys, but less often work in true partnership with staff. The University has a long-established practice of letting students respond to course evaluations, student barometers, alumni surveys, focus group interviews, etc. However, although this is an important means of monitoring student views, it can by no means replace true interaction and dialogue between the University and its students, including the possibility for students to be proactive in their influence.

Since student representatives are on all boards and committees, students are part of all strategic QA/QE projects. Recent examples at the University include the design of a new internal system for systematic review of study programmes, as well as the already mentioned ASP project. The students in the ASP project had more say than in most other enhancement projects at the University, and this meant that they could unleash all their creativity without being stifled by prevailing conventions. During the two-year project period, the ASP team took stock of active student participation at the University, offered workshops and courses on active student participation to students and teachers, and training for student mentors/peer instructors. The team introduced a competition for joint student-teacher projects aiming at improving partnership in learning and teaching, and introduced yearly 'ASP Days', i.e. a university-wide conference dedicated to active student participation. They also coached joint teacher and student projects that had received funding from the University (see Bengtson et al., 2017 as an example), established a wide international network of researchers in the field of student engagement, and presented their insights at international conferences and in international, scientific journals. In summary, the ASP team created a firm knowledge base at the University and inspired other Swedish universities to raise the bar with regard to student participation, and the Swedish Higher Education Authority engaged them as experts and reviewers.

In conclusion, it was a very successful enhancement project, but would it bring about permanent change? When an enhancement project ends, long-term implementation is expected to follow at the meso and micro levels. This step is always a challenge, even in projects that have paid due attention to further implementation and sustainability beyond the project phase. The uptake always varies between faculties and departments. In the ASP project, the continued student engagement was partially secured by hiring two of the students working with the project at the central support unit for academic development (the Unit for Academic Teaching and Learning) at the University. The ASP developers were tasked to continue their work together with the academic developers. In this capacity, the ASP developers have advanced the element of student engagement in the University's teacher training courses and consultations. They have also contributed innovative means of engaging students in the planning, execution and follow-up of reviews within the University's new internal review system for study programmes. Additionally, the Vice Chancellor has decided to direct competitive funding to enhancement projects that are led by student-teacher teams, and that aim at improving active student participation. Thus, the University is becoming well equipped to support the further development of student engagement at the meso level. Still, there is one ambition that has not been realized yet: building a network of ASP developers, i.e. students who, together with teachers, provide support for the further development of student engagement within the different faculties. Maybe there will eventually be such an ASP network, or some alternative way forward that proves to be even more effective in strengthening ASP.

Micro level: students' engagement in their own learning and that of other students

The greatest need for improvement of student participation is probably to be found at the micro level. In some courses, responsible teachers provide the best possible conditions for students to be active, while other courses are still relatively teacher centred. This variation may in part be adequate. It is important that teachers are free to design their courses guided by their own professional experience and in line with the character and tradition of their academic discipline. However, there are also courses where quality could be much improved by adopting a more student-centred perspective on learning and teaching. The same goes for decision bodies. In some department boards students truly co-govern, while they are nearly invisible in others. The reasons for the slow advance of student participation in some parts of the University may be lack of time to change and/or no sense of urgency – or rationale – to do so. There are divided opinions on the value of student participation, and some teachers fear that it will undermine their role, even though that is not at all the intent, as explained by the ASP team:

> Pedagogical literature emphasizes that active student participation is not about replacing teachers, but supplementing the regular curriculum by giving students the opportunity to deepen their knowledge, to train general skills such as oral presentation or leading groups, and to raise awareness about their own and other's learning. The literature about partnership work between teachers and students ('students as partners') emphasizes that the teacher has the ultimate responsibility for teaching and that students' knowledge and skills are not the same as the teacher's. Students have a particular expertise in learning their subject and a partnership approach is not intended to blur the roles of student and teacher, but to learn from and with each other and take joint responsibility for education. (The ASP team)

Although the intention is not to blur the roles, true partnership inevitably changes the traditional student and teacher roles so that everyone is a learner. This does however not diminish the importance of the teacher's expertise in their subject area, but holds the learner expertise of the students as equally important.

There is also a concern that student-centredness means pampering students, including being forced to accommodate all their wishes and lowering the demands on them. This would be at odds with Swedish HEIs' strong impetus to foster independent and capable learners. Some teachers oppose to the very term 'student-centredness' and have suggested the alternative term 'learner-centredness', or even 'learning-centredness'. Consequently, it is a great pedagogical challenge to make clear what student participation means and does not mean. A shift from teacher-centred to student-centred teaching entails a shift in the teacher's role in the classroom, while retaining the responsibility for their courses. It gives teachers creative support in improving the conditions of learning by making it possible for students to be *more* engaged in – and responsible for – their own learning.

> During my many school years up to university, I have seen tendencies towards something that I would call 'study zombies'. [...] A 'study zombie' is someone who is so accustomed to study that he or she is excellent at doing what is required, but in need of reviving some of that natural curiosity and fascination. (Uppsala University student)

Strengthened partnership may also be challenging for students, who also have to seek a new role. As the students in the ASP team describe their collaboration with academic developers: 'We now occupy a liminal space where our perspectives straddle that of an academic developer and a student. This is a curious space to inhabit.'

The ASP project was the first major student-academic developer partnership in Sweden. As such it has been a transformative learning experience for the whole team (Barrineau et al., 2016). Initially, there was great confusion with regard to roles and expectations, leading to a 'crisis' and discomfort, which was resolved by open discussion and joint reflection. At the end of this process, the team found itself 'on the edge of radical collegiality'. According to Fielding, 'radical collegiality' is in place when 'reciprocity and energy of dialogue supersede the monologic exercise of power' (Fielding 1999, p. 28). A similar 'crisis' may well happen when teachers and students get to work in genuine partnership, and the ASP team suggests that academic developers should be active in supporting this conjoint role transition of teachers and students. Thus, to advance student-teacher partnership there is no quick fix. Based on their own pioneering experience, the ASP team gives an ironically comical summary for what lies ahead when starting the journey:

> Staff and students wanted for unpredictable journey. No extra pay or resources, likely discomfort, long periods of complete confusion, constant existential crisis, safe passage possible. Unlikely return to normal teaching. Transformation and lifelong learning in case of success.

Way forward – the importance of leadership engagement

Islands of fruitful partnership in learning and teaching are present in most universities and were present long before we had a term for it. Most often it is a result of individual teachers' and/or students' own initiatives. For the partnership idea to become an integral part of the culture, it has to be supported by the academic leadership at all levels, including collegial bodies, heads of departments, deans and the university management. A study by Gibbs et al. (2009) identified leadership activity associated with excellence in teaching. They investigated two departments in each of eleven world-class, research-intensive universities in eight countries, covering a wide range of disciplines and contexts. In these departments, which were demonstrably excellent at teaching, nine clusters of leadership activity were identified. These included, for example, the leadership identifying teaching problems and turning them into opportunities and supporting change and innovation. Although the presence of different activities varied between departments, two of them were present in *all* of them: the leadership being credible and trusted by staff, and *actively involving students*. In these departments that had proven to be excellent in teaching, effective methods for eliciting students' views and raising their commitment to engage had been developed. Also, students were involved in decision-making about teaching, and in implementing innovations. Students acted as change agents.

Thus, the leadership on all levels – macro, meso and micro – has to provide good conditions for the key actors – teachers and students – to pursue their partnership. It is also important that experimentation and failure are accepted along the way, as long as what is learned is used to inform the further journey. Bringing about change in academia requires a hefty dose of perseverance and a collaborative mindset. Letting things take time and be developed in dialogue increases the likelihood of wise decisions and widespread legitimacy, which most certainly will improve the outcome. When a majority of leaders, teachers and students eventually are on board by their own conviction, the journey will be much smoother and the chances for success greater – and at the end of the day, even the pioneers' struggle may be forgotten.

References

Barrineau, S., Schnaas, U., Engström, A. and Härlin, F. (2016). 'Breaking ground and building bridges: a critical reflection on student-faculty partnerships in academic development', *International Journal for Academic Development*, 21:1, 79–83.

Bengtson, C., Ahlkvist, M., Ekeroth, W., Nilsen-Moe, A., Proos Vedin, N., Rodiuchkina, K., Ye, S. and Lundberg, M. (2017). 'Working as partners: course development by a student–teacher team', *International Journal for the Scholarship of Teaching and Learning*, 11:2, Article 6.

Bovill, C. and Bulley, C. J. (2011). 'A model of active student participation in curriculum design: exploring desirability and possibility'. In: Rust, C. (ed.) *Improving Student Learning (ISL) 18: Global Theories and Local Practices: Institutional, Disciplinary and Cultural Variations*. Series: Improving Student Learning (18). Oxford: Oxford Brookes University: Oxford Centre for Staff and Learning Development, pp. 176–188.

Cook-Sather, A., Bovill, C. and Felten, P. (2014). *Engaging Students as Partners in Learning & Teaching: A Guide for Faculty*. San Francisco: Jossey-Bass.

Fielding, M. (1999). 'Radical collegiality: affirming teaching as an inclusive professional practice', *The Australian Educational Researcher*, 26(2), 1–34.

Gärdebo, J. and Wiggberg, M. (2012). *Students, the University's Unspent Resource. Revolutionising Higher Education Through Active Student Participation*. Uppsala: The Division for Development of Teaching and Learning, Uppsala University.

Gibbs, G., Knapper, C. and Piccinin, S. (2009). *Final Report. Departmental Leadership of Teaching in Research-Intensive Environments*. London: Leadership Foundation for Higher Education.

Healey, M., Flint, A. and Harrington, K. (2014). *Engagement Through Partnership: Students as Partners in Learning and Teaching in Higher Education*. York: The Higher Education Academy.

Hénard, F. (2010). *Learning Our Lesson: Review of Quality Teaching in Higher Education*. Paris: OECD Publishing. doi:10.1787/9789264079281-en

Standards and Guidelines for Quality Assurance in the European Higher Education Area (ESG). (2015). Brussels, Belgium.

Sursock, A. (2015). *Trends 2015: Learning and Teaching in European Universities*. Brussels: The European University Association.

The Swedish Higher Education Act. www.uhr.se/en/start/laws-and-regulations/Laws-and-re gulations/The-Swedish-Higher-Education-Act/ (retrieved on 13 August 2017).

Universitetskanslersämbetet (UKÄ) [In English: The Swedish Higher Education Authority]. (2017a). *Kartläggning och analys av studentinflytandets förutsättningar efter kårobligatoriets avskaffande* [In English: Survey and analysis of student influence following the abolishment of the compulsory student union membership]. www.uka.se/download/18.57b1ff5a15a 444399ff136ab/1487841867116/rapport-2017-02-06-studentinflytande-kartlaggning-o ch-analys.pdf (retrieved 8 August 2017).

Universitetskanslersämbetets (UKÄ) (In English: The Swedish Higher Education Authority) (2017b) *Homepage* http://english.uka.se/ (retrieved on 13 August 2017).

Uppsala University (2008). *Teaching and Learning at Uppsala University. Visions for Educational Activity and Development*. http://regler.uu.se/digitalAssets/14/c_14251-l_1-k_pedagogiskt-p rogram-engelska.pdf (retrieved 16 October 2018).

Uppsala University (2013). *Creative Educational Development 2010–2012.* http://uu.diva-porta l.org/smash/get/diva2:663621/FULLTEXT01.pdf (retrieved 13 August 2017).

Uppsala University (2017a). *The ASP website.* www.uu.se/asp/?languageId=1 (retrieved 13 August 2017).

Uppsala University (2017b). *Homepage.* www.uu.se/en/ (retrieved on 13 August 2017). *World Values Survey* (2017) www.worldvaluessurvey.org/wvs.jsp (retrieved 13 August 2017).

3

STUDENT ENGAGEMENT IN FINNISH HIGHER EDUCATION

Conflicting realities?

Jani Ursin

UNIVERSITY OF JYVÄSKYLÄ

Introduction

Nowadays it seems that governments have become increasingly interested in measuring effectiveness of higher education and students' outcomes where student engagement is often seen as a proxy of quality of teaching and learning. However, governments rarely question the concept of 'engagement', which in research literature is labelled to be very complex and multifaceted including behavioural (teaching practices and student satisfaction), psychological (internal individual processes) and socio-cultural (impact of the broader social context on student experience) elements (Zepke & Leach 2010; Kuh 2009; Fredricks, Blumenfeld & Paris 2004). Kahu (2013) highlights that while discussing engagement it is crucial to acknowledge the importance of the student and the institution, but it is also essential to recognise the critical influence of the socio-cultural context; that is, successful student engagement is a combination of the student, the teacher, the institution and the government. In Finland, discussion of student engagement has been dominated by the behavioural and socio-cultural perspectives, especially because Finnish higher education has become more accountable over the two last decades; therefore, government and higher education institutions (HEIs) have become interested in such questions as whether students are satisfied with their studies, whether teaching practices are effective and whether students complete their studies on time.

How student engagement is understood is naturally related to the history and composition of the whole national higher education system. Finnish higher education is based on the Nordic welfare state ideology where education is considered to be public good and the higher education system is hardly stratified. Therefore, higher education is mainly free for students (no tuition fees except those coming from outside the EU) and all higher education institutions are for the most part funded by the government. This is also why government is steering universities heavily through the funding model (which also includes student engagement as one element). The Finnish higher education system consists of two complementary sectors: 14 universities and 24 universities of applied sciences (UAS) altogether with a little over 300,000 students. The mission of universities is to conduct scientific research and provide instruction and postgraduate education based on it. UASs train professionals in response to labour market needs and conduct research, innovation and development activities, which are expected to promote regional development. Institutional autonomy is secured in the Finnish Constitution and guaranteed by laws governing HEIs (Ammattikorkeakoululaki 351/2003; Universities Act 558/2009).

Evaluation policies for Finnish higher education can be characterised as enhancement oriented. In this approach the focus is not on the accreditation of the programmes but rather on providing support and information to further enhance the quality of the programmes and institutions (Lomas & Ursin 2009; Välimaa 2012). HEIs are responsible for the evaluation of their own operations and outcomes. Such evaluation is supported by the Finnish Education Evaluation Centre (FINEEC). FINEEC's role is to conduct evaluations on HEIs and fields of study and assist HEIs in their own evaluation activities.

Both higher education sectors in Finland have their respective student unions. University students are represented by The National Union of University Students in Finland (SYL), which is an interest organisation defending and improving the educational, financial and social benefits and rights of the students. SYL represents over 130,000 university students, and membership in a student union is compulsory for all students studying for a full degree in Finnish universities. University of Applied Sciences Students in Finland (SAMOK) is an independent nonprofit organisation for students at universities of applied sciences representing about 140,000 students. Both of the student unions, and especially SYL, are influential in affecting education and evaluation policies of Finnish higher education.

How, then, are students engaged in Finnish higher education? The aim of this chapter is to shed light on this issue by describing issues related to student engagement from macro, meso and micro perspectives and highlight the fact that student engagement is more than representativeness in decision-making bodies. In each perspective also a concrete example will be presented.

Student engagement at the macro level: quality audits

Student engagement at the macro level refers to the socio-cultural climate on student experience, which typically is created at the national level. In Finland students are well represented in all the decision-making bodies at the national, institutional and departmental levels. Whenever a reform or any minor developmental activity at the national level is put in place, a steering group or committee always includes a representative from one or both of the student unions. Students are also members of the University Board, which chooses the rector and defines the university's key operational and financial targets, strategy and management principles. Students also have representatives in a University Colloquium, which, for example, decides on the number of members in the University Board, the duration of the term of office for the University Board and its members and elects the University Board members from outside the university community. Students are also represented in Faculty Council and all the department level decision-making and development bodies. All in all, students are considered to be important and equal stakeholders for ministries, higher education institutions, faculties and departments. Next I will give an example of how students are engaged in the national quality assurance of Finnish higher education, that is, in the audit of HEIs.

In an audit, the quality system the HEI has developed from its own needs and goals is evaluated. Typically, students have participated in the development of a quality system in a HEI. Quality system refers to the development of the institution's activities as a whole, comprising quality management organisation, division of responsibility, procedures and resources. The audits assess how well the quality system meets the strategic and operational management needs of the HEI as well as how comprehensive and effective the quality management of the basic duties of the higher education institution is. Moreover, the HEI's quality policy, development of the quality system and how well-functioning and dynamic an entity the system forms are studied. In other words, audit does not evaluate the quality of the education or research of the HEI in question. The aim of the Finnish audit model is to support HEIs in developing quality systems that correspond to the European principles of quality assurance. After passing the audit, the HEI will receive a quality label valid for six years (FINEEC 2015).

The audit is carried out by a trained team of 5–7 members of which one is a student. The audit team visits audited HEIs in order to verify and complement observations made on the basis of the audit materials about the quality system of the HEI. The aim is to make the visit an interactive event, which will support the development of the HEI's operations. During the site visit the audit team also meets and interviews students several times and asks their opinion on possibilities of giving feedback and being heard in university management, for example (FINEEC 2015).

Based on the materials and the visit, the audit team draws up an audit report, in which it also gives its appraisal of whether the HEI should pass the audit or be re-audited. The report highlights the strengths of the HEI's quality system and good practices, as well as making development recommendations to the HEI. FINEEC's Higher Education Evaluation Committee, which has nine members, of which two are students, will make the decision on the audit result. Several audit criteria stress the importance of engaging students in quality assurance procedures of a HEI. The decision is based on the audit report produced by the audit team and the audit team's proposal for the audit result (FINEEC 2015).

As can be seen from this example, students are present at various stages and in various roles in the audit of Finnish HEIs. Students are an integral part of the audit team as well as key stakeholders in giving information on how well quality assurance procedures and processes are working in an audited HEI. Students are also members of the body that will make the decision as to whether an HEI passed the audit or not. Furthermore, whenever the audit model and criteria are revised, a planning group also has student members. This example of quality audits highlights the fact that in Finnish higher education students are always an inherent part of decision-making and assessment of HEIs.

In reality, the student representativeness relies on those who are active in either national or local student unions and as such represents only a very limited body of the whole student population and thus can be argued to be a biased group of people. Therefore, the other, and more important, question is how willing the 'average Joe' students are to be engaged in their studies and in university life. This issue will be discussed in the next section.

Student engagement at the micro level: not everything is what it seems

In Finland, the government has made several reforms trying to engage students more in their studies and to encourage them to complete their studies on time. Behind these reforms is a concern for how long Finnish higher education can be considered a public good – in other words, how long it can be publicly funded. Therefore, government and higher education institutions have tried to rationalise and rebuild study paths so that students would come to higher education younger, graduate on time and transition smoothly to working life. However, students do not always see these initiatives in the same fashion and argue that government is trying to restrict and interfere with students' academic freedom by introducing various managerial measures, such as an upper limit on study times (Ursin, Rautopuro & Välimaa 2011).

The main challenges, which are often interrelated and are considered to have an impact on student engagement, are the issue of a gap year, aimlessness in choosing study places, motivational issues, prolonged study times, the problem of dropouts and entering into the labour market at a (relatively) advanced age (e.g. Uski 1999; Penttinen & Falck 2007; Litmanen et al. 2010). Government worries that too many students have a year off before transitioning from upper secondary school to tertiary education, leading to their entering both higher education and the working life too old (OKM 2010). However, from the point of view of the students, a gap year can provide an opportunity to clear up one's future study plans and fields. Furthermore, research evidence has shown that one gap year really does not have any effect on the future studies as 'gap year' students tend to catch up to those students who have started their studies immediately after high school (Parker et al. 2015).

Students do not always make rational choices when choosing their study place, which can cause unnecessary changes between study programmes and discontinuing or even dropping out of the studies altogether. One of the reasons for this is that students do not get proper career guidance in senior high schools, which makes it difficult for young people under the age of 20 to make rational choices for future studies (Hautamäki et al. 2012). Government and HEIs tend to see this as a waste of resources, whereas for students this is a natural part of exploring one's own field of interest and professional identity. It is true that Finnish graduates enter labour markets at an older age, if compared to peers in OECD countries, for example (OECD 2009). However, this can partly be explained by the differences in educational systems, as Finns typically go to school one year older than in many other countries. Furthermore, in Finland a 5-year Master's degree is typically needed to enter the labour markets; in many other countries a 3-year undergraduate degree is good enough. Although there is no clear evidence, it is often argued in Finland that longer education provides more competent graduates.

Motivation obviously plays an important role in student engagement. Positive stance and motivation towards university studies enhance experiences of engagement (Haggis 2004; Chapman & Pyvis 2005). Motivation is often promoted by positive learning experiences (Korhonen 2007). One of the main reasons for dropping out of the studies among the Finnish students is indeed motivational problems, which lead to poor commitment and engagement in the studies (Penttinen & Falck 2007), which in turn may lead to the experiences of anxiety and exhaustion. Furthermore, in addition to lack of motivation, uncertainty of selected study field, intentions to drop out, lack of prioritising skills, problems in self-regulation and insecurity regarding one's own skills characterise weak engagement in university studies among Finnish students (Törmä, Korhonen & Mäkinen 2012). These features are especially typical for those who proceed slowly in their studies (Haarala-Muhonen 2011).

It seems that the reality of student engagement is very different from the government's point of view and the students' point of view. These two realities often collide in the everyday practices of higher education institutions, which have to deal with the pressure coming from the government and wishes stemming from the students. In the next section, I will present two examples of how a higher education institution can try to enhance engagement of students in a student-centred way and at the same time try to meet the need of the government, too.

Student engagement at the meso level: 'ePortfolios and Goodies'

In Finnish HEIs various measures have been taken to tackle with the challenges of student engagement as presented in the previous sections. Many of these measures are 'soft' ways of promoting students' commitment to their studies. The measures can often be characterised as student-centred practices to support personal development as a student and as a future employee. The University of Jyväskylä, which is a multidisciplinary university of 15,000 students and 2,500 faculty and staff members, has created a concept of 'Student Life' (https://www.jyu.fi/studentlife/studentlife/en/), which aims to create optimal conditions for successful and engaged studies and overall wellbeing for students. The two corner pillars of the model are ePortfolios and the Goodie wellbeing advisers.

ePortfolios

At the University of Jyväskylä, ePortfolio is a tool designed for tracking learning and experiences, planning for personal development and making visible expertise and competencies. The ePortfolio provides students with the possibility of tracking their learning, planning their studies and presenting their learning process or resulting expertise in a multimodal, layered and creative way. From the perspective of guidance and counselling, the ePortfolio can be used for recognising students' skills and objectives, discussing their career goals and supporting them in their study plans. Sharing the portfolios provides opportunities also for peer learning and feedback. The ePortfolio is structured in a way that helps the individual learner align their current experience and skills, their development and their future goals, and make visible their development and learning. Furthermore, it makes it possible to link the experiences to learning and skills development, and to the evidence of that learning or skill (Figure 3.1).

The ePortfolio environment is a combination of a working portfolio, objectives, skills and competences as well as presentation portfolios. The working portfolio helps students to write down what kind of previous skills they have. It also encourages students to think about their extracurricular skills. The working portfolio works as a private environment, where students can add their work experiences, studies, hobbies, voluntary work and international experience, for example. ePortfolio enables students to build their own skill archive in which they can collect different kind of documents, texts and other electronic material. Most importantly ePortfolio is not only a tool where students can gather samples of their skills and demonstrate their previous experience, but students will also be able to plan and design their own studies in a way that is meaningful for the future. Therefore, ePortfolio provides an opportunity to think of one's professional aims and goals.

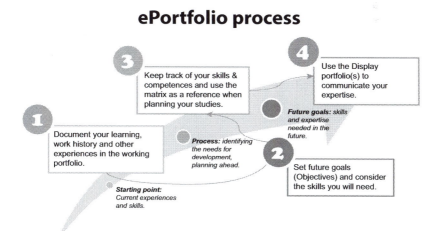

ePortfolio process

3. Keep track of your skills & competences and use the matrix as a reference when planning your studies.

4. Use the Display portfolio(s) to communicate your expertise.

Future goals: skills and expertise needed in the future.

1. Document your learning, work history and other experiences in the working portfolio.

Process: identifying the needs for development, planning ahead.

2. Set future goals (Objectives) and consider the skills you will need.

Starting point: Current experiences and skills.

FIGURE 3.1 ePortfolio process of the University of Jyväskylä
Source: www.jyu.fi/studentlife/en/eportfolio

When setting a new goal, students can use ePortfolio to define what kind of special skills are needed to achieve this goal. This helps to plan studies in a goal-oriented way. A crucial element in ePortfolio is that students are able to tell and recite the skills that they have. In the Presentation portfolio, students are able to practise how to express themselves in the form of shared texts, pictures, videos, blogs, audios etc.

Naturally, the ePortfolio has its challenges as it demands that students be able to reflect the development of their expertise in the course of the studies, to make this development explicit and to be very target-oriented in their studies. At its best an ePortfolio can help students to become consciously engaged with their studies and to compose a narrative which shows the development of student identity through time.

'Goodies'

The aims of the Goodie operating model are to ensure that students have easily accessible wellbeing counselling for every need and phase of their studies, to support students in taking care of their study ability and to overcome any difficulties, and to help students find motivation to study and meaningfulness in their studies. The Goodie wellbeing advisers are voluntary university staff members who have been selected and trained to support the wellbeing of students, but they are not therapists or psychologists. A student can come with any issue or problem and discussions are always kept confidential. Indeed, the whole idea of the Goodie operating model is student centredness in which the student is the one who approaches a Goodie when s/he needs advice on any student-related matter. Goodie advisers can help students find information on how to promote and enhance their own wellbeing, put them in touch with available peer support groups and share ideas regarding how to build their own support network.

The Goodie operating model is not only important from the point of view of enhancing student engagement. It also increases faculty members' and departments' understanding and awareness of those issues that might be problematic from the student's point of view and thus helps to react to any challenging issues as soon as possible. As is the case with ePortfolio, the Goodie model requires students to be active in seeking help.

These two models from the University of Jyväskylä show alternative ways of trying to engage students in their studies. Traditional ways, such as engagement surveys, are also used in some Finnish universities as complementary information. However, in the Finnish context typically students are invited to be engaged through student-centred ways. This kind of inclusive higher education is in line with the idea of intentionally offering incentives, opportunities and reinforcements for broadened student learning experiences (Sandeen 2004; Harper & Quaye, 2009).

Conclusion

In Finnish higher education, student engagement seems to have two layers or realities. First, at the level of representativeness, students are well engaged and students have strong voices in decision-making bodies and strategy development (macro level). Naturally, we can always pose critical questions like who the student representatives actually represent and is student engagement then seen as a form of activism and policy rather than development-oriented activity. Therefore, it is crucial to see beyond the 'official student agenda' in order to be able to see the big picture of student engagement. Secondly, at the level of everyday practices (micro level), students are less engaged and therefore HEIs (meso level) in collaboration with students have developed various initiatives to tackle these issues. There has been a tendency to move from external support systems (like a student's financial aid) to internal support models and structures of which the ePortofolio and Goodies wellbeing advisors are examples. Hence, when improving student engagement, individual students are not only to be seen as the customers of the university teaching or counselling services, but rather as active constructors of their own lives, careers and employment (Stuart, 2005; Sallinen, 2006). This indeed is a way to move forward and close the gap between the two, occasionally conflicting realities of student representativeness and actual student engagement in their studies.

Korhonen (2012) has presented a model of inclusive and student-centred higher education in which student engagement is seen to be constructed in the triangle of the meaning of the studies, learning identity and social practices of guidance, which in turn can create a sense of belongingness, artistry of academic learning and participation in various relevant communities during the studies (Figure 3.2).

The *sense of belongingness* is pivotal when considering engagement in studies and communities in education. Students may anticipate a range of objectives and outcomes for their studies, from personal growth to more practical and vocationally oriented objectives. When a student experiences the studies as meaningful through his/her objectives, the sense of belongingness will also be stronger. On one hand, the sense of belongingness is also very personal, but on the other hand, the community can also strengthen or weaken it socially with its own practices and expectations. *Proceeding participation* refers to the

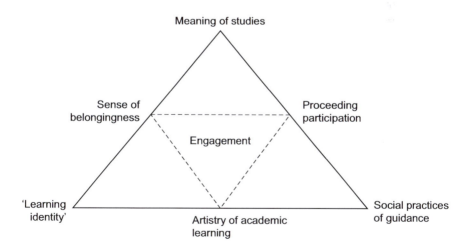

FIGURE 3.2 The elements of student engagement
Source: Korhonen 2012

'memberships' in various communities during students' studies, such as a student peer community. The dimensions of proceeding participation are constructed around a joint enterprise, a mutual engagement and a shared repertoire of those practices, knowledge and values. The studying process can be at its best a multi-membership in intersecting and simultaneous communities, where knowledge is shared and constructed, and where meaningful experiences can arise. In the worst case, when contacts and participation remain superficial, or they are totally missing, studying can be a lonely grind without meaningful engagement and memberships in any community of practice (Korhonen 2012).

The artistry of academic learning is connected to academic studying competence and how capable students perceive themselves to be in the higher education environment. Artistry in an academic learning setting is connected to the learner's self-conception, but also to those social, emotional and physical learning abilities that are needed for academic achievement and success in a higher education context. The barriers to student engagement may depend on a weak self-concept of 'learning identity' or relate to concrete deficiencies or difficulties in academic studying competence (Korhonen 2012).

Although there seem to be conflicting views, especially between government and students, on how engaged Finnish students are in their studies, higher education institutions have, nonetheless, implemented several novel and student-centred ways to get students to be more committed to their studies. How successful these initiatives will be remains to be seen as current globalised and occasionally turbulent higher education environments can pose new and unforeseen challenges, which may or may not underline already existing differences in views of student engagement.

References

Ammattikorkeakoululaki (351/2003). *Polytechnics Act (351/2003)*. FINLEX: The Finnish Ministry of Justice. Retrieved from www.finlex.fi/fi/laki/ajantasa/2003/20030351 (accessed 11 October 2018).

Chapman, A. & Pyvis, D. (2005). Identity and social practice in higher education. *International Journal of Educational Development*, 25(1), 39–52.

FINEEC. (2015). *Audit manual for the quality systems of higher education institutions 2015–2018*. Tampere: Finnish Education Evaluation Centre Publications.

Fredricks, J. A., Blumenfeld, P. & Paris, A. (2004). School engagement: potential of the concept, state of the evidence. *Review of Educational Research*, 74: 59–109.

Haarala-Muhonen, A. (2011). *Oikeustieteen ensimmäisen vuoden opiskelijoiden haasteet opiskelussa* [First year law students' challenges in studying]. Helsingin yliopisto: Käyttäytymistieteellisiä tutkimuksia 237.

Haggis, T. (2004). Meaning, identity and 'motivation': expanding what matters in understanding learning in higher education? *Studies in higher Education* 29(3), 335–352.

Harper, S. R. & Quaye, S. J. (2009). Beyond sameness, with engagement and outcomes for all: an introduction. In: S. R. Harper & S. J. Quaye (Eds.) *Student Engagement in Higher Education*. New York: Routledge, 1–16.

Hautamäki, J., Säkkinen, T., Tenhunen, M-L., Ursin, J., Vuorinen, J., Kamppi, P. & Knubb-Manninen, G. (2012). *Lukion tuottamat jatkokoulutusvalmiudet korkeakoulutuksen näkökulmasta* [Evaluation of the competencies for higher education of upper secondary school students]. Jyväskylä: Koulutuksen arviointineuvoston julkaisuja 59.

Kahu, E. R. (2013). Framing student engagement in higher education . *Studies in Higher Education* 38(5), 758–773.

Korhonen, V. (2007). Opiskelijoiden merkittävät oppimiskokemuksen opintopolun eri vaiheissa [Students'significant learning experiences in different phases of the study path]. In M. Lairio & M. Penttilä (Eds.) *Opiskelijalähtöinen ohjaus yliopistossa.* Jyväskylän yliopisto: Koulutuksen tutkimuslaitos, 129–146.

Korhonen, V. (2012). Towards inclusive higher education? Outlining a student-centered counselling framework for strengthening student engagement. In S. Stolz & P. Gonon (Eds.) *Challenges and Reforms in Vocational Education – Aspects of Inclusion and Exclusion.* Bern: Peter Lang, 297–320.

Kuh, G. D. (2009). What student affairs professionals need to know about student engagement. *Journal of College Student Development,* 50, 683–706.

Litmanen, T., Hirsto, L. & Lonka, K. (2010). Personal goals and academic achievement among theology students. *Studies in Higher Education,* 35(2), 195–208.

Lomas, L. & Ursin, J. (2009). Collegial or managerial? Academics' conceptions of quality in English and Finnish universities. *European Educational Research Journal* 8(3), 447–460.

OECD. (2009). *Education at Glance 2008.* Paris: OECD Publications.

OKM. (2010). Ei paikoillanne, vaan valmiit, hep! Koulutukseen siirtymistä ja tutkinnon suorittamista pohtineen työryhmän muistio. [Not ready but go! A memorandum of the group deliberating transiting to education and completing a degree] *Opetusministeriön työryhmämuistioita ja selvityksiä 2010:11.* Helsinki: Opetusministeriö.

Parker, P. D., Thoemmes, F., Duineveld, J. & Salmela-Aro, K. (2015). I wish I had (not) taken a gap-year? The psychological and attainment outcomes of different post-school pathways. *Developmental Psychology,* 51(3), 323–333.

Penttinen, L. & Falck, H. (2007). Mutkia opintopolulla: keskeyttämistä harkitsevien ohjaustarpeet ja haettu ohjaus. [Twists in study paths: needs for guidance and acquired guidance of those who considers dropping out] In M. Lairio & M. Penttilä (Eds.) *Opiskelijalähtöinen ohjaus yliopistossa.* Jyväskylän yliopisto: Koulutuksen tutkimuslaitos.

Sallinen, A. (2006). The role of the university in promoting HE guidance policy and practice. In: R.Vuorinen & S. Saukkonen (Eds.) *Guidance services in Higher Education.* University of Jyväskylä: Institute for Educational Research, 67–74.

Sandeen, A. (2004). Educating the whole student. the growing academic importance of student affairs. *Change,* May/June, 28–33.

Stuart, M. (2005). What price inclusion? Debates and discussions about learning and teaching to widen participation in higher education. In: G. Layer (Ed.) *Closing the equity gap. The impact of widening participation strategies in the UK and the USA.* Leicester: NIACE (the National Institute of Adult and Continuing Education), 155–182.

Törmä, S., Korhonen, V. & Mäkinen, M. (2012). Miten arvioida yliopisto-opiskelijoiden kiinnittymistä opintoihin? [How to assess university students' engagement with their studies] In V. Korhonen & M. Mäkinen (Eds.) *Opiskelijat korkeakoulutuksen näyttämöillä.* Tampereen yliopisto: Kasvatustieteiden yksikkö. Campus Conexus – projektin julkaisuja A:1, 163–191.

Universities Act (588/2009). FINLEX, The Ministry of Justice. Retrieved from www.finlex. fi/en/laki/kaannokset/2009/en20090558 (accessed 11 October 2018).

Ursin, J., Rautopuro, J. & Välimaa, J. (2011). Opiskelijoiden syrjäytymisriski korkeakoulupoliittisessa keskustelussa. [Students' risk of being excluded in higher education policy discussions] In M. Mäkinen, V. Korhonen, J. Annala, P. Kalli, P. Svärd & V-M. Värri (eds.) *Korkeajännityksiä – kohti osallisuutta luovaa korkeakoulutusta.* Tampere: Tampereen yliopistopaino, 19–35.

Uski, E. (1999). *Eksyneet lampaat. Selvitys Tampereen yliopiston opiskelijoiden opintojen pitkittymisestä.* [Lost sheeps. A study on the prolonged study times of the students of the University of Tampere] Tampereen yliopisto. Opinto –- ja kansainvälisten asiain osaston julkaisusarja. Tutkimuksia ja selvityksiä 40.

Välimaa, J. (2012). The corporatization of national universities in Finland. In B. Pusser, K. Kempner, S. Marginson, & I. Ordorika (Eds.), *Universities and the public sphere. Knowledge creation and state building in the era of globalization.* New York, NY: Routledge, pp. 101–120.

Zepke, N. and Leach, L. (2010). Beyond hard outcomes: 'soft' outcomes and engagement as student success. *Teaching in Higher Education,* 15, 661–673.

4

STUDENT ENGAGEMENT IN QUALITY IN UK HIGHER EDUCATION

More than assurance?

Stuart Brand and Luke Millard

BIRMINGHAM CITY UNIVERSITY

Introduction

The United Kingdom higher education sector comprises some 164 institutions and 2.28 million students of whom 1.75 million are undergraduates and 0.53 million postgraduates. Just fewer than 20% of these students are from outside the UK: 30% of the overseas students are from within the European Union (EU) and 70% from non-EU countries (Universities UK, 2016). The Higher Education Initial Participation Rate (HEIPR), an estimate of the likelihood of a young person participating in higher education by the age of 30, grew steadily from 42% in 2006–07 to 49% in 2011–12, but fell sharply in 2012–13 before recovering in the following years. In 2014–15 it had risen again to 48%. Indeed the figures for 2011–12 and 2012–13 can now be interpreted as a disturbance to the steady rise over nearly ten years. This disturbance was almost certainly associated with a tuition fee change in 2012 (Gov.uk, 2016).

In any discussion of student roles in quality assurance in the UK there are a number of issues to consider. The first of these relates to tuition fees. These were first introduced in 1998 with a maximum annual fee of £1,000. This was subsequently trebled to £3,000 in 2004 and again in 2012 to a maximum of £9,000. Associated with this rise in fees, manifested for many as the acquisition of student debt, has been a tendency to cast students as customers or consumers (Freeman, 2013). The challenge with this consumerist notion is that the role is relatively passive (McCulloch, 2009). Indeed it can be argued that those interested in a more constructive student role, that goes further than merely a customer survey approach, have had to recast the position of students into roles as partners and co-creators to engage them effectively in quality assurance and enhancement processes. This in turn is growing the potential role of students as influencers in quality processes.

There is, then, a backcloth of a growing debate over the last ten to fifteen years around the role of students in higher education and consequently their actual and potential contribution to quality processes is changing. As recently as nine years ago the Higher Education Academy (HEA), the principal professional development body for the UK sector, published an important paper that sought 'to support institutions in addressing an increasing external attention on quality enhancement' (Higher Education Academy, 2008). This publication, jointly produced with the Quality Assurance Agency (QAA) and the Higher Education Funding Council for England (Hefce), had a lot to say about quality assurance processes and kept a welcome focus on the need to shift focus to enhancement activity, yet interestingly there was relatively little to be found about students' roles in enhancement. There was reference to an emergent consumerist focus however and there was a single page on 'Student Involvement in QE'. This brief section in a sixty-page document made reference to student roles in audit and on programme approval panels. It also referred to: staff anxieties about student involvement; the traditional role of students being to provide feedback but not to participate as full members of panels; and to the difficulty of securing high quality student input to quality processes. Revisiting this article in preparation for writing this chapter has not left us surprised as we recall just how limited student involvement was ten years ago!

Here at Birmingham City University (BCU), when we started our own work on Student Academic Partners, we were seen as either eccentric or dangerously radical by a number of senior colleagues. It is, we suggest, no exaggeration to assert that there has been a profound change in the last ten years in sector-wide perception of student roles, not only in quality processes but also relating to their own learning. The journey is however not yet complete and in this chapter we will seek to suggest future developments as well as reporting on change thus far.

The macro level

In the UK the QAA, an organisation independent of government and providers of higher education, carries responsibility for 'Safeguarding standards and improving the quality of UK higher education'. As part of their description of role they are clear that they 'will continue to put students and the public interest at the centre of everything we do'. One of their major areas of work is the publication of UK Quality Code for Higher Education, which has three sections:

(A)   A – Setting and Maintaining Academic Standards
(B)   B – Assuring and Enhancing Academic Quality
(C)   C – Information about Higher Education Provision

There are a total of nineteen expectations in the three sections of the Quality Code and individual providers of higher education have to be able to demonstrate how they meet these expectations. It is clear that students are much more prominent in enhancement than was the case in 2008. Indeed one clear manifestation of this is the existence of a chapter (B5) in the Code, specifically focussed upon student engagement (QAA, 2017). It is worth viewing the overall expectation that underpins this chapter: 'Higher education providers take deliberate steps to engage all students, individually and collectively, as partners in the assurance and enhancement of their educational experience.'

Seven indicators of sound practice underpinned delivery against this expectation and provided a comprehensive document as to that which HE providers would be required to demonstrate. These included promoting the range of learning opportunities; maintaining an environment for staff-student discussion; effective student representation; effective training of students and staff to underpin quality assurance and enhancement; effective dissemination of evidence of enhancement; and a requirement to monitor and review the effectiveness of student engagement.

It is interesting to note, ten years later, that the QAA has been, during 2017–18, undertaking a review of the UK Quality Code for Higher Education with a view to streamlining the documentation. The consultation associated with this review identified 'Student Engagement' with the following themes:

- student engagement was supported as a key principle of UK HE
- expectations in relation to practice in student engagement must be fully articulated
- students as active partners, closely involved in quality assurance, were seen by many as fundamental to the Quality Code's principles
- collaborative student engagement was perceived as important for ensuring the UK-wide applicability of the Quality Code, given its importance in the Scottish and Welsh systems.

When published the UK Quality Code (2018) identifies as a requirement of universities, within its expectations for quality, that 'the provider actively engages students, individually and collectively, in the quality of their educational experience'.

This prominent role for student engagement in quality assurance is, we would contend, only part of the story of student involvement and the focus is now considerably about enhancement. An interesting, relatively early, example of this was the Student Learning and Teaching Network (Freeman and Wilding, 2009), which emerged from government-funded Centres for Excellence in Teaching and Learning (CETLs); for background on CETLs, see Trowler, Ashwin and Saunders (2013). A number of these well-resourced Centres developed the network to share good practice in student engagement in the enhancement work being pursued.

Over the ten-year period since 2008, there has been an explosion of activity that has been variously described as partnership working and/or student engagement. We will explore aspects of these developments later in this chapter but some useful context can be found in Ratcliffe and Dimmock (2013) and also Millard et al. (2013). These publications emerge from the University of Exeter and BCU respectively: two institutions who were among the earliest developers and adopters of these notions of partnership.

It should be noted that, in relation to individual institutional mission statements in the UK, student engagement or student centred learning now appears in virtually all of them; this signals the seriousness with which universities now take student perspectives. For some of course it may be lip service but the language is embedded and adopted across the sector.

Another key development in the way in which quality assurance is delivered in England is the formation of the Office for Students (OfS) from April 2018. This body fulfils a regulatory function and carries responsibility for: helping students get into and succeed in higher education; helping students stay informed; making sure students get a high-quality education that prepares them for the future; and protecting students' interests (Office for Students, 2018a). There is a student member of the Board at OfS and a twelve-strong Student Panel, chaired by a former President of the National Union of Students (NUS). The Student Panel has the following purpose:

> Meaningful student engagement is a top priority for the OfS and members of its panel. The student panel, established by the OfS, will ensure that students' views inform the OfS's decision-making processes. The student panel will therefore play a critical role in informing the OfS's strategy and activity, and in that way will help the OfS shape the higher education agenda for years to come.

A further significant development in quality assurance is the advent of the Teaching Excellence Framework (TEF), which has been developed through a government ministry, the Department for Education (Office for Students, 2018b). The TEF has been operated thus far at institutional level, but in 2017–18 there have been pilots of subject-level TEF assessments. The role for students in the TEF is in two principal ways.

Students are involved, as members of TEF Assessment Panels, in the decision making process as to which category of excellence a provider may be awarded: gold, silver or bronze. In addition, data from the wider student population contributes to the metrics used, alongside narrative statements, in determining outcomes. This data is obtained from the National Student Survey, which will be discussed in the next section of this chapter.

At a national level, a key way in which the student voice is heard is through the National Union of Students, which has over 600 affiliated institutional students' unions (National Union of Students, 2018). In recent years the National Union of Students has become significantly involved in student engagement work and partnership working. It houses The Student Engagement Partnership (TSEP, 2013) a formal group formed in 2013 which describes its aspirations thus:

> Student engagement is about empowering students to shape their own educational experience and creating excellent teaching and learning within a connected and cohesive higher education community. The Student

Engagement Partnership (TSEP) champions and develops student engagement practice in the English higher education sector.

Through our work, we provide expertise and insight, bringing together established and emerging knowledge and practice in order to equip student engagement professionals, practitioners and decision-makers across the sector with the knowledge and skills they need to make a success of student engagement in their context.

The changing regulatory landscape in the UK has seen the QAA, OfS and NUS coming together in a variety of guises to promote ideas and investigate practices as they determine areas of influence and priority in the evolving UK regulatory sector.

The meso level

Quality assurance processes within the United Kingdom higher education sector have for many years involved student representation at institutional and programme level. At institutional level it is usual to find one or more student representatives on the governing body and also on a range of senior-level committees, such as Senate/ Academic Board. This student representation would usually be delivered through the students' union and most often delivered through their elected officers. For many years the evidence of such involvement of students in decision-making has been a significant requirement of audits of quality assurance and was often seen as sufficient to tick the regulatory student engagement box.

The QAA, the body responsible for institutional audits and reviews, has used students as members of teams carrying out those events since 2009 when 45 students were recruited and trained. It currently has a pool of 82 such students for its review work.

At programme level staff-student committees, which exist with a variety of nomenclatures, have provided the formal mechanism whereby the student voice is heard. However, this formal representation has been fraught with challenges. Many institutions, and indeed their students' unions, would describe difficulty in securing the election of student representatives to serve on such committees and in securing their subsequent attendance at meetings. It is, we believe, also the case that some of these committees may operate in a kind of customer feedback mode with the almost unavoidable consequence that staff may take somewhat defensive approaches in meetings that are commonly dominated by the staff agenda. That of course is something of a 'worst case scenario' and it would be possible to find many examples of good practice in this area. However we would propose that there is a significant distance from the 'students as customers feedback approach' to one of true partnership working.

One feature of the 'student as customer' approach historically was that an adversarial relationship between students' unions and their institutions was often generated with perhaps more of a focus on negative feedback rather than development of solutions to problems. However the climate in these relationships has significantly shifted over the last ten years. One manifestation of a new collaborative approach was the instigation of a joint HEA-NUS Partnership Award from 2013. Interestingly the first two winners of this award were BCU (HEA, 2013) and the University of Exeter (HEA, 2014). In this way it can be seen that two of the early adopters of partnership working with students had developed approaches in collaboration with their students' unions. Further information concerning collaboration between the National Union of Students, the HEA and BCU can be found at Bols and Freeman (2011), who describe the journey from traditional methods of canvassing student opinion towards partnership working thus: Consultation – Involvement – Participation –Partnership.

The development of partnership working approaches is well documented in the literature and has often been led at institutional level. For example, at BCU, a three-layered approach was used: micro-level work using projects as a vehicle for enhancement that also sought culture change; at the meso level student engagement in curriculum design; and also at the macro level, institutional level arrangements to underpin student–staff partnership (Brand et al., 2013). A theme running through all three layers was the desire to generate a greater sense of 'belonging' in a learning community. We will return to the project based work in the micro-level section in this chapter.

At a meso level, in relation to curriculum redesign, we had learned important lessons from a 2008–10 major redesign initiative at BCU. External evaluation of that work led us to conclude that student involvement, although signalled as a priority, was largely tokenistic. Student aspirations for participation were relatively low and did not include any expectation of making real contributions to decision making. We therefore set out to require greater evidence gathering by programme teams from students before decisions were made and we used enhancement funding to promote mechanisms for this to be enacted (Bartholomew et al, 2010).

Secondly, in relation to institutional change we built much of our work on partnership activity with our students' union. Our motivation had been to change the culture of the University with greater emphasis on collaborative working and sense of learning community. D'Andrea and Gosling (2005) draw interesting comparisons in this context between whole institution approaches and the perhaps relatively isolated position of individual change agents.

A number of excellent initiatives in the UK make a powerful case for institutional change via partnership working. For example, the 'Student as Producer' initiative, which commenced at the University of Lincoln in 2010, was unusual in that it set out an approach that was institutionalised as a whole university strategy and subsequently from 2012 underpinned all aspects of the University's approach to quality assurance and, importantly, enhancement. A comprehensive discussion of its impact can be found at Neary (2013).

A further example can be found at HEA (2013). Here there is a description of 'Students as Partners Change Academy', an initiative led by the HEA bringing nine universities together to explore how they could further develop their partnership working. The Change Academy operated through a combination of plenary development sessions and the work of mentors who made two or three visits per institution during the academic year 2012–13. Additionally, other networks have been generated to foster discussion amongst practitioners. The RAISE network offers an excellent example of a collaborative institutional approach to enhancing engagement practices (RAISE, 2018).

We have in this section so far described a number of ways in which students are involved in quality assurance at both programme and institutional level in the UK higher education sector. However there is another key mechanism operating at both institutional and programme level: the collection data concerning firstly student satisfaction and secondly performance, through progression and retention data. In his insightful recent book on 'A University Education' the former Minister for Universities and Science from 2010 to 2014, David Willetts, discusses the National Student Survey, which operates across undergraduate provision (Willetts, 2017). This survey measures how satisfied students are with various aspects of their academic experience. The core questions fit under eight categories: The Teaching on my Course; Learning Opportunities; Assessment and Feedback; Academic Support; Organisation and Management; Learning Resources; Learning Community; Student Voice. Undergraduates undertake the survey in the spring of their final year. In 2017, over 300,000 students took part representing a response rate for those eligible of around 68 per cent (HEA, 2017). For UK universities this is a high stakes survey as results are published and contribute significantly to a variety of league tables for universities; for a summary see Which? (2018). This contrasts markedly with the National Survey of Student Engagement (NSSE) in the USA (see Felten, Chapter 5 in this publication) from which data are not publicly released. Another invaluable difference between NSS and NSSE is that NSSE actually asks students to reflect upon their own activities, in a way that the NSS does not. Indeed, it is interesting that the sections on Learning Community and Student Voice were only added to the NSS in 2017.

The micro level

As mentioned earlier in this chapter there has been an almost exponential growth in the student role in quality developments over the last ten years. Although much of that which has been discussed at institutional and sector levels refers to quality assurance, there has been an even fuller focus on enhancement work in recent times. A useful context to consider is the very influential 'What Works? Student Retention and Success' initiative, which reported in 2012 (Thomas, 2012). This sector-wide work, comprising seven projects across 22 universities, concluded: 'At the heart of successful retention and success is a strong sense of belonging in HE for all students'. A further key finding was that: 'Relationships between staff and students and peers promote and enable student engagement and success in HE.'

It can be argued that much of the work on student engagement has been aimed at quality enhancement through partnership working that greatly improves the students' sense of belonging and in turn generates a sense of learning community. There are multiple examples of good practice in the UK sector:

- Kay et al. (2012) explore the nature of the role of students as Change Agents at the University of Exeter.
- Millard et al. (2013), in their introduction to a book produced through partnership between staff and students at BCU, discuss how student engagement is a driver for both institutional and individual development.
- Freeman et al. (2014) consider the Student Academic Partners initiative at BCU offering principles as to how an institutional culture for such work might be achieved.
- Bovill (2013) provides an overview of work on students working with staff on co-creation of curricula; she also considers how Chickering and Gamson's seven principles for good practice in undergraduate teaching are demonstrated in such work.
- Carey (2013), at Liverpool John Moores University and also in the area of curriculum design, evaluates the engagement of students in the process and suggests that engagement needs to be a consistent feature of the student experience, rather than just associated with particular activities such as curriculum design.
- Martin and McKenna (2012) present an account of a 'Science Shop' at Queen's University Belfast through which student learning and community engagement are enhanced.
- Asghar (2016) reports on the lived experience of dialogue days at York St John University as a way of capturing the student voice with involvement of more interaction. The reflections of participants, both staff and students, identified not only the 'reduction of barriers that might normally exist in the classroom', but also for some 'an opportunity to get back to the broader focus of higher education'.

One field in which much development work in student engagement has taken place in recent years is that of peer education. Ody and Carey (2013) present an excellent overview of the various developments in this area at the University of Manchester, where recognised structures for peer support have been in place since 1995. A model of peer support is provided, together with six case studies. A particularly interesting case study is that relating to Peer Assisted Study Sessions (PASS), an approach adapted from the international Supplemental Instruction (SI) model. At the time of writing the authors referred to the existence of PASS in 29 disciplines and with around 750 student leaders. Evaluation of PASS work suggests not only an improvement in academic performance but also confidence building, deeper learning and community development. The peer support work at Manchester has also exerted wide influence around the sector. Interestingly, since 2002, peer support schemes have operated on an 'opt out' rather than 'opt in' basis, indicating the extent to which this activity has grown. Further discussion of peer learning as a vehicle for change at the University of Plymouth can be found at Hilsdon (2014).

The extent of this growth in peer support at Manchester raises another interesting question concerning student engagement at the micro level, namely the extent to which such developments involve the majority of students and staff or in contrast a minority of enthusiasts. There are challenges to face when adopting staff-student partnership approaches. Bovill et al. (2016) address these challenges in an analysis using case studies. They conclude with a discussion as to how benefits of co-creation merit trying to overcome the risks. Curran and Millard (2016) also discuss two important areas where challenge may be encountered: blurring of roles can be a source of ambiguity particularly where, as at BCU in the Student Academic Partners scheme, students have a role as an employee alongside their position as a student. This perhaps suggests a spectrum of student engagement that sees students as co-workers contributing to university life at a pedestrian level, through jobs on campus programmes, or engaging in challenging academic development initiatives at the higher end of the spectrum. The way in which students in such varied roles impact on the quality of the student experience throughout the university may be worthy of further investigation. Additionally, there is a need to demonstrate the value and impact of such partnership working in a sector in the UK that is bedevilled with the use of quantitative metrics to construct league tables of universities.

Conclusion

In this chapter we have seen how the role of students in the UK higher education sector quality assurance and enhancement has developed substantially over the last ten years. The focus has also shifted to be considerably about forward-looking enhancement rather than retrospective assurance alone. There has been considerable sharing of good practice across the UK sector and there is now a wealth of literature in this area, for examples see Bryson and Hardy (2012), Bryson (2014) and also the seminal HEA report (Healey et al, 2014).

References

Asghar, M. (2016). Staff and Student Experiences of Dialogue Days, a Student Engagement Activity. *Innovations in Education and Teaching International*, 53(4), 435–444.

Bartholomew, P., Brand, S. and Cassidy, D. (2010). Distributed Approaches to Promote Stakeholder Ownership of Postgraduate Programme Design. In Nygaard, C., Frick, L. and Courtney, N. (Eds.) *Learning and Teaching in Higher Education: Postgraduate Education – Form and Function* (pp. 59–76). Faringdon, UK: Libri Publishing.

Bols, A. and Freeman, R. (2011). Engaging Students in Shaping Their Curriculum. *Education Developments*, 12(2) 5–9. London: SEDA. Accessed at: www.seda.ac.uk/past-issues/12. 2 (accessed 7 May 2018).

Bovill, C. (2013). Students and Staff Co-creating Curricula: An Example of Good Practice in Higher Education? In Dunne, E. & Owen, D. (Eds.) *The Student Engagement Handbook: Practice in Higher Education* (pp. 461–476). Bingley, UK: Emerald Publishing Group.

Bovill, C., Cook-Sather, A., Felten, P., Millard, L. and Moore-Cherry, N. (2016). Addressing Potential Challenges in Co-creating Learning and Teaching: Overcoming Resistance, Navigating Institutional Norms and Ensuring Inclusivity in student–staff Partnerships. *Higher Education*, 71(2), 195–208. doi:10.1007/s10734-015-9896-4

Brand, S., Millard, L., Bartholomew, P. and Chapman, P. (2013). Students as Partners; A Three-Layered Approach for Enhancement In Dunne, E. & Owen, D. (Eds.) *The Student Engagement Handbook: Practice in Higher Education* (pp. 477–491). Bingley, UK: Emerald Publishing Group.

Bryson, C. (Ed.) (2014). *Understanding and Developing Student Engagement*. Abingdon, UK: Routledge.

Bryson, C. and Hardy, C. (2012). The Nature of Academic Engagement: What the Students Tell Us. InSolomonides, I., Reid, A. and Petocz, P. (Eds.) *Engaging with Learning in Higher Education* (pp. 25–45). Faringdon, UK: Libri Publishing.

Carey, P. (2013). Student as Co-Producer in a Marketised Higher Education System: A Case Study of Students' Experience of Participation in Curriculum Design. *Innovations in Education and Teaching International*, 50(3), 250–260.

Curran, R. and Millard, L. (2016). A Partnership Approach to Developing Student Capacity to Engage and Staff Capacity to be Engaging: Opportunities for Academic Developers. *International Journal for Academic Development*, 21(1), 67–68.

D'Andrea, V. and Gosling, D. (2005). *Improving Teaching and Learning in Higher Education: A Whole Institution Approach*. Milton Keynes: SRHE/Open University Press.

Freeman, R. (2013). Student Engagement in Practice: Ideologies and Power in Course Representation Systems. In Dunne, E. & Owen, D. (Eds.) *The Student Engagement Handbook: Practice in Higher Education* (pp. 145–161). Bingley, UK: Emerald Publishing Group.

Freeman, R. and Wilding, D. (2009). The Student Learning and Teaching Network: Bringing Together Students Engaged in Learning and Teaching. *Education Developments*, 10(3) 5–9. London: SEDA. Accessed at: www.seda.ac.uk/resources/files/publications_113_Educational%20Developments%2010.3%20v3%20(final).pdf (accessed 7 May 2018).

Freeman, R., Millard, L., Brand, S. and Chapman, P. (2014). Student Academic Partners: Student Employment for Collaborative Learning and Teaching Development. *Innovations in Education and Teaching International*, 51(3), 233–243.

Gov.uk (2016). *Participation Rates In Higher Education: Academic Years 2006/2007–2014/2015 (Provisional)*. Accessed at: www.gov.uk/government/uploads/system/uploads/attachment_data/file/552886/HEIPR_PUBLICATION_2014-15.pdf (accessed 7 May 2018).

HEA (2013). *HEA and NUS Joint Students' Union and Institution Partnership Awards 2013 – Winning Entry*. Birmingham City Students' Union and Birmingham City University. Accessed at: www.heacademy.ac.uk/system/files/downloads/winner_2013_birmingham_city_university.pdf (accessed 7 May 2018).

HEA (2014). *HEA and NUS Students' Union and Institution Partnership Award 2014*. University of Exeter: Strategies for Partnership. Accessed at: www.heacademy.ac.uk/system/files/downloads/winner_2014_university_of_exeter.pdf (accessed 7 May 2018).

HEA (2017). *National Student Survey 2017 Results Show High Levels of Student Satisfaction and Engagement*. Accessed at: www.hefce.ac.uk/news/newsarchive/2017/Name,115244,en.html (accessed 7 May 2018).

Healey, M., Flint, A. and Harrington, K. (2014). *Engagement Through Partnership: Students as Partners in Learning and Teaching in Higher Education*. York, UK: The Higher Education Academy.

Higher Education Academy (2008). *Quality Enhancement and Assurance – a changing picture?* York, UK: The Higher Education Academy.

Hilsdon, J. (2014). Peer Learning for Change in Higher Education. *Innovations in Education and Learning International*, 51(3), 244–254.

Kay, J., Owen, D. and Dunne, E. (2012). Students as Change Agents: Student Engagement with Quality Enhancement of Learning and Teaching. InSolomonides, I., Reid, A. and Petocz, P. (Eds.) *Engaging with Learning in Higher Education* (pp. 359–380). Faringdon, UK: Libri Publishing.

Martin, E. and McKenna, E. (2012) The Science Shop at Queen's University Belfast: Embedding Community Engagement in the Curriculum. In Mason O'Connor, K. and McEwen, L. (Eds.) *Developing Community Engagement*. London: SEDA.

McCulloch, A. (2009). The Student as Co-producer: Learning from Public Administration about the Student-University Relationship. *Studies in Higher Education*, 34, 171–183.

Millard, L., Bartholomew, P., Brand, S. and Nygaard, C. (2013). Why Student Engagement Matters. In Nygaard, C., Brand, S., Bartholomew, P. and Millard, L. (Eds.) *Student Engagement: Identity, Motivation and Community* (pp. 1–15). Faringdon, UK: Libri Publishing.

National Union of Students (2018). *Students' Unions*. Accessed at: www.nus.org.uk/en/students-unions/ (accessed 7 May 2018).

Neary, M. (2013). Student as Producer: Radicalising the Mainstream in Higher Education. In Dunne, E. & Owen, D. (Eds.) *The Student Engagement Handbook: Practice in Higher Education* (pp. 587–601). Bingley, UK: Emerald Publishing Group.

Ody, M. and Carey, W. (2013). Peer Education. In Dunne, E. & Owen, D. (Eds.) *The Student Engagement Handbook: Practice in Higher Education* (pp. 291–312). Bingley, UK: Emerald Publishing Group.

Office for Students (2018a). *Welcome to the Office for Students*. Accessed at: www.officeforstudents.org.uk (accessed 7 May 2018).

Office for Students (2018b). *What is the TEF?* Accessed at: www.officeforstudents.org.uk/advice-and-guidance/teaching/what-is-the-tef/ (accessed 7 May 2018).

QAA (2017). *Quality Code, Chapter B5: Student Engagement*. Accessed at: www.qaa.ac.uk/en/quality-code/the-existing-uk-quality-code/part-b-assuring-and-enhancing-academic-quality (accessed 7 May 2018).

RAISE (2018). *RAISE: Researching, Advancing and Inspiring Student Engagement. History*. Accessed at: www.raise-network.com/about/history/ (accessed 7 May 2018).

Ratcliffe, A. and Dimmock, A. (2013). What Does Student Engagement Mean to Students. In Dunne, E. & Owen, D. (Eds.) *The Student Engagement Handbook: Practice in Higher Education* (pp. 59–76). Bingley, UK: Emerald Publishing Group.

Thomas, L. (2012). *Building Student Engagement and Belonging in Higher Education at a Time of Change: Final Report from the What Works? Student Retention and Success Programme*. Accessed at: www.heacademy.ac.uk/system/files/what_works_final_report.pdf (accessed 7 May 2018).

Trowler, P., Ashwin, P. and Saunders, M. (2013). *The Role of HEFCE in Teaching and Learning Enhancement: A Review of Evaluative Evidence*. York, UK: The Higher Education Academy. Accessed at: www.heacademy.ac.uk/system/files/downloads/The_role_of_HEFCE_in_TL_Enhancement_final_report.pdf (accessed 7 May 2018).

TSEP (2013). *TSEP: What We Do*. Accessed at: http://tsep.org.uk/what-we-do/ (accessed 7 May 2018).

Universities UK (2016). *Higher Education in Numbers*. Accessed at: www.universitiesuk.ac.uk/facts-and-stats/Pages/higher-education-data.aspx (accessed 1 February 2017).

Which? (2018). *Choosing a Course. What Do University League Tables Really Tell You?* Accessed at: https://university.which.co.uk/advice/choosing-a-course/what-do-university-league-tables-really-tell-you (accessed 7 May 2018).

Willetts, D. (2017). *A University Education* (pp. 203–221). Oxford, UK: Oxford University Press.

5

STUDENT ENGAGEMENT IN THE UNITED STATES

From customers to partners?

Peter Felten

ELON UNIVERSITY

Introduction

Student engagement in U.S. higher education has focused primarily on the micro-level of teaching and learning. Many institutions employ high-impact practices and active learning pedagogies to engage students in the classroom and the curriculum, although inequities persist within the system. At the meso-level of quality assurance, U.S. students tend to be sources of data used by institutional decision-makers, but partnership approaches have begun to spread from the micro- to the meso-level to involve students in assessment processes. U.S. institutions rarely engage students seriously in macro-level strategic activities; this absence of student voices reinforces a broader student-as-customer ethos in American higher education. Within this environment, a partnership framework for student engagement offers the possibility of enhanced educational quality and equity for all undergraduates.

The U.S. higher education context

Higher education in the United States is both vast and decentralized. More than 20-million undergraduates enroll in some 4,700 colleges and universities each year. Compared to other higher education systems globally, the U.S. is distinct in at least four ways. First, U.S. higher education is characterized by a wide diversity in institutional types, ranging from small, private, liberal arts colleges and sprawling, public, research universities to work-oriented community colleges and entirely on-line, for-profit institutions. Second, these institutions operate with relatively limited supervision and control from governmental bodies, particularly the national government. Third, the majority of funding for U.S. higher education comes from private (not governmental) sources, and many institutions are highly dependent on tuition revenue from students. Finally, this diverse and decentralized system has produced intense competition among colleges and universities, including struggles to attract students, recruit faculty, raise funds, win sporting competitions, and rise to the top of various measures of rank and reputation (Bok, 2015).

This scale, complexity, and diversity has contributed to dynamic growth and change in the U.S. higher education sector and, more broadly, in the nation's economy (Goldin & Katz, 2008); however, these same factors contribute significantly to persistent struggles with inequities of access to and outcomes of higher education (Arum & Roksa, 2011). These weaknesses are being magnified by the financial, technological, demographic, and accountability pressures currently straining higher education. Some contemporary critics have called for an "unbundling" of U.S. higher education to allow students more flexibility than traditional curricula and institutions permit (e.g., Craig, 2015), yet research clearly demonstrates that "systematically underserved students fare worse in unstructured, do-it-yourself learning environments, and they succeed in environments with strong advising, mentorship, and clear pathways to their goals—all of which require continued guidance from faculty and staff" (Schneider, 2016, p. vi). In this context, questions of student engagement are central both to the present and to the future of higher education in the United States.

Student engagement in the U.S.

The concept of student engagement emerged from deep veins of research into undergraduate learning and experiences in the United States. Boiled down to its essence, as Kuh (2001) explains, student engagement involves two inter-related factors:

1.   What students do: The time and effort students spend on educationally purposeful activities.
2.   What institutions do: The environment institutions create that prompt students to spend time and effort on educationally purposeful activities.

This simple framework has guided a significant amount of reform in higher education over the past two decades, and it also has spawned an influential student survey used by many U.S. institutions (NSSE, the National Survey of Student Engagement) that will be addressed further in the "meso" section below.

One of the results of this focus on student engagement, and a byproduct of the NSSE survey, has been the identification of ten "high-impact educational practices" (often referred to as high-impact practices or simply HIPs) that research demonstrates yield particularly positive outcomes for students (Table 5.1).

Recently, other scholars have asserted – and Kuh has agreed – that reflective portfolios should be considered an eleventh HIP (Hubert, Pickavance, & Hyberger, 2015; Eynon & Gambino, 2016). Despite the diversity of these eleven practices, all of the HIPs share a common set of design principles:

TABLE 5.1 High-impact educational practices

First-year seminars and experiences	Learning communities
Common intellectual experiences	Writing-intensive courses
Collaborative assignments and projects	Undergraduate research
Service-learning/community-based learning	Diversity/global learning
Capstone courses and projects	Internships

Source: Kuh, 2008

> HIPs immerse students in authentic learning environments with relatively few cues and structures to guide them in deciding what and how they should transfer what they learned in the classroom into a new context. This dynamic uncertainty ... leads students to be thoughtful and creative about how they adapt and apply their existing knowledge. (Felten, 2017, p. 54)

Although the HIPs model has received considerable attention across U.S. higher education, the systematic adoption of high-impact practices is more of an aspiration than a reality for most institutions and students (Kuh & O'Donnell, 2013). Some colleges and universities have integrated HIPs into all undergraduate programs, requiring students to complete one or more of these experiences to be eligible to graduate (Felten et al., 2016). However, first-generation and low-income students tend to engage in HIPs at lower rates than their peers who have college-educated parents (Finley & McNair, 2013). Equity remains a central challenge to student engagement in U.S. higher education.

Micro: students as actors in high-impact practices and active learning pedagogies

Herbert Simon, one of the most influential American academics of the 20th century, succinctly described the micro-level of student engagement: "Learning results from what the student does and thinks and only from what the student does and thinks. The teacher can advance learning only by influencing what the student does to learn" (quoted in Ambrose et al., 2010, p. 1).

What precisely should the student *do* and *think* when they are engaged? My synthesis of the research is that to be fully engaged learners, students need to *do* five things:

- Time: Students need to spend time focused on educationally purposeful activities.
- Effort: Students need to put forth considerable effort in these activities, persisting through confusion and challenging themselves to move beyond their existing knowledge.

- Feedback: Students need to receive and respond constructively to feedback on their knowledge and performance so they can adjust their effort in ways that maximize their learning.
- Practice: Students need to practice applying and using what they are learning in different contexts so that they become fluent with their new knowledge and skills.
- Reflect: Students need to reflect on both what and how they have learned so that they can develop the metacognitive capacities that will allow them to learn even more deeply in the future.

As they act in these ways, to be fully engaged students also need to *think* three things:

- "I belong here": Students need to believe that they belong in higher education and within their discipline of study to learn effectively; students who lack a sense of belonging are likely to interpret normal academic struggles as evidence that they cannot be successful as undergraduates.
- "I can learn this": Students need to have a growth mindset in order to persist through the difficult stages of learning.
- "I find this meaningful": Students who value what they are learning are more motivated and persistent because they find meaning in their work, even when it is difficult.

Highly engaged students will experience these factors as mutually reinforcing; they willingly put in time and effort on academic work that they find meaningful, and they will deepen their sense of belonging as they respond to constructive feedback and practice what they are learning in diverse contexts. In short, engagement creates a virtuous cycle that fosters continued and deepened engagement.

To influence students towards this kind of engagement – towards thinking and doing in these ways – faculty and institutions in the United States have focused on three general approaches over the past decade: high-impact practices (HIPs), active learning pedagogies, and student-faculty partnerships.

Kuh's (2008) identification of ten high-impact practices sparked a groundswell of interest across U.S. higher education. Despite the widespread attention, many institutions have struggled to move HIPs from the margins to the center of the undergraduate student experience. An analysis of the 400,000-student California State University (CSU) system, for instance, noted that institutional focus on enrollment growth and additional degree production has meant that HIPs are available to most students but that few undergraduates actually engage in them. To expand access to high-quality HIPs, CSU has aimed to make HIPs both "visible, credit-bearing, and funded, so they count toward our degrees" (O'Donnell, 2013, p. 16) and also portable, so students who plan to transfer from a community college in California (where some 2.4-million students enroll each year) into a CSU institution will see HIPs as a viable path towards graduation. These efforts have gotten off to a promising start. CSU students report that the real-world and complex learning experienced in most HIPs prompt them to do and think in ways that enhance their learning and increase their motivation to complete an undergraduate degree (O'Donnell, 2013).

Research on active learning pedagogies, particularly in STEM (Science, Technology, Engineering, and Mathematics) classrooms, has produced an even more influential movement towards engaged learning in U.S. higher education over the past decade. Prominent scientists such as Nobel-winner Carl Wieman (2007) have challenged their faculty peers to adopt active learning pedagogies by asking: "Why not try a scientific approach to science education?" The scholarship that has emerged to answer that question has demonstrated that a variety of active learning interventions, from group problem-solving to peer instruction and two-stage exams, consistently produce better student performance and deepened student learning. Indeed, an influential meta-analysis that compared lecturing to active learning in undergraduate STEM classrooms concluded:

> If the experiments analyzed here had been conducted as randomized controlled trials of medical interventions, they may have been stopped for benefit – meaning that enrolling patients in the control condition might be discontinued because the treatment being tested was clearly more beneficial. (Freeman et al., 2014, p. 8413)

Although lecturing continues to be a common form of undergraduate instruction in STEM and other fields, a long-term pedagogical shift seems to be underway toward more active learning within courses across the disciplines. A widespread institutional commitment to faculty development and also to redesigning classrooms to foster engaging pedagogies is likely to ensure this trend takes root across U.S. higher education (Adams Becker et al., 2017).

Finally, a rapidly growing movement toward student-faculty partnerships aims to reconfigure traditional roles in undergraduate education, enabling deeper and more sustained engagement. Partnership has emerged recently as a new approach to engagement in many parts of the world (Matthews, 2016). In the U.S., student-faculty partnerships are "a collaborative, reciprocal process through which all participants have the opportunity to contribute equally, although not necessarily in the same ways, to curricular or pedagogical conceptualization, decision making, implementation, investigation, or analysis" (Cook-Sather, Bovill, & Felten, 2014, pp. 6–7). Within that broad framework, students and faculty work together on a variety of tasks that traditionally have been the exclusive domain of instructors, including assignment or course design, consulting about classroom practices, and inquiring into student learning (Bovill et al., 2016). Faculty typically initiate partnerships, but then they work side-by-side with their student partners toward common goals, paying particular attention to processes and practices that cultivate shared respect, reciprocity, and responsibility. A growing body of research documents the positive outcomes of partnerships for student – and faculty – engagement, metacognition, and learning (Mercer-Mapstone et al., 2017).

In all three of these approaches to student engagement – HIPs, active learning, and partnerships – an instructor or the institution assume responsibility for creating conditions that encourage students to act in educationally purposeful ways. Students are not able to remain passive witnesses to the educational process as they can in many traditional lecture settings; instead, students become active agents of their own and their peers' learning. These approaches have not yet become ubiquitous in U.S. higher education, and strong cross-winds are blowing that could divert institutions and students from their path towards deeper engagement. However, sustained movement towards more engagement for more students at the micro-level seems likely in the U.S. over the next several years.

Meso: from students as data sources to evaluation partners

In the U.S. most student involvement with quality assurance occurs in indirect ways as students respond to questionnaires about their experiences and perspectives. Perhaps the most influential example of this is the National Survey of Student Engagement (NSSE), a tool developed by Kuh and colleagues that is used regularly by many U.S. institutions and that has spun off a number of related surveys including one for faculty and another for pre-enrollment undergraduates. Data from NSSE are *not* publicly released so students and others are not able to easily compare engagement at different institutions; instead, individual institutions that participate in NSSE receive detailed results from their own students along with aggregated data from clusters of other institutions that illustrate how an institution's scores relate to comparison groups. Many administrators use these data for strategic planning, but students typically encounter NSSE results only when an institution has positive scores that are useful in marketing efforts. Indeed, scholars who have looked for relationships between NSSE data and popular forms of institutional ranking in the U.S. recently concluded that "educational quality, as indicated by engagement, seems to have little to do with institutional rank" (Zilvinskis & Rocconi, 2018, p. 266). In short, students provide data to NSSE and similar surveys that are used by institutions for improvement but that are rarely available to assist students in making informed decisions about their own educational choices.

To complement this type of indirect evidence of student engagement, U.S. institutions often also use student-generated academic work to evaluate progress toward institutional and departmental learning outcomes. As with NSSE and other surveys, students produce the data in this approach to quality assurance. Staff and faculty use rubrics or other tools to assess the quality of this student work, and then, ideally, those judgments inform decision-making about curricula, pedagogy, and institutional resource allocation (Rhodes, 2010). Unfortunately, many institutions have developed compliance-oriented practices and cultures around quality assurance, employing scientifically rigorous methods to generate results for external accreditors but not using the results of this process to improve student learning.

One large multi-institutional study, for instance, concluded: "It is incredibly difficult to translate assessment evidence into improvements in student learning" (Blaich & Wise, 2011, p. 11). Concerns about the lack of connection between data and decision-making have become so common that leading scholars now advocate re-thinking methodologies:

> Consequential validity posits that assessment must be valid for the purposes for which it is used, consistent with relevant professional standards, and – this is the key point here – that the *impacts or consequences of its use* should be factors in determining its validity. (Hutchings, Kinzie, & Kuh, 2015, p. 41, emphasis in original)

This attention to the uses and users of quality assurance has contributed to efforts to involve undergraduates more systematically in the collection and analysis of, and the institutional strategic actions based on, data about student engagement (Cain & Hutchings, 2015). The Wabash-Provost Scholars program at North Carolina A&T State University is an exemplary model of students-as-partners in quality assurance. For the past decade, each year a pair of faculty have trained a cohort of 15–20 undergraduates, who are paid to serve in this role, to dig deeply into the institution's assessment results. After they are trained, these Wabash-Provost Scholars analyze various kinds of student data, conduct focus groups with peers to probe more deeply into questions, and then write up and present their findings to diverse institutional groups, including student organizations, academic departments, and university trustees. The Wabash-Provost Scholars have contributed to institutional decisions about consequential curricular and policy issues, but the results of this program extend beyond quality assurance; as one Scholar explained:

> What has surprised me most about this program is how much of a role we play as a student. Although we were told on numerous occasions that this was our project and our research, I truly did not understand it until we were put directly in the midst of everything. From the forming of the questions, to conducting the focus groups, and even to the summarization of the data and final presentation (to the department), we truly were in charge of this research project … I believe that I can use the skills I learned to not only develop better relationships with others but also to apply those skills to other "real world" situations and settings in my career. (quoted in Cook-Sather, Bovill, & Felten, 2014, p. 78)

Engaging students as partners in quality assurance remains the exception to the rule in U.S. higher education. However, programs like the Wabash-Provost Scholars are beginning to spread because they are not only an effective way to critically and deeply evaluate student engagement, but they also are a means of cultivating further student engagement – both in the students who participate directly in quality assurance and among the broader community of students who see their peers as significant actors on campus.

Macro: students as customers

The United States does not have a significant tradition of direct student involvement in strategic decision-making at either the institutional or governmental levels (Bok, 2015). Some institutions have students who serve in roles on governing boards and on key institutional committees. Occasionally, this positions students to have a meaningful voice in university operations and management. More often, these roles are more-or-less tokens, filling a seat but not providing real guidance. A recent report by an influential higher education association illustrated this orientation when it recommended that institutional leaders:

> find ways outside the formal governance structure to incorporate the voices of all faculty, staff, and students in the campus discourse on issues of importance, to take those voices seriously, and to include those voices in ways that the stakeholders themselves find valuable. (AGB White Paper, 2017, p. 8)

In short, U.S. higher education rarely involves students directly in macro-level considerations, except as one of many stakeholders to be consulted by institutional leaders and policy-makers.

Unfortunately, these customs of student exclusion from macro-level decisions about engagement reinforce the all-too-common tendency to view students as customers. Because U.S. higher education institutions compete fiercely for students, many colleges and universities allocate substantial resources to marketing and branding (Guilbault, 2018). Admissions materials often feature glossy images of attractive students interacting in vaguely academic ways in architecturally appealing settings, with nary a reference to the effort and time necessary for engagement and learning. The misalignment between the advertised images of college life and the realities of academic work does little to encourage serious student engagement (Felten et al., 2016). The high cost of tuition at many U.S. institutions reinforces the perception that higher education is a transaction between a student customer and an institutional service provider.

Market-based competition rooted in image and price will only become more intense as U.S. higher education institutions struggle with demographic, economic, and technological changes on the horizon. Integrating students into macro-level decision-making could be one way to counter the many forces that position students as customers. Serious and sustained attention to student engagement, particularly the micro-level work of learning and teaching and the meso-level of educational quality, would help keep institutional leaders focused on the transformational – not merely the transactional – purposes of higher education. Engaging students as real partners in institutional governance would be a practical, and a symbolic, step towards deepening engagement for all undergraduates.

Conclusion

Over the past two decades, U.S. higher education has made significant strides towards more systematic student engagement, particularly through micro-level initiatives on high-impact practices and active learning pedagogies. This is a positive movement that clearly contributes to more students learning more deeply. Since high-impact practices and active learning have been demonstrated to have especially positive outcomes for students who have traditionally been underserved by American colleges and universities (Finley & McNair, 2013), there is reason to hope that these developments will ameliorate some of the inequities that have plagued U.S. higher education.

However, these same developments unintentionally could bolster the undergraduate-as-customer ethos that values student satisfaction and institutional revenue-generation more than either student learning or the civic mission of higher education. Indeed, many U.S. institutions now feature high-impact practices in their marketing materials, promising study abroad in exotic locales and internships with prestigious corporations. Similarly, active learning sometimes is portrayed as more fun than a traditional class, and technological "solutions" are sold to make learning available (and easy!) to students while working out at the gym or relaxing at home. These messages may attract students, but they also create false expectations about the undergraduate experience. If students expect to be treated like customers, they are not prepared to be challenged, to work hard, or to persist through difficulties.

Partnership offers a path out of this consumer-oriented engagement framework. When institutions and faculty engage with students as partners in learning, quality assurance, and decision-making, they create an environment characterized by dynamic reciprocity: "a process of balanced give-and-take not of commodities but rather of contributions: perspectives, insights, forms of participation" (Cook-Sather & Felten, 2017, p. 181). Reciprocal relationships do *not* require all involved to offer or to receive exactly the same things; instead, the exchange is rooted in the different knowledge, experiences, and perspectives that each brings to the relationship. Like student engagement, reciprocity is based in a notion of collective responsibility for education; what the student contributes matters just as much as what the institution does. Yet this is not simply an exchange of goods where the student pays the tuition and the university bestows a credential that certifies the student has been educated. Instead, students become partners in an educational process that is explicitly different from what they have experienced in earlier schooling. They are the primary actors of their own learning, working alongside faculty, staff, and peer partners who challenge them to engage and grow more deeply.

By embracing partnership, student engagement aligns with the broader purposes of higher education to transform students and develop communities. Without deliberate and sustained focus on these purposes, engagement can become a customer-oriented framework that aims for student satisfaction and economic efficiency. Partnership offers the possibility of re-orienting engagement towards preparing students – and their faculty and staff partners – to not only develop:

> a craft or skill or a way of being in the world that frees us to act with greater knowledge or power. But [also to] remind us of obligations we have to use our knowledge and power responsibly … exercising our freedom in such a way as to make a difference in the world for more than just ourselves. (Cronon, 1998, p. 79)

References

Adams Becker, S., Cummins, M., Davis, A., Freeman, A., Hall Giesinger, C., & Ananthanarayanan, V. (2017). *NMC Horizon Report: 2017 Higher Education Edition.* Austin, TX: The New Media Consortium.

AGB White Paper. (2017). *Shared Governance: Changing with the Times.* Washington, DC: Association of Governing Boards of Universities and Colleges

Ambrose, S., Bridges, M., DiPietro, M., Lovett, M., & Norman, M. (2010). *How Learning Works: Seven Research-Based Principles for Smart Teaching.* San Francisco, CA: Jossey-Bass.

Arum, R., & Roksa, J. (2011). *Academically Adrift: Limited Learning on College Campuses.* Chicago, IL: University of Chicago Press.

Blaich, C., & Wise, K. (2011). *From Gathering to Using Assessment Results: NILOA Occasional Paper #8.* Urbana, IL: University of Illinois.

Bok, D. (2015). *Higher Education in America.* Princeton, NJ: Princeton University Press.

Bovill, C., Cook-Sather, A., Felten, P., Millard, L., & Moore-Cherry, N. (2016). Addressing potential challenges in co-creating learning and teaching: Overcoming resistance, navigating institutional norms and ensuring inclusivity in student–staff partnerships. *Higher Education,* 71(2), 195–208.

Cain, T., & Hutchings, P. (2015). Faculty and students: Assessment at the intersection of teaching and learning. In *Using Evidence to Improve Higher Education,* by G. Kuh, S. Ikenberry, N. Jankowski, T. Cain, P. Ewell, P. Hutchings, & J. Kinzie. San Francisco: Jossey-Bass.

Cook-Sather, A., Bovill, C., & Felten, P. (2014). *Engaging Students as Partners in Learning and Teaching.* San Francisco: Jossey-Bass.

Cook-Sather, A., & Felten, P. (2017). Ethics of academic leadership: Guiding learning and teaching. In *Cosmopolitan Perspectives on Academic Leadership in Higher Education,* edited by F. Su & M. Wood. New York, NY: Bloomsbury.

Craig, R. (2015). *College Disrupted: The Great Unbundling of Higher Education.* New York, NY: St. Martin's.

Cronon, W. (1998). Only connect…: The goals of a liberal education. *American Scholar,* 67 (4), 73–80.

Eynon, B., & Gambino, L. (2016). *High-Impact ePortfolio Practice: A Catalyst for Student, Faculty, and Institutional Learning.* Sterling, VA: Stylus.

Felten, P. (2017). Writing high-impact practices: Developing proactive knowledge in complex contexts. In *Understanding Writing Transfer: Implications for Transformative Student Learning in Higher Education,* edited by J. Moore & R. Bass. Sterling, VA: Stylus.

Felten, P., Gardner, J., Schroeder, C., Lambert, L., & Barefoot, B. (2016). *The Undergraduate Experience: Focusing Institutions on What Matters Most.* San Francisco, CA: Jossey-Bass.

Finley, A., & McNair, T. (2013). *Assessing Underserved Students' Engagement in High-Impact Practices.* Washington, DC: Association for American Colleges and Universities.

Freeman, S., Eddy, S., McDonough, M., Smith, M., Okoroafor, N., Jordt, H., & Wenderoth, M. (2014). Active learning increases student performance in science, engineering, and mathematics. *Proceedings of the National Academy of Science of the United States of America*, 111 (23), 8410–8415.

Goldin, C., & Katz, L. (2008). *The Race Between Education and Technology.* Cambridge, MA: Harvard University Press.

Guilbault, M. (2018). Students as customers in higher education: The (controversial) debate needs to end. *Journal of Retailing and Consumer Services*, 40, 295–298.

Hubert, D., Pickavance, J., & Hyberger, A. (2015). Reflective e-portfolios: One HIP to rule them all? *Peer Review*, 17(4), 15–18.

Hutchings, P., Kinzie, J., & Kuh, G. (2015). Evidence of student learning: What counts and what matters for improvement. In *Using Evidence to Improve Higher Education*, by G. Kuh, S. Ikenberry, N. Jankowski, T. Cain, P. Ewell, P. Hutchings, & J. Kinzie. San Francisco: Jossey-Bass.

Kuh, G. (2001). Assessing what really matters to student learning. *Change*, 33(3), 10–17.

Kuh, G. (2008). *High-Impact Educational Practices: What They Are, Who Has Access to Them, and Why They Matter.* Washington, DC: Association for American Colleges and Universities.

Kuh, G., & O'Donnell, K. (2013). *Ensuring Quality and Taking High-Impact Practices to Scale.* Washington, DC: Association for American Colleges and Universities.

Matthews, K. (2016). Students as partners as the future of student engagement. *Student Engagement in Higher Education Journal*, 1(1), 1–5.

Mercer-Mapstone, L., Dvorakova, S., Matthews, K., Abbot, S., Cheng, B., Felten, P., Knorr, K., Marquis, E., Shammas, R., & Swaim, K. (2017). A systematic literature of students as partners in higher education. *International Journal for Students as Partners*, 1(1), 1–23.

O'Donnell, K. (2013). Bringing HIPs to scale: Turing good practice into lasting policy. In *Ensuring Quality and Taking High-Impact Practices to Scale*, by G. Kuh & K. O'Donnell. Washington, DC: Association for American Colleges and Universities.

Rhodes, T., ed. (2010). *Assessing Outcomes and Improving Achievement: Tips and Tools for Using Rubrics.* Washington, DC: Association of American Colleges and Universities.

Schneider, C. (2016). Foreword. In *Open and Integrative: Designing Liberal Education for the New Digital Ecosystem*, by R. Bass & B. Eynon. Washington, DC: Association of American Colleges and Universities.

Wieman, C. (2007). Why not try a scientific approach to science education? *Change*, 39(5), 9–15.

Zilvinskis, J., & Rocconi, L. (2018). Revising the relationship between institutional rank and student engagement. *The Review of Higher Education*, 41(2), 253–280.

6

OLD TECHNOLOGIES, NEW OPPORTUNITIES

Rethinking traditional approaches to student engagement in Australia

Ryan Naylor

LA TROBE UNIVERSITY

Introduction

The Australian higher education sector has changed dramatically over the last 25 years, and particularly over the last decade (Harvey et al. 2016; James et al. 2015; Kemp and Norton 2014). This has created unprecedented pressure on the system—in terms of academics' pastoral and educative interactions with students, in the nature of academic work and in university governance—but these changes have also created new opportunities to rethink how students engage with their institutions and their student experience—even in well-established technologies.

Twenty-five years ago, there were only 27 universities in Australia and 485,075 students, including 28,993 international students (Department of Education, Employment and Training (DEET) 1993). Following the Dawkins reforms of 1989–1990, colleges of adult education were reorganised and incorporated into the university system, with several undergoing mergers with existing universities or other colleges to create new universities (James et al. 2013; Naylor and James 2015). Further diversification and growth ensued—by 2015, Australia had around 130 non-university higher education providers, and the number of students had increased to 1,313,766, including 328,392 international students (Department of Education and Training 2015). This represents a 2.7-fold increase in the total number of students (much of it in the last decade due to the introduction of the so-called demand–driven system) and an 11-fold increase in the number of international students (due to the increasing international reputation of many Australian universities, and economic growth in Asia—Kemp and Norton 2014).

Australia has transitioned from an elite higher education system to a near–universal system, which has occurred against the emergence of neoliberalism as arguably the dominant model of university governance (Giroux 2002; Olssen and Peters 2005) and alongside considerable debate about the nature of academic work and the relationship between students, academics and universities (Bexley et al. 2011; James et al. 2015). Despite this, a student from 25 years ago would perhaps find few differences in the ways many institutions engage students in aspects of their education, such as feedback on teaching, governance and quality assurance. For many years and in many institutions, the stalwart technologies for allowing students to engage with academic business have been through two major mechanisms: student representatives on university committees and governance bodies, and feedback and evaluation surveys. This is not to say that some institutions are not developing novel and innovative mechanisms for involving students as co-creators of knowledge and in enhancing their educations (Bell 2016; Lizzio and Wilson 2009); however, these examples are too often piecemeal and reliant on 'champions' rather than being a part of everyday business.

This chapter will summarise the history and current practice of the two major methods of engaging students in quality assurance of education in Australia: the use of student representatives and student surveys to gather feedback. These methods are near-universally used to collect feedback at the micro, meso and macro levels (Healey et al. 2010), although (particularly in the case of surveying students), complexities in which level of feedback a particular instrument is meant to collect has created difficulties in the ways they are used. It will then argue that, nationally and internationally, universities must do more to interact with students on an individual level and allow them to shape their own curricular and co-curricular experiences as co-creators rather than subjects (or even objects) of university activities. While well-established technologies remain potentially powerful, we cannot operate a universal higher education system by simply stretching decades-old conceptualisations from the elite era further and further. New attitudes and understandings about the roles of students, academics and university leaders must be adopted instead.

Student representation in Australia

This section will examine student engagement with university quality assurance through student participation in formal and informal student representation. Australian universities have a long history of these types of student representation, which has been used to inform decisions at typically the meso and macro levels of Healey et al. (2010)'s framework. Given this long history, it is perhaps unsurprising that a diversity of forms of student engagement has arisen. These range from informal meetings with student volunteers to provide feedback on individual subjects or courses; to the invited presence of students (again, typically volunteers) on formal academic committees for the same purpose; to formal, legislated positions for salaried or volunteer representatives from formal student associations on major governance committees (Lizzio and Wilson 2009; Lodge 2005). Indeed, the founding statues of many universities recognise student associations in legislation, and formalise funding arrangements and inclusion in university governance (Rochford 2014). Legal understanding holds that these associations exist 'primarily to further the education purposes of the educational institution with which it is associated' (*Australian National University Union and Commissioner for ACT Revenue* [1997] in Rochford 2014) and to provide services, support and representation to students (*University of Queensland Act* 1998 (Qld), also in Rochford 2014).

Despite this long involvement and apparently clear legislative requirement for student participation in academic business, the role of students is still contested and contestable. The Tertiary Education Quality and Standards Agency (TEQSA), the federal agency responsible for monitoring university quality and compliance with the Australian qualifications standards, recognises the role of students and student associations in advocacy but does not require student participation in governance bodies such as the University Council and Academic Board (Rochford 2014). Indeed, TEQSA's audits of university governance systems have largely been silent on student engagement with these systems. In contrast to countries such as the UK (and particularly Scotland), TEQSA does not engage with students or student associations during re-accreditation of Australian higher education providers (Rochford 2014; Shah 2012).

The efficacy of student representation in influencing academic work is variable. Lizzio and Wilson (2009) report that the student representatives themselves perceive the overall effectiveness of their role as being dependent on the willingness and ability of academics and managers to listen to their input rather than simply providing 'lip service' or 'box ticking' consultation. Within academic hierarchies, students' views are sometimes marginalised, their legitimacy questioned (as superficial, immature, redundant, self-interested or adversarial) and staff input privileged (Little et al. 2009; Lizzio and Wilson 2009; Ratsoy and Bing 1999). Connor (1999) draws the distinction between input which is noted, as opposed to that which is valued. Clearly, this is not a simple dichotomy; a spectrum exists on which not valuing student input at all falls on one end, and authentic and systematic partnerships with students at every level sits at the other, with various degrees of 'noting' or 'valuing' consultations sitting between them. Although several Australian institutions have attempted to shift towards the partnership model in recent times, most areas in most Australian institutions remain towards the middle of the spectrum, despite the long history of student representation in Australia.

This insensitivity towards student representatives is unexpected given the emphasis modern higher education places on student centredness, sense of belonging and developing graduate attributes, all of which are positively affected by student representations (at least for the representatives themselves). Student representatives report more positive views of their university and peers, and representation increases their sense of engagement with the institution (Carey 2013; Lizzio et al. 2011). These are important concerns in the modern era of institutional reputation and national interest in retention rates and quality of student experiences.

Almost all Australian universities claim some form of citizenship as a graduate attribute—framing it, for example, as 'ethical and inclusive engagement with communities' (Oliver 2011). Oliver (2011) notes that measurement and quality assurance of this graduate attribute is uncommon, and calls for new, efficient and effective ways of developing and assuring the development of these skills. Given many graduates will go on to work in medium-to-large bureaucracies or have professional experience of committee decision making, it seems that student representatives offer an effective and authentic experience that could be used for quality assurance of their developing citizenship skills (albeit one where only a limited number of students are typically involved at any one time). Unlike in the US, service learning—which might otherwise have filled this gap—is relatively uncommon in Australia. As well as being valuable to universities, student representation and other forms of organised citizenship and participation could be valuable to students as learning experiences. That is, participation can serve universities at the meso and macro levels, while students benefit from the same process at the micro level (Healey et al. 2010). If this is to be the case, universities must make representation and participation a genuine teaching experience, by, for example, formalising the role through organising formal hand overs between representatives and written role descriptions in the same way that they do currently for staff (Lizzio and Wilson 2009). Setting aside the problem of institutional responsiveness to students' feedback, leaving students to figure out an informal role's expectations and how to manage the system's expectations places too much burden on them in a way that would be unthinkable in any other aspect of their interaction with university structures (Lizzio and Wilson 2009). Representation and participation offers a new opportunity for formal learning of skills that are otherwise difficult to embed and assess in curricula as well as an opportunity for institutional research and quality assurance; as a minimum professional standard, however, student representatives then require training for the role.

These findings underline the conclusions drawn in Tanaka (Chapter 11, this volume). In contrast to Japan, Australia has a long history of engagement with students through representative bodies at both the meso and macro levels. However, successful engagement is clearly not simply a matter of maturity. It requires a determined shift in perspective to see students as legitimate stakeholders and partners, rather than simply a source of data for academics and university bodies to paternalistically draw on to shape practice. As Rothenburg famously observed, privilege is often invisible to those who hold it (Rothenberg 2000), and most university structures are unquestionably structured to privilege academic positions and minimise or de-legitimise the perspectives of students, even when they are allowed 'inside the tent' as student representatives.

Student feedback surveys and quality assurance

Student feedback surveys (SFSs) were widespread in Australia by the 1980s, although the 1990s saw a rapid growth in the design and development of data collection instruments, and the last decade has seen an increased emphasis on quality assurance in their usage—led to in large part by government policy (Coates 2010; Darwin 2016; Shah et al. 2016). The now-ubiquitous surveys developed out of similar trends in the USA, and have remained influenced by American developments ever since (Darwin 2016). In Australia, SFSs have typically been used at the micro and meso levels of Healey et al.'s framework (2010). Indeed, using the same instruments to provide data at both levels has led to considerable tensions around SFS usage.

Academic development units originally led the development of SFSs to provide feedback on learning at the micro level, to enhance quality and retention at the level of individual subjects (Darwin 2016). The motive for use at this level was to encourage the use of effective, evidence-based pedagogies and high quality teaching practices. However, SFSs quickly became used in the institutional quality assurance of teachers, standards and curricula, and frequently linked to the promotion prospects of individual academics (Darwin 2016; Shah et al. 2016; Shah and Sid Nair 2012)—sometimes, in direct conflict with institutional policy stating how survey results should be used. Academic anxiety about the performance review aspects of SFSs appears to be widespread (Carey 2013; Darwin 2016; Hirschberg et al. 2015; James et al. 2015; Shah et al. 2016; Shah and Richardson 2016; Southwell 2012).

With the introduction of the Australasian Survey of Student Engagement (AUSSE) in 2007, which evolved into the University Experience Survey (UES) and then the Student Experience Survey in 2015, greater emphasis was placed on the quality assurance aspects of survey data. The AUSSE's introduction coincided with a federal review of the Australian higher education system (Bradley et al. 2008) and the transition to the so-called demand-driven system for university funding. The increased focus on access and participation for disadvantaged students in the demand-driven system and the Bradley review, and therefore an increased public and policy focus on engagement and retention, led to further entangling between SFS results, quality assurance and institutional profile (through websites such as the Quality Indicators for Learning and Teaching website (qilt.edu.au) and news articles naming the universities with the lowest-ranked student satisfaction). These in turn influenced university strategic priorities (Shah and Richardson 2016)—the macro level of Healey et al. (2010)'s framework—albeit typically at a relatively crude level of setting targets for average survey results and university rankings.

As with student representation, universities have shown themselves to be relatively unresponsive to feedback from students via surveys in terms of quality enhancement, although not in terms of the importance given to institutional rankings and scores. Shah et al. (2016) report that the collection, analysis and reporting of SFS data is systematic, but there has been only limited work done to use this data to inform improvements in pedagogy. Quality assurance audits performed by the federal Australian university regulator between 2009 and 2012 commended only 7 out of 43 institutions for their commitment to monitoring student feedback and then acting on it, and most students see limited or no improvements in their learning experience despite providing feedback (Kember et al. 2002; Shah et al. 2016). Although academics may be penalised for low SFS results, they are rarely rewarded for implementing improvements suggested or inspired by student feedback. This continues the pattern previously discussed of noting but not valuing student feedback. Again, although policy emphasises student centredness, practice more often focuses on managing the student body as a whole rather than responding to their experiences (Lizzio and Wilson 2009), particularly at an individual level.

Poor response rates are often cited as a reason for minimising the role of SFSs in academic work (Adams and Umbach 2012). Several researchers link poor response rates to a failure of students to see any effect arising from their feedback, which also leads students to vent frustration rather than provide constructive feedback (Coates 2010; Kember et al. 2002; Shah et al. 2016; Shah and Sid Nair 2012). Williams and Brennan (2003) warn that 'student cynicism may endanger the potentially very valuable functions that student feedback data can perform'. A positive feedback cycle is therefore potentially created, where unresponsiveness to student feedback breeds this cynicism, which creates further unresponsiveness and the de-legitimisation of student views discussed above.

Other undesirable behaviour and perverse outcomes can be driven by conceptualisations of students and other university stakeholders. If students are viewed as customers of the university (as through the lens of neoliberalism), then their satisfaction becomes important, which may create conflict with educational outcomes or quality of engagement and lead to poor pedagogy and undermine academic rigor (Carey 2013; Shah et al. 2016). Recent research has cast doubts on the relationship between satisfaction and conceptual understanding (Uttl et al. 2016), which suggests that the two are not equivalent, and that the difference should be kept in mind when interpreting and applying these constructs in quality assurance processes.

This is not to say that students should never be conceived of as customers or consumers. There are some services provided by universities where this may indeed by the appropriate role for students to assume. However, the traditional SFS model places students as sources of data, rather than agentive stakeholders in their own educational experience. There are clearly aspects of the student experience in which active input from students would be valid and productive, which would not lead to perverse outcomes sometimes associated with the current use of SFSs. Recasting this role will unquestionably require a redefinition of the academic role as well, and particularly the concept of academic autonomy (which has arguably been under threat for some time in any case—Shah and Sid Nair 2012).

Feedback surveys are sometimes seen as a low level of student engagement. Their often-managerial nature and potential for driving perverse incentives for individual academics has created resentment in the academy and driven institutional insensitivity to the feedback itself beyond the use (and perhaps misuse) of simple indicators. However, these are artefacts of usage, rather than inherent to the instruments themselves. Coates (2010) argues that participation in the AUSSE provides an intrinsic benefit to students to reflect on their studies and wider university experiences, and that this benefit is lost if they don't feel that their voices are heard. While it is questionable whether students genuinely do internalise their experience of completing the AUSSE or other SFSs as a reflective educational experience, there is no intrinsic reason why this should not be the case through subtle changes in the delivery or design of the instrument, or through how results are fed back to students (for example, through student dashboards). Similarly, the developmental aspect of SFSs for individual academics at the micro level is often undermined by the weight given to the results by quality assurance at the meso and macro levels, but academics who visibly 'close the loop' for students—where student feedback is valued and acted on—can harness a powerful tool for engaging students. This can provide a springboard for further participation, where students have input into solving the issues they have raised through student representatives on academic-led committees, student-led working groups, or opportunities to volunteer feedback on the feedback. As noted above, this will require a shift in how the academy views academic autonomy and the role of students as consumers or co-creators of their experience, but SFSs remain a powerful but largely under-used tool in this process.

Student engagement as more than quality assurance

It has been argued that conceptions of the roles students—and academics—play within university hierarchies and governance structures has profoundly affected the ways students have been permitted to take part in their educational experiences, and particularly in quality assurance and enhancement. These roles—first, as peripheral members of the academy, whose input is often ignored or de-legitimised compared to the privileged input of academics; and second, as members of a mass student body to be managed rather than as individual agents to be engaged—have blunted the impact of long-lasting, well-intentioned systems to harness student voices to improve the quality of teaching and university experience across the Australian higher education sector. With the exception of some areas in some institutions, genuine, responsive engagement with students seems elusive, despite the potential power and scope of even such 'old-fashioned' mechanisms as student representation and student feedback surveys.

The solution to these problems may not be simple to achieve. First, academics, university leaders and students must all be convinced that student engagement in governance and standards of education is genuinely valuable to themselves and their institutions, rather than a simply tokenistic effort. This debate in universities echoes similar conversations about public engagement in politics and public health, and even research funding (Andersson 2014; Holland et al. 2008; Miller 2014; Ocloo and Matthews 2016). It is clear than genuine engagement in any of these fields is not a simple process. It requires all stakeholders to be involved in and value the process, and a shift in the perceptions of their various roles, and perhaps even the purpose of universities.

Are academics, for example, gatekeepers for their disciplines and arbiters of academic standards? In which case, it makes sense that students are seen primarily or exclusively as a source of data—they have no legitimate claim to be able to be involved in assessing standards and have little stake in participating in extra-curricular quality assurance processes. It also makes sense here that academics see quality assurance processes as an unwelcome intrusion into their autonomy, and engage only superficially with them. The very positioning of students as the locus of action—*student* engagement in *university* business—highlights again the role of academic privilege in this discourse. Academics are identified with and made invisible within university governance or teaching structures, while students are othered. The shortfalls in genuinely engaging academics in conversations about quality assurance are often ignored in favour of the 'problem' of engaging students (Shah et al. 2016).

Alternatively, are universities places where communities of practice are developed through the participation of both core and peripheral members? In this conception, quality assurance is the responsibility of all members of the community; there is little practical distinction between students, academics and university leaders because all members contribute to the community and are benefitted by an enriched and robust community. Although recent moves towards consultation and engagement and changing theoretical understandings of university governance (including the work of this volume) suggest that this is an emerging or minority view, it is in fact closer to the legal understanding of students' 'status' membership of the university due to the nature of universities' founding legislation (Rochford 2014). It thus has a strong precedent as a legitimate conceptualisation of the student role.

Both conceptions here are intentionally limited to provide contrast. They are to some extent exaggerations of existing views, and neither begins to examine the co- and extra-curricular aspects of university life or even university outcomes beyond the purely academic (although it could be argued that making the distinction between curricular and co-curricular activities is a hallmark of the first model rather than the second). It is not argued that people adopt one or the other exclusively; it is possible to adopt and discard several competing conceptions of stakeholder roles depending on the situation. Shifting positions are part of the nature of complex organisations and agents' interactions within them—usually implicitly, and sometimes without the agent being aware of the change in position (Davies and Harré 1990; Harre and van Langenhove 1999). However, with the advent of open access education through massive open online courses (MOOCs), YouTube videos, Google books and other online repositories, academics no longer have monopoly power over disciplinary knowledge. While the forecast disruptive power of MOOCs has yet to materialise, universities must consider the value proposition they offer students in a world where access to vast amounts of declarative knowledge can be accessed with trivial ease. Higher education institutions are still able to operate a near-monopoly on access to particular skilled professions through awarding credentials, and it is clear that there is still value there—87% of Australian first-year students reported that improving their job prospects was an important reason for them enrolling in university, while 77% reported that they wanted to get training for a specific job (Baik et al. 2015). However, purely transactional understandings of the value of higher education seem to imply an impoverished understanding of what university life has to offer. In this case, being part of a community dedicated to learning and creating knowledge, in which one is an active partner, potentially offers a strong value proposition that retains a competitive edge for institutions while being consistent with their intellectual heritage and goals.

To examine this point, first-year students studying allied health and health science degrees in one Australian university were invited to participate in a study of factors contributing to student success. Two hundred and one participants, from entry-to-practice qualifications in vocational fields such as nursing, physiotherapy and dietetics, as well as more generalist degrees, such as a bachelor of health sciences or of exercise science, completed the online questionnaire. Students were asked to consider what having a successful experience at university would mean to them. They were then asked to rate the importance of the following factors in contributing to a successful experience (Naylor 2017):

- Sense of belonging (making friends, feeling part of a community) [*Belonging*]
- Having new opportunities or experiences (exchange, trying new things, broadening your horizons) [*Opportunity*]
- Developing your personal traits or 'soft skills' (e.g. leadership, integrity, ethics, entrepreneurism) [*Identity*]
- Developing connections (internships, meeting scholars or professionals) [*Connection*]
- Learning or discovering new things (intellectual engagement or interest) [*Discovery*]
- Achievement (getting good grades) [*Achievement*]
- Completion (passing subjects, completing your degree) [*Completion*]
- Flexibility (being able to accommodate your needs and other commitments, studying when it suits you) [*Flexibility*]
- Personalisation (being able to accommodate your interests, electives, choices on assessment, personalised LMS etc) [*Personalisation*]

A short title is given in square brackets for each factor after the question stem. These factors were based on a modification of the framework established in Coates, Kelly and Naylor (2016). The results are provided in Table 6.1.

It is clear that intellectual engagement remains an important part of the university experience for the vast majority of students. While the ultimate benchmark for success remains completing the qualification (Naylor et al. 2016), over three-quarters of students are motivated by getting good grades and intellectual engagement with their studies. As Kift and Field (2009) observed, motivation for intellectual engagement continues to unite students regardless of diversity in socio-demographic background. The increased diversity of a universal higher education system is potentially underlined by the importance given to flexibility, which allows students who may not be able to pursue 'traditional' face-to-face, full-time studies the ability to complete their qualification. This finding indicates that the

TABLE 6.1 Importance of different factors to having a successful university experience

Factor	% impor-tant/ very important	95% Confidence interval	Mean	SD
Completion	95.3	91.3–97.5	4.46	1.14
Achievement	81.8	75.7–86.6	4.03	1.18
Flexibility	75.5	69.3–80.8	3.98	1.14
Discovery	75.5	69.0–81.1	3.89	1.19
Personalisation	63.5	56.5–70.0	3.74	0.97
Belonging	61.5	54.4–68.1	3.50	1.29
Connection	58.3	51.3–65.1	3.49	1.20
Opportunity	52.6	45.6–59.5	3.39	1.16
Identity	51.6	44.5–58.5	3.33	1.14

trend towards blended learning is well founded; there is no way back to traditional modes of learning in a universal higher education system. The relatively low importance given to 'self-discovery' factors such as opportunity and identity may also represent the increased proportion of mature-aged students in the system, who may not see these factors as important as school leavers.

It also appears that there is an appetite for personalisation among a majority of students. Thus, while many students are motivated by a desire for intellectual engagement, they also want to be able to interact with curricula in ways that are personally meaningful to them. Many also seek to belong to the university community—a finding which is consistent with improved academic outcomes and student retention (Bennett et al. 2015; Gale 2012; Kift and Field 2009; Naylor et al. 2013; Naylor and James 2015). These findings present a powerful case for treating students as members of a community of practice alongside academics, rather than as a different 'kind' of stakeholder. There is clearly a desire in at least three-fifths of students to interact with disciplines in engaging, personally meaningful ways and to belong to a community. Even those students who did not rate the importance of belonging highly may be convinced by the impact of belonging on completion rates and academic achievement.

Those who resist reconceptualising universities as communities of practice as a mechanism for student engagement may still find value in these results. It remains important to understand what students expect from university if one wishes to provide a satisfactory experience (Appleton-Knapp and Krentler 2006). Traditionally, institutions have been limited by technological limitations—particularly processing time—in how they respond to stakeholder feedback, which has led to analysis being restricted to the level of particular groups (Coates et al. 2016). This is arguably the reason student representatives and surveys are so widely used, because they offer methods for managing feedback without requiring too much processing. Considerable work has been done to identify particular typologies of students based on their attitudes, behaviour or demographic factors (Astin 1993; Bahr 2011; Cheong and Ong 2014; Hackman and Tabor 1976; Hu et al. 2011; Kuh et al. 2000; Stage 1988; Zhao et al. 2003).

However, institutions now have the technology to respond to individuals as individuals, rather than anticipating the needs of blocks of students, despite increasing student numbers. For example, Figure 6.1 provides the survey responses for two individuals alongside the cohort averages. Although in both cases the average scores across all the categories were equal to the average across the cohort as a whole, making them relatively representative examples, they show substantial individual variation.

In both cases, completing is considered extremely important in university success, and both are about average in how they see the importance of intellectual engagement and flexibility. However, student 1 values a sense of belonging considerably more than the cohort average, while not being as interested in creating professional connections or undertaking internships. In contrast, student 2 is less interested in belonging or having new experiences while at university, and more focused on developing soft skills, undertaking internships and being able to personalise their studies.

Student satisfaction could be improved simply by having algorithms respond to particular triggers, to promote community events more strongly to student 1 and opportunities for 'resume building' to student 2. Indeed, the same events could be marketed in different ways to different individuals to improve uptake for particularly valuable events. In this case, there is clear value to both the institution and the student for engaging in university feedback processes. Beyond this trivial responsiveness, value in participating can be conveyed by making participation an educationally purposive task in itself. What does it mean to an individual student if they rate belonging more important than most of their peers, or that they were less satisfied with a particular subject? How should they go about their studies, or

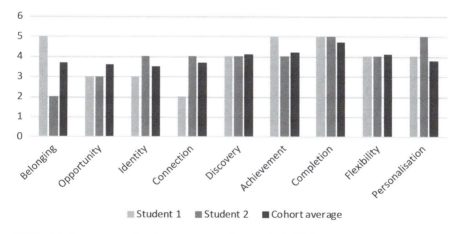

FIGURE 6.1 Factors contributing to success for two individuals

interpret messages from the university or academics in the light of this benchmark? How do their attitudes change over the course of their studies, and how does that reflect their changing understanding of their progress? Would that progress help them build a resume or portfolio to help them get a job after graduation? As Coates (2010) observed, self-reflection is important, and engagement in quality assurance mechanisms potentially offer an opportunity for students to reflect. However, these instruments currently offer no path to follow or scaffold for understanding how to contextualise this reflection. Providing meaning and value for students through their engagement with quality assurance or governance instruments can only improve participation, and therefore provide better data for institutions. Given the importance afforded to intellectual engagement in the survey results above, integrating quality assurance with the academic curriculum—particularly a personalised and individually relevant integration—seems an obvious opportunity to renew and reinvigorate well-established student engagement approaches such as student representation or feedback surveys.

Conclusion

Australia, in many ways, led the field in gathering data on the student voice through large-scale and longitudinal surveys of the student experience such as the AUSSE (now Student Experience Survey) or the First Year Experience survey (Baik et al. 2015; Coates 2010) and in pursuing programs to engage students in their studies and in university feedback and governance mechanisms (Kift and Field 2009; Rochford 2014). However, although student-based quality assurance instruments such as student representative and feedback surveys are relatively well established and widespread in Australian higher education, they are typically (although not universally) at what Kift et al. (2010) call a first-generation approach, where the mechanisms for encouraging student and academic engagement are piecemeal, poorly integrated with university business and offer few incentives to close the loop for academics or students. In both cases, only a small number of students are involved (sometimes despite considerable effort), despite benefits for all stakeholders in widening participation in these instruments.

Considerable difficulties remain around the perceived role of students in university governance and institutional responsiveness to student feedback. Partly, this may be because academics are not rewarded for acting on student feedback, while individual students rarely see the benefits of providing feedback when it is responded to, which has led to disenchantment with the process on both sides. The process may also have led to perverse outcomes and gaming the system in terms of balancing academic rigour and standards against pressure to avoid dissatisfied students providing negative feedback, reducing the benefits at the micro level and shifting emphasis at the macro level (Quinlan 2014).

There has been some focus recently, including in this volume, on new methods, processes and programs for engaging students in university governance, quality assurance and education. It is argued here, however, that traditional mechanisms for engagement are not necessarily inferior to newer approaches, and—because they are so well established and widespread, with strong historical datasets and institutional experience—they retain considerable power. What is needed is not new technologies, although modern analytics and processing power do offer the opportunity to engage and react responsively to students on an individual level. What is needed is a renegotiation of the role of students as legitimate partners and co-creators of their university experience. This necessarily involves some redefinition of academic privilege within university governance and their monopoly power as discipline experts (although critics of neoliberalism in universities may argue that the academic role is already being redefined).

There can be no doubt that universities are places for creating new knowledge, whether the corpus of disciplinary knowledge, through research; knowledge of a discipline, through teaching and learning; or knowledge of the self, through personal growth and development. Within the context of open access to online knowledge for much of the global population, universities must reconsider students as partners and members of an academic community of practice, rather than sources of data to paternalistically respond to. This implies that the feedback loop should be closed, so that students can see the value in providing feedback for them personally, as well as their institution, although this value may be in terms of personal development and opportunities to reflect on progress as well as direct impact in curriculum development. There is clearly an appetite for intellectual engagement, personalisation and community development in the majority of first-year students which can be powerfully harnessed for the benefit of all stakeholders. Fully integrating these processes into university life in educatively purposive and individually meaningful ways may well be key to making this transition to a community of practice-based method of student engagement.

References

Adams, M. J., and Umbach, P. D. (2012). 'Nonresponse and online student evaluations of teaching: understanding the influence of salience, fatigue, and academic environments.' *Research in Higher Education*, 53(5), 576–591.

Andersson, E. (2014). *Engagement in health: roles for the public and patients*, Switzerland: World Health Organisation.

Appleton-Knapp, S. L., and Krentler, K. A. (2006). 'Measuring student expectations and their effects on satisfaction: the importance of managing student expectations.' *Journal of Marketing Education*, 28(3), 254–264.

Astin, A. W. (1993). 'An empirical typology of college students.' *Journal of College Student Development*, 34(1), 36–46.

Bahr, P. R. (2011). 'A typology of students' use of the community college.' *New Directions for Institutional Research*, 2011(S1), 33–48.

Baik, C., Naylor, R., and Arkoudis, S. (2015). *The First Year Experience in Australian Universities: Finding from Two Decades, 1994–2014*, Melbourne: Centre for the Study of Higher Education.

Bell, A. (2016). 'Students as co-inquirers in Australian higher education: opportunities and challenges.' *Teaching & Learning Inquiry*, 4(2), 1–10.

Bennett, A., Naylor, R., Mellor, K., Brett, M., Gore, J., Harvey, A., Munn, B., James, R., Smith, M., and Whitty, G. (2015). *The Critical Interventions Framework Part 2: Equity Initiatives in Australian Higher Education: A Review of Evidence of Impact*, Newcastle: The University of Newcastle.

Bexley, E., James, R., and Arkoudis, S. (2011). *The Australian Academic Profession in Transition: Addressing the Challenge of Reconceptualising Academic Work and Regenerating the Academic Workforce*. Melbourne: Centre for the Study of Higher Education.

Bradley, D., Noonan, P., Nugent, H., and Scales, B. (2008). *Review of Australian Higher Education: Final Report*, Canberra: Department of Education, Employment and Workplace Relations.

Carey, P. (2013). 'Representation and student engagement in higher education: a reflection on the views and experiences of course representatives.' *Journal of Further and Higher Education*, 37(1), 71–88.

Cheong, K., and Ong, B. (2014). 'Pre-college profiles of first year students: a typology.' *Procedia-Social and Behavioral Sciences*, 123, 450–460.

Coates, H. (2010). 'Development of the Australasian survey of student engagement (AUSSE).' *Higher Education*, 60(1), 1–17.

Coates, H., Kelly, P., and Naylor, R. (2016). *New Perspectives on the Student Experience*, Melbourne: Melbourne Centre for the Study of Higher Education.

Connor, H. (1999). 'Collaboration or chaos: a consumer perspective.' *Australian and New Zealand Journal of Mental Health Nursing*, 8(3), 79–85.

Darwin, S. (2016). 'The emergence of contesting motives for student feedback-based evaluation in Australian higher education.' *Higher Education Research & Development*, 35(3), 419–432.

Davies, B., and Harré, R. (1990). 'Positioning: the discursive production of selves.' *Journal for the Theory of Social Behaviour*, 20(1), 43–63.

Department of Education and Training. (2015). *Review of Research Policy and Funding Arrangements*. Canberra: Department of Education and Training.

Department of Education Employment and Training. (1993). *National Report on Australia's Higher Education Sector*. Canberra: Department of Education Employment and Training.

Gale, T. (2012). 'Towards a southern theory of student equity in Australian higher education: enlarging the rationale for expansion.' *International Journal of Sociology of Education*, 1 (3), 238–262.

Giroux, H. (2002). 'Neoliberalism, corporate culture, and the promise of higher education: The university as a democratic public sphere.' *Harvard Educational Review*, 72(4), 425–464.

Hackman, J., and Tabor, T. (1976). 'Typologies of student success and nonsuccess based on the College Criteria Questionnaire (OIR 76R007).' Yale University, Office of Institutional Research.

Harre, S. R., and van Langenhove, L. (1999). *Positioning Theory: Moral Contexts of Intentional Action*, London: Blackwell.

Harvey, A., Bernheim, C., and Brett, M. (2016). *Student Equity in Australian Higher Education: Twenty-five Years of A Fair Chance for All*, New York: Springer.

Healey, M., O'Connor, K. M., and Broadfoot, P. (2010). 'Reflections on engaging students in the process and product of strategy development for learning, teaching, and assessment: an institutional case study.' *International Journal for Academic Development*, 15(1), 19–32.

Hirschberg, J., Lye, J. N., Davies, M., and Johnston, C. G. (2015). 'Measuring student experience: relationships between teaching quality instruments (TQI) and course experience questionnaire (CEQ).' Available at SSRN 2563326.

Holland, S., Renold, E., Ross, N., and Hillman, A. (2008). *Rights, 'Right On' or the Right Thing to Do? A Critical Exploration of Young People's Engagement in Participative Social Work Research*, Cardiff: Cardiff University.

Hu, S., Katherine, L., and Kuh, G. D. (2011). 'Student typologies in higher education.' *New Directions for Institutional Research*, 2011(S1), 5–15.

James, R., Baik, C., Millar, V., Naylor, R., Bexley, E., Kennedy, G., Krause, K., Hughes-Warrington, M., Sadler, D., and Booth, S. (2015). *Advancing the Quality and Status of Teaching in Australian Higher Education: Ideas for Enhanced Professional Recognition for Teaching and Teachers*, Sydney: Office of Learning and Teaching.

James, R., Karmel, T., and Bexley, E. (2013). 'Participation', in G. Croucher, (ed.), *The Dawkins Revolution 25 Years on*, Melbourne: Melbourne University Press, pp. 357–365.

Kember, D., Leung, D. Y., and Kwan, K. (2002). 'Does the use of student feedback questionnaires improve the overall quality of teaching?' *Assessment & Evaluation in Higher Education*, 27(5), 411–425.

Kemp, D., and Norton, A. (2014). *Review of the Demand Driven Funding System: Report*, Canberra: Commonwealth of Australia.

Kift, S., Nelson, K. J., and Clarke, J. A. (2010). 'Transition pedagogy: a third generation approach to FYE: a case study of policy and practice for the higher education sector.' *The International Journal of the First Year in Higher Education*, 1(1), 1–20.

Kift, S. M., and Field, R. M. (2009) 'Intentional first year curriculum design as a means of facilitating student engagement: some exemplars.' In 12th Pacific Rim First Year in Higher Education Conference. "Preparing for Tomorrow Today: The First Year Experience as Foundation." Conference Proceedings, 29 June–1 July, Townsville, Queensland.

Kuh, G. D., Hu, S., and Vesper, N. (2000). '"They shall be known by what they do": an activities-based typology of college students.' *Journal of College Student Development*, 41(2), 228–244.

Little, B., Locke, W., Scesa, A., and Williams, R. (2009). *Report to HEFCE on Student Engagement*, Bristol: HEFCE.

Lizzio, A., and Wilson, K. (2009). 'Student participation in university governance: the role conceptions and sense of efficacy of student representatives on departmental committees.' *Studies in Higher Education*, 34(1), 69–84.

Lizzio, A., Dempster, N., and Neumann, R. (2011). 'Pathways to formal and informal student leadership: the influence of peer and teacher–student relationships and level of school identification on students' motivations.' *International Journal of Leadership in Education*, 14(1), 85–102.

Lodge, C. (2005). 'From hearing voices to engaging in dialogue: problematising student participation in school improvement.' *Journal of Educational Change*, 6(2), 125–146.

Miller, G. (2014). 'Public engagement and the national enabling technologies strategy.' *Chain Reaction* (121), 46.

Naylor, R. (2017). 'First year student conceptions of success: what really matters?' *Student Success*, 8(2), 9–20.

Naylor, R., and James, R. (2015). 'Systemic equity challenges: an overview of the role of Australian universities in student equity and social inclusion', in M. Shah, A. Bennett, and E. Southgate (eds.), *Widening Higher Education Participation: A Global Perspective*, USA and UK: Chandos Publishing, pp. 1–13.

Naylor, R., Baik, C., and James, R. (2013). *Developing a Critical Interventions Framework for Advancing Equity in Australian Higher Education*, Melbourne: Centre for the Study of Higher Education.

Naylor, R., Coates, H., and Kelly, P. (2016). 'From equity to excellence: renovating Australia's national framework to create new forms of success', in A. Harvey, C. Bernheim, and M. Brett, (eds.), *Student Equity in Australian Higher Education: Twenty-five Years of A Fair Chance for All*, New York: Springer, pp. 257–274.

Ocloo, J., and Matthews, R. (2016). 'From tokenism to empowerment: progressing patient and public involvement in healthcare improvement.' *BMJ Quality & Safety*, doi:2015–004839.

Oliver, B. (2011). *Good Practice Report: Assuring Graduate Outcomes.* Sydney: Australian Learning and Teaching Council.

Olssen, M., and Peters, M. A. (2005). 'Neoliberalism, higher education and the knowledge economy: from the free market to knowledge capitalism.' *Journal of Education Policy*, 20(3), 313–345.

Quinlan, K. M. (2014). 'Leadership of teaching for student learning in higher education: what is needed?' *Higher Education Research & Development*, 33(1), 32–45.

Ratsoy, E. W., and Bing, Z. (1999). 'Student participation in university governance.' *The Canadian Journal of Higher Education*, 29(1), 1.

Rochford, F. (2014). 'Bringing them into the tent – student association and the neutered academy.' *Studies in Higher Education*, 39(3), 485–499.

Rothenberg, P. S. (2000). *Invisible Privilege: A Memoir about Race, Class, and Gender*, Lawrence, KS: University Press of Kansas.

Shah, M. (2012). 'Ten years of external quality audit in Australia: have audits improved quality assurance in universities.' *Assessment and Evaluation in Higher Education*, 37(6), 761–772.

Shah, M., and Richardson, J. T. (2016). 'Is the enhancement of student experience a strategic priority in Australian universities?' *Higher Education Research & Development*, 35(2), 352–364.

Shah, M., and Sid Nair, C. (2012). 'The changing nature of teaching and unit evaluations in Australian universities.' *Quality Assurance in Education*, 20(3), 274–288.

Shah, M., Cheng, M., and Fitzgerald, R. (2016). 'Closing the loop on student feedback: the case of Australian and Scottish universities.' *Higher Education*, 1–15.

Southwell, D. (2012). *Good Practice Report: Revitalising the Academic Workforce.* Sydney: Australian Learning and Teaching Council.

Stage, F. K. (1988). 'Student typologies and the study of college outcomes.' *Review of Higher Education*, 11(3), 247–257.

Uttl, B., White, C. A., and Gonzalez, D. W. (2016). 'Meta-analysis of faculty's teaching effectiveness: Student evaluation of teaching ratings and student learning are not related.' *Studies in Educational Evaluation*, 54, 22–42.

Williams, R., and Brennan, J. (2003). *Collecting and Using Student Feedback on Quality and Standards of Learning and Teaching in Higher Education.* Bristol: HEFCE.

Zhao, C., Gonyea, R., and Kuh, G. (2003) 'The psychographic typology: toward higher resolution research on college students.' Presented at Annual Forum of the Association for Institutional Research, Tampa, FL.

7

STUDENT ENGAGEMENT IN BRAZILIAN HIGHER EDUCATION AND ITS SOCIOPOLITICAL DIMENSION

Bernardo Sfredo Miorando

UNIVERSIDADE FEDERAL DO RIO GRANDE DO SUL

Introduction

In this chapter, I explore different phenomena that can be activated to speak about student engagement (SE) in Brazilian higher education to highlight the relation between SE and quality assurance (QA). The national context of Brazil—inserted in the Latin American regional context—produces a peculiar form of student life that is dissimilar to the Northern/Western transatlantic tradition, for which the concept of SE was initially coined. There are differences in both the materiality of life and the institutional superstructure, with its respective set of disciplines and theories used to interpret student phenomena. Presently, SE barely exists as a concept in Brazilian higher education studies. An unaddressed concept is an unproblematised phenomenon or something that is not politically framed as a question. To speak about SE is to name a problem to construct it. In fact, SE still has to be constructed in the Brazilian higher education lexicon. Other phenomena and theorisations—such as student representation and student activism—occupy connected discursive spaces and may be used to consider SE, apprehend it as a practice, and incorporate it as theory.

Approaching SE in international comparative work requires some specific cautions. There are limits to narrowing a concept in international work, as concepts are not equally available across national contexts. The focus on SE must be adapted according to the higher education traditions in which it is being deployed. This focus becomes especially important if one heeds Buckley's (2017, p. 729) consideration that 'there should be more explicit discussion[s] of the political implications of research into students' participation in decision-making' and that 'at a policy level, the current highly politicised nature of higher education means that clarity about the political implications of engagement research is crucial'.

Likewise, when paying close attention to the links between SE and QA, one must acknowledge that QA [*garantia da qualidade* or, less frequently, *asseguramento da qualidade,* in the Portuguese language spoken in Brazil] is not a commonly used term in Brazilian higher education discussions. This activity is usually comprehended within the umbrella notion of evaluation [*avaliação,* a word that can signify both evaluation and assessment] (Felix, Bertolin, Polidori, 2017). From a critical stance, one must also perceive the political character of quality as a negotiation of conflicting ideas and assurance as an exercise that involves differential powers. Thus, speaking about SE and QA requires recognising the sociopolitical dimension of learning processes.

I opt to approach SE and underscore its sociopolitical dimension; thus, I show how the social phenomenon of language points to a close association in the Brazilian usage of Portuguese language. If SE is not a stable term in the Brazilian higher education lexicon, 'engagement' [*engajamento*] is a politically loaded word that is more related to the context of social movements and labour unions than it is to the study of learning processes. One definition of the word *engajamento* found in a classic Brazilian dictionary illustrates this association:

> Condition of one who knows to be solidary with the social, historical and national circumstances in which one lives, and seeks, therefore, to be cognizant of the moral and social consequences of one's principles and attitudes (in opposition to the liberal-bourgeois individualistic attitude) (Buarque de Hollanda Ferreira, 1975)

As a critical scholar, I feel the need to address an important matter: I write from a specific position within the Brazilian field of higher education. Brazil has a very diversified educational system. I speak as one who works in a traditional public research university, Universidade Federal do Rio Grande do Sul (UFRGS). I do not suppose that my experience can operate as a metonymy for the system, but I understand that it carries some representativeness, as this flagship university is the paragon for higher education institutions (HEIs) in Brazil. In accordance with this book's proposal, I understand that 'the best way to improve the quality of university education is to activate dialogue with students'.

Brazil's higher education system

In 2016, eight million undergraduate students (Inep, 2017a) were enrolled in Brazilian higher education (HE) programmes, and more than 347,000 postgraduate students in Brazil were enrolled in master's, professional master's, and doctoral programmes (Capes, 2018). In Brazil's diversified system, public HEIs are but one part of the system. According to the most recent data available from the Higher Education Census of 2016 (Inep, 2017a), 75.3% of the undergraduate enrolment is in private institutions, which are not necessarily organised as universities. The dispute for hegemony between the public and private sectors is a long-lasting trait of Brazilian HE. The most recent calculation of the net enrolment rate in HE showed that only a small part of Brazilian youth could enjoy this level of education (i.e. 18.1%). Brazil's HE system is in transition from elite to mass (Caregnato et al., 2018), and it is clearly experiencing the tensions related to this change.

Many of these tensions are also related to inequalities which are constitutive in the Brazilian context: geographical disparity, uneven distribution of programmes among disciplines, and quality gaps. The richest regions of the country have a higher concentration of doctors and research funding, which translate to differentials in opportunities for SE in research and other knowledge-producing activities. The private sector, especially the for-profit HEIs, target their supply in more marketable, 'inexpensive' programmes in the applied social sciences, frequently offered at night with few or no activities for students other than traditional classes. Although quality as measured by the evaluation system indices cannot apprehend variations in students' experiences, even this simplified appraisal of HE reality shows that public universities offer better learning opportunities than for-profit faculties.

Brazil's HE system is quite young. Until the arrival of the Portuguese royal family in Brazil in 1808, HE was prohibited by Portuguese colonial rule. The first HEIs were founded in the 19th century. There have been attempts to establish universities since 1920, but the HEIs that opened soon closed and resumed their status as isolated facilities. An initial University Act was passed in 1931. The first university in continuous operation was established in 1934.[1] In the 1960s, during a brief democratic stint, intense debate was carried out by academic society about the need to democratise universities, as can be seen in the works of Álvaro Vieira Pinto (1962) and Ernani Maria Fiori (2014 [1962]). Students were important players in this process. However, the HE system would only be reorganised when the country was under dictatorial military rule and passed the University Reform of 1968 (Brasil, 1968). Since this reform, students can take part in the election of university rectors and elect representatives to the collegiate bodies of public universities. This representation, however, is designed to be minority, as professors should always make up at least 75% of every collegiate body, including the superior collegiate that chooses the rector and vice-rector. This legal disposition was renewed by decree in the 1990s (Brasil, 1996)—when democracy had been restored—and has not been questioned by rectors.

Brazilian HE has expanded continuously amid tensions between the Napoleonic and Humboldtian traditions (Sguissardi, 2006). Brazil is also influenced by the Latin American model of a university. This model incorporates values espoused by the Cordoba Reform—most noticeably, student activism and co-governance. As theorised by Ribeiro (1975, p. 111), it comprises, among other elements, 'student activism, as a reflex of the national conscience, nonconformist and critical of the social reality' and 'student co-governance, as a conquest of such activism, and as a force virtually able to act in the direction of [a] university's structural reform but paralyzed by the lack of a project of renewing action'.

Since the period of redemocratisation in Latin America in the late 1980s, this model has received renewed attention; it has also been reclaimed as a 'model of democratisation'. It considers university an institution tasked with political critique, aimed at transforming the social order through extension [*extensão*][2] activities and interaction with the social movements. This inspirational model has its basis in the national universities of Hispano-American countries, centred in a public, gratuitous, autonomous, and democratic institution that is co-governed by current students and graduates. It places as references the collective dimension and intellectual organicity (Leite & Morosini, 1992; Mollis, 2006; Morosini, 2006).

In terms of QA and evaluation systems, new legislation on these matters was developed in subsequent decades, assuming a central role in the governance of national HE. Further structuring of dispositions and characterising of Brazilian HE can be found in its undergraduate and postgraduate evaluation systems. Evaluation is a powerful steering force in Brazil, as it has regulatory character and determines if HEIs and programmes are accredited to operate. It also defines if programmes are eligible to receive public resources. Evaluation is one of the few mechanisms for gauging and enforcing attention to SE. However, the mode of operation is dichotomised between undergraduate and postgraduate education.

The National System of Higher Education Evaluation [Sistema Nacional de Educação Superior, or SINAES] accredits institutions and programmes. It was established in 2004, and it incorporates contradictions regarding how the QA debate took place in Brazil; the context is a dispute for public education during the rise of neoliberalism. SINAES is operated by the National Institute for Educational Research and Studies Anísio Teixeira [Instituto Nacional de Estudos e Pesquisas Educacionais Anísio Teixeira, or Inep], an autarchy linked to the Ministry of Education. The system gives 10 dimensions for evaluation, among which are 'planning and evaluation', including institutional self-evaluation, and 'policies for student support' (Brasil, 2004, art. 3). Among the tools used for QA by SINAES, two are distinctive features for the consideration of SE: the National Examination of Student Performance [Exame Nacional de Desempenho do Estudante, or Enade] and the Institutional Evaluation Commissions [Comissões Próprias de Avaliação, or CPAs].

Enade is a test given to students in their last year of undergraduate studies. It has two components: the first group of questions assesses generic skills and the second one assesses knowledge pertaining to the programme's specific professional area. Alongside Enade, a student questionnaire is used to survey students about the conditions in which they pursued their education. Responses to some of these questions are the only available data nationwide that may be used to gauge SE.

CPAs are collegiate bodies tasked with organising the institution's internal evaluation processes and gathering, systematising, and accounting for the information requested by Inep to proceed with external evaluations. By law, CPAs must ensure the participation of all segments of the university community; further, they must not have a composition that favours the absolute majority of any segment, and they must be autonomous in relation to other HEI collegiate bodies. The law is based on the intention that evaluation will be a democratising force in HE.

As of 2018, the evaluation of postgraduate education is under reform. Former laws—now suspended but not yet replaced (Brasil, 2018)—were established in 1998. The National System of Postgraduate Education [Sistema Nacional de Pós-Graduação, or SNPG] is managed by the Coordination for the Enhancement of Higher Education Personnel [Comissão de Aperfeiçoamento de Pessoal de Nível

Superior, or Capes], an autarchy linked to the Ministry of Education. Through eva-luations, funding is assigned to postgraduate programmes. The system now under revision reserved no space for student participation. Only one of its indicators could to lead to any insight on SE: the participation of students in research projects. Evaluation has steered postgraduate education towards fabricating publication-producing researchers. No concern has been shown towards the human formative process beyond that, eschewing any attention to the development of ethical, political, socio-affective, cultural-aesthetic, or physical dimensions—that is, for the well-being of stu-dents or the promotion of a good and fair existence. Legally, some student repre-sentation is required, such as in the commissions that distribute grants (Brasil, 2010), but that does not mean students hold any sway over institutional policy.

Student engagement (SE) in Brazil

As stated previously, in Brazil, SE as an object of knowledge cannot be constructed without considering the related phenomena of student activism and student representa-tion. Student organisations in Brazil usually follow a pattern that builds upon student representation in programme administration to form a national collective organisation. Thus, at the undergraduate level, students usually organise through academic directories [*diretórios acadêmicos*, or *DAs*] that make political action possible within the scope of pro-grammes or academic units (i.e. faculties, colleges, schools, institutes within HEIs). In parallel, a students' central directory [*diretório central dos estudantes*, or *DCE*] responds for the articulation of representation in HEIs' collegiate bodies and for the organisation of extracurricular activities. There is, finally, a national undergraduate student union [União Nacional dos Estudantes, or UNE]. At the postgraduate level, there is usually no orga-nisation in local academic directories, and representation is exerted directly in the units' committees. A postgraduate students' association [*associação de pós-graduandos*, or *APG*] may be present at major research universities, interacting with a national association [*associação nacional dos pós-graduandos*, or *ANPG*].

   At each level, elections are held to choose student representatives. I believe that involvement in these political activities is an important dimension of SE and that par-ticipation in HEIs' elections is a possible indicator to be studied in future research on the issue. Furthermore, this structure of political organisation and representation is reflected within evaluation mechanisms. In this section, I follow Tanaka's (Chapter 1 in this book) review and characterise SE as it operates across the three interconnected levels proposed by Healey, Mason-O'Connor, and Broadfoot (2010), also considering the experiences I have witnessed at my institution (UFRGS).

Micro-level engagement: students' engagement in their own learning and that of other students

In Brazil, SE at the micro level may be adopted as a key variable for studies regarding university pedagogy, considering the pedagogical gaps that hamper learning in HE. The precariousness of Brazilian secondary education leads students to HE without the necessary preparation to follow advanced classes. Better trained students have access to elite universities. At the same time, there is a persistent indefiniteness to institutional policies of university pedagogy to better adapt teaching to non-traditional students. As a result, although new and diverse audiences have entered HEIs, straining their dynamics, traditional teaching methods have not changed significantly.

Students develop coping mechanisms to deal with such deficits, such as organising *study cells*. There is a long-lasting tradition in Brazilian universities of students gathering in small groups to read and discuss theoretical literature they deem politically interesting. This practice is especially noticeable in relation to Marxian theory, but it has grown in scope to approach formulations which are identified with 'new social movements', such as feminism and black critiques. Furthermore, students may organise lectures and 'public classes'—speeches in the public spaces of universities to discuss candent issues associated with contemporary politics. Aside from the public approach, students also organise subaltern 'counterpublics' (Fraser, 1990) as support spaces. With advances in information and communication technologies, it has become increasingly popular to set up groups on instant messaging apps to debate class matters. Moreover, students who are subjects of affirmative action (black and indigenous people and people with disabilities), as well as students considered political minorities (e.g. women and members of the LGBT community), have promoted meetings to debate their situations within the university. Such constellations of actors may call themselves 'collectives' and follow logic that is only partially akin to that exercised by traditional and 'new' social movements (Gohn, 2016).

A number of innovations that were introduced for Brazilian HE flourished between 2004 and 2014 (Leite et al., 2016). These include the expansion and creation of apprenticeship grants [*bolsas de iniciação*] that support the engagement of students in extracurricular activities. They induct students in activities of teaching, research, extension, technological development, and institutional internships. According to the HEI, there may be special programmes that support the learning of international students and students who enter a university because of affirmative action criteria. Major research universities, such as UFRGS, organise an annual event for students to reveal the results of their work. There are specific expositions for each activity. As of 2018, a new modality is to be included in which students will present their experiences with institutional evaluations.

There is, however, an acute interference of the sociopolitical context in the possibilities represented by such opportunities. Student assistance and scientific training are in crisis: because of a decrease in the public budget, the current Brazilian government has fixed public expenditures at their nadir for the next 20 years. Even traditional student assistance resources, such as subsidised meals, are under constraint. It is impossible to live on undergraduate grants. In return for 20 hours of work per week, students receive a monthly stipend of 400 reais (approximately 110 US dollars). Moreover, among the graduating students who took part in the 2016 edition of Enade, only 23.2% had received any kind of apprenticeship grant during their studies (Inep, 2017b). Graduate students may compete for research grants ranging from 1,500–2,200 reais (412–605 US dollars), which makes for a challenging livelihood. Many students have to work during their HE studies to support themselves and their families, thus compromising their possibilities for SE. Among the students surveyed by Enade 2016, 21% worked 40 hours/week or more, and 22.6% worked variable hours (Inep, 2017b). Thus, we point out that to discuss SE, especially in an international comparative perspective, one must consider the political and domestic economies of student life.

The latest data available from Enade's Student Questionnaire further illustrate this reality. There were 195,448 respondents in 2016 (Inep, 2017b); from the 68 questions they answered, a small sample may be used to express some dimensions of SE (Table 7.1).

A certain scenario poses dilemmas for both students and teachers: almost half (45.6%) of the students surveyed indicated that they did not dedicate enough time outside of class to studying. How can teaching be enhanced when students devote such little time to extra-class study? Is meaningful SE limited to students who can rely on grant apprenticeships? From the case of UFRGS, a traditional and elite public research university, students in HEIs seem to have a more favourable position. They do not have to pay for tuition and have more chances of finding opportunities for on-campus apprenticeships. By attending a traditional, elite university, they have more chances of conquering internships in the extra-academic environment and networking with more influential actors within society. But this kind of elite HEI does not represent the totality of Brazilian higher education. Also drawing on data from Enade's Student Questionnaire, Table 7.2 shows how Brazilian students perceive some opportunities of engagement to be enabled in their HEIs.

Among the selected questions, the one with the least favourable results was the one dealing with students' political engagement in institutional life, which leads us to the next levels of SE. Students perceived this dimension as not being favoured by HEIs; they also appeared to be less informed about it.

TABLE 7.1 Undergraduate students' study hours per week

Study hours per week, excluding in-class hours	% of answers
None	2.8
1–3	42.8
4–7	29.8
8–12	12.9
More than 12	11.6

Source: Inep (2017b)

TABLE 7.2. Micro level student engagement according to Enade

Questions	% of answers							
	1	2	3	4	5	6	7	8
Academic activities inside and outside the classroom allowed for reflexivity, conviviality and respect to diversity.	1.0	1.6	3.0	8.0	18.5	66.3	0.8	0.7
The program offered conditions for students to participate in events in the institution or in other institutions.	2.5	3.3	4.7	10.1	18.1	59.3	1.0	1.0
The students were offered opportunities to take part in extension programs, projects, or activities.	3.5	3.4	4.7	9.9	17.1	58.5	1.4	1.5
The students were offered opportunities to take part in scientific apprenticeship project and activities that fostered academic research.	4.2	3.9	5.3	10.1	16.8	56.7	1.5	1.6
The institution provided culture, leisure and social interaction activities.	4.8	4.7	5.9	11.1	17.0	53.0	1.8	1.7
The institution offered opportunities for students to act as representatives in collegiate bodies.	5.7	4.5	5.9	11.6	16.6	46.4	2.8	6.5

Source: Selected items from Enade 2016 (Inep, 2017b)

Note: Scale: 1 to 6 from I fully disagree, to I fully agree. Answer 7 means 'I do not know' and answer 8, 'Not applicable'.

Meso-level engagement: students' engagement in QA and enhancement processes

The meso level of SE in Brazil can be explored by resorting to yet another analytical device: the idea of social fields of action (Bleiklie and Kogan, 2006). According to this view, HE can be seen from the angles of academic work, educational institutions, and national policy. Making use of these delimitations, one can approach the categories of political action that are involved in SE in QA and quality enhancement (QE).

In the social field of action pertaining to academic work, students are informants in surveys about the quality of the courses they attend—a procedure required by SINAES. However, as part of their civil liberties, students cannot be compelled to answer questionnaires. Participation rates fluctuate. For instance, in 2017, UFRGS obtained answers from 51% of the undergraduate students and 30% of the postgraduate students (UFRGS, 2018). By engaging with these tools, students provide quantitative and qualitative information that can be used for QE by teachers, programmes, and departments. The question is, 'Is it'? There is resistance from many players to incorporate evaluation data in HE planning, and much of this resistance is because such data comes from student critiques. Consequently, HEIs do not always treat internal QA with proper respect.

In this field of social action, the institution's evaluation activity may become perfunctory. The hard work of compiling and analysing institutional data may not be appropriated by top managers. In such cases, CPAs would play a ritualistic role, with the token participation of students. Thus, even if students have *de jure* places to occupy in the institutional structure, they are not always present in them. Students often suspect that the time and effort they put into evaluations will not be properly considered. Nonetheless, this situation does not dismiss the potential for student action in CPAs. Student representatives may voice their concerns and make propositions just like any other member of the CPA. At UFRGS's CPA, student representatives have been instrumental in reforming internal evaluation instruments. For instance, they have made respect for sociocultural diversity a topic for assessment in undergraduate work, and they drafted a questionnaire that would later be implemented to evaluate postgraduate education.

As mentioned, the system reserves places for students in policy discussions but not in policy or decision making. Although undergraduate evaluation by SINAES at least offers students a space to voice their approval, discontent, or suggestions regarding their programmes, it gives them no say about the system itself. Postgraduate evaluation by Capes supposes no participation by students in QA or QE. Unlike other countries, in Brazil, there is no recognition that students may act as peer evaluators in visiting accrediting committees by SINAES or evaluating teams working with Capes by knowledge area.

Macro-level engagement: students' engagement in strategy development

At the macro level, students may engage in strategic university planning by acting in collegiate bodies as student representatives. In the case of UFRGS, these collegiate bodies include the University Council; the Council for Teaching, Research and Extension; and the chambers of Undergraduate Studies, Postgraduate Studies, Research, and Extension for the university as a whole and also in the corresponding instances within each academic unit or faculty.

Nevertheless, because of federal rulings, students in this capacity will always be in the political minority, continually needing to form coalitions to defend their propositions. They will most often contest decisions that harm their categories and enforce accountability matters. In more positive terms, they will strive for student rights and push for an agenda that broadens the space of participation and enforces student assistance.

In strategy development, SE may depend on other sociopolitical variables that need to be explored through the lenses of political science and sociology. Particularly in a 'cordial' (Buarque de Hollanda, 1995) society such as Brazil, students' possibilities for negotiating influence in strategy development may rest on the ability to network their personal influence through individual ties of trust and dependence. Alternatively or concomitantly, students may draw on their ability to form coalitions between class fractions inside the university polity. Either way, the political climate of grassroots organisations in Brazil has been calling for greater organicity, and 'collective' and 'horizontality' have become leitmotifs in social movements (the student movement included). This development, of course, shocks the vertical logic of organisation in a hierarchic institution, such as a university.

If regularly enrolled, a student can vote in a rector election. The totality of student votes in the last election at UFRGS, however, was limited to a weight of 15%, because of a decision by the University Council, which, by law, must be dominated by professors. The fact that rectors are elected in Brazilian universities adds another opportunity to engage students in strategy development, as they can be co-authors of administrative plans. This ideal, however, seldom occurs. For instance, students have not been included in the steering committee for the Institutional Development Plan [Plano de Desenvolvimento Institucional, or PDI]. Of course, things may play out differently at the diverse levels of institutional governance, and some academic units, such as faculties, may seek greater engagement from students in their planning efforts.

At the macro level, there is a layer of political complexity that must accompany the analysis. Thus, SE is a complex phenomenon and more so in very complex and unequal societies such as Brazil. Student activism and student representation become conflated with students' involvement in partisan politics. Students running for representation are often affiliated with political parties and may be as interested in promoting their agenda in HEIs as they are in promoting SE. Students are not a homogeneous political totality and may have different views on the role of HE in society. This tension is stressed especially as a country lives through the fierce opposition between left-wing and right-wing political ideologies. It is inevitable, therefore, to question the possibilities of SE at a macro level within the limits of representation (an interrogation that further crosses the theories of democracy).

The challenging 'other' face of SE

As can be seen, both the social context and institutional structure have—at best—an ambiguous effect on SE in Brazil. The combination of the authoritarian tradition of Brazilian academia with a Latin American tradition of student activism makes up for a difficult balance that periodically breaks at its seams when difficult issues are faced. In these times, a different type of SE arises beyond the delimited spaces of student representation: a broad-range political activism, linked to the 'wicked problems' of inequality/unfairness. As the political structure of the public university is inefficient in ensuring students a place and a voice to express their demands to the administration, students' political pressure creates other channels for expressing discontent. One such channel has been the occupation of university buildings by students. This sort of political pressure was resorted to during the years of military dictatorship and later revived in the 2010s.

At UFRGS, some briefer experiences of this kind took place as students demanded space in the Faculty of Education, denounced corruption in the Faculty of Law, and required a proper ruling regarding affirmative action. However, in 2016, many units of the university were occupied by students, and the same happened in other HEIs—to the point that the majority of federal universities were seized by students. This situation was prompted by the national conjuncture, and the movement united students who were not usually involved in student representation or other forms of institutional engagement.

The year 2015 marked an inflexion in the growth of public investments that had taken place for a decade. In 2016, after a *coup d'état*, the national government initiated a reform of upper secondary education (by decree) and proposed a constitutional amendment to freeze public expenditures—including educational investments—for 20 years. At the same time, conservative politicians presented 'gag laws', which were legislative propositions to censor what teachers could say in class. This combination of regressive attacks on social rights to education magnified student discontent. Public HEIs, like UFRGS, publicised reports on how academic activity would be harmed by austerity policies (UFRGS, 2016). Large demonstrations were held in major Brazilian cities and repressed by the police. When the national chamber of representatives moved to vote on the constitutional amendment, HE students rallied in assemblies to promote the occupation of universities—the only public space with which they were familiar—in protest.

All over the country, the experience of occupation put people who would not otherwise talk to each other in contact with one another. In occupied buildings, students developed organisational routines to preserve the security and integrity of the facilities. They hosted a variety of debates, workshops, and public classes. In the specific case of UFRGS, from the worries about university life, a new form of academic solidarity emerged—one between students and outsourced workers. Outsourced workers engage in support services, occupying the most subaltern position in academic organisations, having no direct legal rapport with the university and having no voice in its political processes. Students reached out to them and invited them to organise in unions. In practice, they forced a temporary merger between the traditional public space of universities and the place of its subaltern counterpublics.

The occupation movement eventually waned after the constitutional amendment passed, but it left as a legacy a testimony to the pedagogical power of student political organisation. It is important to underscore the kind of civic engagement associated with occupying a university in Brazil. The infrastructure was poor, making it difficult for students to sleep, shower, or cook on universities' premises. Insecurity was also a factor during the occupation, as police repression and the menace of attacks by right-wing militias were constant. Occupying students were also subject to bullying by classmates, prosecution by university authorities, and even penal suits. In occupations, students claimed protagonism and took SE beyond HE; to engage with a university was to contest the very social order and political framing in which academic work takes place. They did so by endangering their own physical well-being.

From activism to partnership to effect change

Although an orthodox approach could discard these experiences of student activism from the repertoire of phenomena represented by SE, I would argue otherwise. I have tried to show that in societies like Brazil, the sociopolitical context plays a forceful conditioning role in students' opportunities to engage with HE. I further argue that these sociopolitical experiences are an important part of learning in HE. As the Brazilian Constitution recalls, one of the aims of education is to prepare individuals to exert their citizenship (Brasil, 1988, art. 205).

Thus, one of the contributions from the Brazilian context to studies on SE is to emphasise that SE demands not only knowledge about sociopolitical conditions that conform to HE; it also requires further learning about the development of dispositions to engage with sociopolitical structures. This exercise is deeply pedagogical, since it deals with conscientisation (Freire, 1970) and the development of political subjectivities (Genro, 2011)—that is, they are about social consciousness and political learning (Leite, 1990; 1992).

Education deals with emergence, with the dialectics of tradition and innovation. In Latin America, students have traditionally been innovative actors in the political scene. If one takes a more distant perspective, one can see this link between SE and political activity as a radical constitutive feature of HE. Since its medieval roots, the university has been linked to the notion of youth that conflicts with the status quo and reclaims new relations between society and state, giving way to emergent actors/agents (Suárez Zozaya, 2017).

As the literature shows, it is difficult to frame what fits into the category of SE. Likewise, it is difficult to frame a movement for the occupation of universities. I suggest this approximation. Occupants wove new collaborative ties with each other and made allies for institutional policy based on a shared belief in radical democracy—one that was always promised but never experienced in the nation or in HEIs. Since 1988, Brazil struggled to come to terms with its history and lay the foundations for democratic citizenship. Educators are, collectively, a paramount piece of this struggle, and they succeeded in instilling Brazilian law with some republican and democratic dispositions, trying to progressively universalise primary and secondary education and expand tertiary education. However, these efforts took place in the context of an authoritarian and colonial society wherein cultural development was muffled for decades by repressive regimes.

As a result, in Brazil, students are not expected to be agents, but rather actors. Of course, not all of them conform to this role. Student agency in Brazilian society—more so after 2016—refers to a 'competent rebel' (Santos, 2017) engaging in a struggle against an oppressive order. Hence, students organise in collectives (Gohn, 2016) that may coalesce around identities (black, indigenous, women, LGBT), classes (unions, representation), and other political issues (housing, health).

Considering the representation presented in Chapter 1 of this book, it is my understanding that the Brazilian system of HE—through institutional practices and state policies—positions students somewhere between the vertices of disciples (at the micro level) and clients (at the meso level). Furthermore, there is ambiguity regarding what is intended and projected for students in strategic development (macro level). At this level, the role reserved for students as stakeholders is undefined. There is hardly any space or say reserved for them at all, though this matter is open to dispute. Whereas students are hardly invited by HEIs and professors to be partners in strategy decisions, when matters become pressing, they may force their way into determinations and occupy.

Again, the Brazilian case involves reading SE against a backdrop in which students wage a constant struggle for recognition in the face of a lack of recognition by HEI authorities. Change in HE is also mobilised by the innovation imparted by the renewed tradition of SE in politics. This dimension of action bolsters the stasis towards the vertex of partners through the exercise of citizenship, which, in turn, demands the construction of the 'collective self' of students as a class identity or *lato sensu* party—in Gramscian terms—inside HE polity. After all, there is not a consolidated position of students as an organised and homogeneous totality; students differ greatly in attitudes (Ribeiro, 1975; Leite, 1990). What can happen—and in many cases, does happen—is that students coalesce to form a collective agent with a provisional consensus involving proposals related to different levels of SE and fields of social action. In these cases, through assertive and anticipatory action, their agency sets up students as partners in HEI politics.

In the microcosm of UFRGS's Postgraduate Program in Education, student agency was not directly fostered by the administration; rather, it emerged from grassroots work. In this programme, research grant recipients are required to attend at least two monthly administrative meetings. One is a meeting of the programme council, in which students have one vote per five professors' votes, regardless of the number of students. The other is a self-organised meeting in which students share information and deliberate on how to respond to the Steering Commission's demands. This venue has also been used to choose postgraduate student representatives required by university law to serve in the collegiate bodies of the Faculty of Education.

Over time, student collectivism has gained more organicity and a more protagonistic character. Since 2017, student representatives have organised as the Collective of Student Representation [Coletivo de Representação Discente],[3] drawing inspiration from experiences during the occupation of 2016. The Coletivo has presented student demands to the programme Steering Commission, dealing with all three levels of SE mentioned by Healey, Mason-O'Connor, and Broadfoot (2010). At the micro level, students have proposed and organised courses and seminars, trying to build momentum for curricular reform that enhances their training as both researchers and teachers. At the meso level, they have engaged in evaluative discussions, questioning the way national evaluations are appropriated by the programme and taking part in activities of the UFRGS CPA's associated unit in the Faculty of Education. At the macro level, they have called for sounder pedagogical and administrative programme planning, proposing axes for debate. Overall, attention has been paid to specific segments, such as international students and students who are subject of affirmative action. Furthermore, postgraduate students have become important interlocutors in the elaboration of the Faculty of Education's institutional development plan.

What does this kind of SE require? As a basic requirement, students must acquire an understanding of the 'rules of the game' by reading not only relevant legislation and policy documentation, but also discerning the set of social relations that supports them, its players, and institutions. Students must proceed with intensive networking. The Coletivo thus works as a 'broadened collective', activating allies among students who are not representatives but who are interested in performing certain tasks and joining work groups. Discussions take place not only in the monthly assemblies, but also in extraordinary meetings and via e-mail and instant messaging. As with many kinds of political activity, this kind of SE supposes the subjects' disposition to overwork—that is, to go beyond normal work hours to organise for political-pedagogical action. Who are these students? They are young adults who grew up with the promise of citizenship rights and democracy put forth in the Brazilian Constitution of 1988. Many are engaged in social movements, where other forms of collegiate deliberation are practised. They understand that democracy building is a bottom–up exercise that must permeate all public institutions.

By operating according to this set of symbolic and material relations, students have struggled for recognition in an effort to become partners. Of course, they are still partners in the precarious position of a subaltern group. However, they can participate in a level of discourse and political representation by which it would be unacceptable for professors to disregard their suggestions or not use them in their own discourses inside the university as they relate to the pedagogical categories set forth by students. This phenomenon by which SE merges with student activism and student representation may show how subaltern counterpublics slowly infiltrate the public arena to create new agents with a wider understanding of democracy.

Notes

1 This is, to date, the most prestigious Brazilian HEI: Universidade de São Paulo (USP). It is a public research university, owned by the state of São Paulo and headquartered in the city of São Paulo, the country's most populous and wealthiest metropolitan area. I would like to acknowledge that my own institution, UFRGS, was also founded later in 1934 as a technical university.

2 The Portuguese word *extensão* designates activities that in other contexts have labels, such as 'service', 'third mission', or 'societal engagement'. A national forum of provosts once reached the following definition: 'university extension [*extensão universitária*] is a scientific, cultural, and educative process that indissociably articulates teaching and research and enables the transformative relation between university and society. Extension works both ways, ensuring transit to the academic community, who will find in society the opportunity to elaborate the praxis of academic knowledge. Back to the university, teachers and

students will bring a learning which, submitted to theoretical reflexivity, will be added to that knowledge. This flux, which established the exchange of systematised forms of knowledge, academic and popular, will have as consequences: knowledge production resulting from the confrontation with the regional and Brazilian reality; democratisation of academic knowledge; and effective participation of community in the University's activities' (Forproex, 1987, p. 11).

3　In Portuguese, the word 'student' [*estudante*] has three possible forms: *aluno, estudante, discente*. All words have Latin origins, designating, respectively, one who needs to be nourished, one who studies, and one who learns. Although the word *aluno* is very common, it is considered by many as slightly demeaning. *Estudante* is a more neutral form. *Discente* is the preferred form in legislation, and taking up this title may embody an attitude of recognising one's place as an active subject both in the learning process and in an educational institution's polity.

References

Bleiklie, Ivar, & Kogan, Maurice (2006). Comparison and theories. In M. Kogan, M. Bauer, I. Bleiklie, & M. Henkel (Eds.) *Transforming higher education: A comparative study* (pp. 3–22). 2nd ed. Dordrecht: Springer.

Brasil (1968). *Lei N° 5.540, de 28 de novembro de 1968. Fixa normas de organização e funcionamento do ensino superior e sua articulação com a escola média, e dá outras providências.* Retrieved June 18, 2018 from www2.camara.leg.br/legin/fed/lei/1960-1969/lei-5540-28-novembro-1968-359201-publicacaooriginal-1-pl.html

Brasil (1988). *Constituição da República Federativa do Brasil de 1988.* Retrieved May 15, 2018 from www.planalto.gov.br/ccivil_03/constituicao/constituicao.htm

Brasil (1996). *Decreto N° 1.916, de 23 de maio de 1996. Regulamenta o processo de escolha dos dirigentes de instituições federais de ensino superior, nos termos da Lei n° 9.192, de 21 de dezembro de 1995.* Retrieved May 15, 2018 from www.planalto.gov.br/ccivil_03/decreto/d1916.htm

Brasil (2004). *Lei N° 10.861, de 14 de abril de 2004. Institui o Sistema Nacional de Avaliação da Educação Superior – SINAES e dá outras providências.* Retrieved May 15, 2018 from www. planalto.gov.br/ccivil_03/_ato2004-2006/2004/lei/l10.861.htm

Brasil. Ministério da Educação (2018). *Portaria N° 321, de 5 de abril de 2018. Dispõe sobre a avaliação da pós-graduação stricto sensu.* Retrieved June 18, 2018 from www.capes.gov.br/images/stories/download/legislacao/06042018-Portaria-MEC-n-321-de-5-de-a bril-de-2018.pdf

Brasil. Ministério da Educação. Coordenação de Aperfeiçoamento de Pessoal de Nível Superior (2010). *Portaria N° 76, de 14 de abril de 2010. (Regulamento do Programa de Demanda Social – DS).* Retrieved June 18, 2018 from www.capes.gov.br/images/stories/download/legislacao/Portaria_076_RegulamentoDS.pdf

Buarque de Hollanda, Sérgio (1995). *Raízes do Brasil.* 26th edn. São Paulo: Companhia das Letras.

Buarque de Hollanda Ferreira, Aurélio (1975). *Novo Dicionário da Língua Portuguesa.* Rio de Janeiro: Nova Fronteira.

Buckley, Alex (2017). The ideology of student engagement research. *Teaching in Higher Education*, 23(6), 718–732.

Capes – Coordenação de Aperfeiçoamento de Pessoal de Nível Superior (2018). *GEO-CAPES – Sistema de Informações Georreferenciadas Capes.* Retrieved June 18, 2018 from http s://geocapes.capes.gov.br/geocapes/

Caregnato, Célia Elizabete, Raizer, Leandro, Grisa, Gregório, & Miorando, Bernardo Sfredo (2018). New audiences and new educational stratifications in Brazilian higher education in the 21st century. *AISHE-J: The All Ireland Journal of Teaching and Learning in Higher Education*, 10, 350. 1–350. 13.

Felix, Glades Tereza, Bertolin, Julio Godoy, & Polidori, Marlis Morosini (2017). Avaliação da educação superior: um comparativo dos instrumentos de regulação entre Brasil e Portugal. *Avaliação*, 22(1), 35–54.

Fiori, Ernani Maria (2014 [1962]). Aspectos da reforma universitária. In E. M. Fiori, *Educação e política* (pp. 25–56). 2nd edn. Porto Alegre: Editora da UFRGS.

Forproex – I Encontro de Pró-Reitores de Extensão das Universidades Públicas Brasileiras (1987). *Conceito de extensão, institucionalização e financiamento*. Brasília: UnB.

Fraser, Nancy (1990). Rethinking the public sphere: A contribution to the critique of actually existing democracy. *Social Text*, 25/26, 56–80.

Freire, Paulo (1970). *Pedagogy of the oppressed*. New York: Seabury.

Genro, Maria Elly Herz (2011). Educação do sujeito político na universidade. In D. Leite, M. E. H. Genro, & A. M. S. Braga (Eds.), *Inovação e pedagogia universitária* (pp. 139–151). Porto Alegre: Editora da UFRGS.

Gohn, Maria da Glória Marcondes (2016). Manifestações de protesto nas ruas no Brasil a partir de Junho de 2013: novíssimos sujeitos em cena. *Revista Diálogo Educacional*, 16(47), 125–146.

Healey, Mick, Mason-O'Connor, Kristine, & Broadfoot, Patricia (2010). Reflections on engaging student in the process and product of strategy development for learning, teaching, and assessment: An institutional case study. *International Journal for Academic Development*, 15(1), 19–32.

Inep – Instituto de Estudos e Pesquisas Educacionais Anísio Teixeira (2017a). *Sinopses Estatísticas da Educação Superior – Graduação*. Retrieved May 29, 2018 from http://portal.inep.gov.br/web/guest/sinopses-estatisticas-da-educacao-superior

Inep – Instituto de Estudos e Pesquisas Educacionais Anísio Teixeira (2017b) *Sinopses Estatísticas do Enade*. Retrieved May 29, 2018 from http://portal.inep.gov.br/web/guest/sinopses-estatisticas-do-enade

Leite, Denise (1990). *Aprendizagem e consciência social na universidade (Doctoral dissertation)*. Porto Alegre, Brazil: Universidade Federal do Rio Grande do Sul.

Leite, Denise (1992). A aprendizagem política do estudante universitário. *Educação e Realidade*, 17, 25–31.

Leite, Denise, & Morosini, Marilia (1992). Universidade e Integração. In M. Morosini & D. Leite (Eds.), *Universidade e Integração no Cone Sul* (pp. 17–26). Porto Alegre: Editora da Universidade.

Leite, Denise et al. (2016). Brasil: tendencias emergentes y de cambio en la educación superior, 2000–2015. In A. Didriksson Takayanagui, C. I. Moreno Arellano (Eds.), *Innovando y construyendo el futuro: La universidad de América Latina y el Caribe: Estudios de caso* (pp. 43–73). Guadalajara: Universidad de Guadalajara; Global University Network for Innovation.

Mollis, Marcela (2006). Geopolítica del saber: Biografías recientes de las universidades latinoamericanas. In H. Vessuri (Ed.), *Universidad e Investigación Científica* (pp. 85–101). Buenos Aires: CLACSO.

Morosini, Marilia (2006). Modelo Latino-Americano. In M. Morosini (Ed.), *Enciclopédia de Pedagogia Universitária: Glossário* (pp. 227–228). Brasília: Inep.

Ribeiro, Darcy (1975). *A universidade necessária*. 2nd edn. Rio de Janeiro: Paz e Terra.

Santos, Boaventura de Sousa (2017). The resilience of abyssal exclusions in our societies: Toward a post-abyssal law. *Tilburg Law Review*, 22, 237–258.

Sguissardi, Valdemar (2006). Universidade no Brasil: Dos modelos clássicos aos modelos de ocasião? In M. Morosini (Ed.), *A universidade no Brasil: Concepções e modelos* (pp. 275–289). Brasília: Instituto Nacional de Estudos e Pesquisas Educacionais Anísio Teixeira.

Suárez Zozaya, María Herlinda (2017). Juventud de los estudiantes universitarios. *Revista de la Educación Superior*, 46(184), 39–54.

UFRGS – Universidade Federal do Rio Grande do Sul. Pró-Reitoria de Planejamento (2016). *A UFRGS e a PEC 241.* (Public report) Retrieved June 18, 2018 from www. assufrgs.org.br/wp-content/uploads/2016/11/A-UFRGS-e-a-PEC-241.pdf

UFRGS – Universidade Federal do Rio Grande do Sul. Secretaria de Avaliação Institucional (2018). *Painel da qualidade.* Retrieved May 29, 2018 from www.ufrgs.br/sai/dados-resulta dos/painel-qualidade

Vieira Pinto, Álvaro (1962). *A questão da universidade.* Rio de Janeiro: UNE, Editora Universitária.

8

THE RELEVANCE OF STUDENT ENGAGEMENT IN AFRICAN HIGHER EDUCATION

The Mozambican case

Nelson Casimiro Zavale and Patrício V. Langa

EDUARDO UNIVERSITY AND INCHER-UNIVERSITY OF KASSEL, AND EDUARDO MONDLANE UNIVERSITY AND UNIVERSITY OF WESTERN CAPE

Introduction

Since the mid-1980s, a body of literature has consistently demonstrated that students' engagement is more relevant to students' academic success than their socio-economic background or the type of institution or degree they attend (Astin, 1984; Kuh, 2003; Kuh et al., 2005; Pascarella and Terenzini, 2005). As voiced by Kuh (2003), what students actually do, i.e. the time and effort they devote to (extra) curricular activities, is more relevant to their academic success than what they bring to higher education (HE). As a result of these claims, this literature has argued that expanding access to HE seems to be as important as assuring their access to relevant knowledge and learning.

In Sub-Saharan Africa (SSA), interest in students' engagement has emerged in a context of rapid expansion of HE. Following a global trend of massification, HE in SSA has expanded in the number of HEIs and students. The number of HEIs has increased from about 30 by the late 1960s to over 600 by the late 2000s (Zeleza, 2016). These HEIs are of different typologies: university-type vs non-university institutions (e.g. higher institutes, polytechnics); public vs private institutions. The number of students has increased as well, from less than 200 thousands in 1970s to over 5 million by 2008 (Mohamedbhai, 2014). This expansion enabled access to HE by significant segments of population whose access to HE has been neglected since the colonial period.

However, the rapid pace of expansion of HE in SSA raises concerns regarding the quality of teaching-learning, research and outreach provided by African HEIs (Materu, 2007), particularly if one considers that the expansion has not been accompanied by proportional inflow of resources. According to the World Bank (2010), students' enrolments in SSA have increased at an annual average rate of 16%, but funding has only increased at annual average rate of 6%. UNESCO

(2015)'s scientific report indicates that SSA's share on world's gross expenditure in R&D has increased from 1.1% in 2007 to 1.3% in 2013, while during the same period, South Asia and Latin America registered an increase from 3.1% to 3.4%. As Schendel and McCowan (2016) noticed, universities in developing countries are grappling with the challenge of maintaining quality in face of rapid expansion and budget constraints.

Therefore, interest on students' engagement in SSA emerges amidst some shift of focus regarding HE, from expanding access to assuring quality. As Hornsby and Osman (2014) refer, it is important to interrogate the impact that increased enrolments in HE are having on the learning environment. Signs of this shift are at least twofold. Firstly, with the repositioning of HE into the heart of SSA (World Bank, 2009), literature has emerged to examine the contribution of African HE to SSA's socio-economic development (Zavale, 2017; Cloete et al., 2015; Bloom et al., 2014; Bennell, 1996). This literature interrogates the degree to which the expansion of HE has impacted SSA's socio-economic development. Secondly, the emergency of literature which maps and examines QA processes in African HE (Ansah, 2016; Zavale et al., 2015; Odhiambo, 2014; Ogachi, 2009; Materu, 2007). This literature calls policy-makers to pay more attention to the quality, not just to the quantity, of HE provided in SSA.

Despite these changes, students' engagement is still an incipient field of study in SSA. While literature has widely documented the increasing numbers and types of students entering into the African HE system (Zeleza, 2016; Mohamedbhai, 2014), studies addressing what students actually do at universities are still scarce but emerging. In this chapter, we provide an overview of the emerging literature on students' engagement in African HE. We begin by discussing the state-of-the-art about student engagement in African HE. Then, based on the Mozambican case, we discuss students' engagement in light of three levels. In the micro-level, based on available research findings, we discuss how some students enrolled in some universities engage with some selected aspects of their own learning. In the meso level, based particularly on data from the oldest and largest HEIs – the Eduardo Mondlane University – we discuss the extent to which the voice of student is considered within the recently established quality assurance (QA) system in Mozambique. At the macro level, we examine how student participation is framed at the national and institutional (i.e. Eduardo Mondlane University) legislative and organizational apparatus. We conclude by arguing that the focus on HE policy in Africa should shift from merely expanding access, to expanding effective access to learning and knowledge.

The state-of-the-art of students' engagement in African higher education

The emerging literature on students' engagement in African HE can be grouped into two main clusters. The first cluster focuses on broad or macro issues of social, civic and organizational participation of students into the social and academic life of the university. The second cluster focuses on the degree of students' learning while at university.

The integration of student voice into the governance of African HEIs

A significant body of literature has examined the way students are integrated into the governance of African HE at national and institutional levels (Luescher-Mamashela, 2005; Luescher-Mamashela and Magume 2014; Mulinge and Arasa, 2017). Of particular interest are research outputs produced in a context of a project entitled *Student Representation in Higher Education Governance in Africa*. The project has brought together several scholars to map out the mechanisms through which the voice of the student is considered in the governance of African HEIs. Two publications produced by this project are worth mentioning. The first is a special issue entitled "*Student Power in Africa*" published in the *Journal of Student Affairs in Africa* (Klemenčič et al., 2015). The issue explores the manifestation of student power in African HE. The second publication is an edited book (Luescher-Mamashela et al., 2016), that assembles chapters which document and analyse student representation and participation in the governance at national and institutional levels in several African countries.

Historical evolution of student engagement in governance of African HE

In the book edited by Luescher-Mamashela et al. (2016), two chapters have provided an historical overview of the evolution of student engagement in university governance in SSA. The first is a chapter written by Oanda (2016), in which, based on studies focusing on Ghana, Kenya, Uganda and Tanzania, the author traces the historical context within which student participation in university governance has evolved in SSA. The second chapter, written by Bianchini (2016), undertakes similar analysis for the Francophone SSA, with special focus on Senegal and Burkina Faso. Both chapters identify three main phases of student representation in African universities.

The first phase began with the establishment in SSA of universities by colonial powers. During this phase, despite restrictions imposed by colonialism as regards to participation – and perhaps because of these limitations – African students were engaged in universities in radical, activist and nationalist manners. This *anti-colonial* engagement has led to the birth of nationalisms and then independence of African states, with some former student leaders being promoted to political leaders of their countries.

After independence, the second phase emerged in the 1970s, with the transformation of former colonial universities into national institutions. However, African students continued to have limited space in university governance and wider political arena. A natural consequence of this restriction was systematic and direct confrontation between post-colonial student leaders with political leaders, who were former student leaders during the colonial period. The conflictual relationship between student leaders and university (and national) leaders in the 1970s up to the late 1980s was due to bad governance at institutional and national levels which in turn hampered the emergence of a strong student governance system. During this period, African political and university elites have often subverted the original nation-building ideals, emanated during the struggle for independence, into a search for personal gains. As a result, authoritarian regimes emerged, which curtailed the democratic participation of students in governance, either through severe restrictions or through manipulating student leaders.

The third phase has begun from the 1990s onwards. It is characterized by fragmentation of student organizations due to the intensification of neoliberal policies, ethnicisation of student politics, manipulation of student leaders through political influence and corruption. This fragmentation has deteriorated the quality of student representation, particularly the capacity to defend students' interests in decision-making circles. It is not surprising that student protests are still systematic in SSA (Oanda, 2016; Bianchini, 2016).

Student engagement in governance of African HE: an overview

At the national level, findings document the existence of two systems of student representation in SSA (Klemenčič et al., 2016). Most countries (e.g. Botswana, Burundi, Cameroon, Ghana, Nigeria, Kenya, Uganda) have neo-corporatist systems, i.e., have recognized national student associations that are autonomous, at least formally. In some cases, like in Kenya, Burundi and Botswana, there is latent or no national student association; students are often represented, at the national level, by the national flagship university in the capital. There are also cases (e.g. Uganda, Ghana) in which student representatives have seats on national HE commissions/councils (Klemenčič et al., 2016; Bailey, 2015; Luescher-Mamashela and Magume 2014). Countries like South Africa and Zimbabwe display pluralist system, i.e. students at the national level are represented by several student associations (Klemenčič et al., 2016).

Despite the existence of student representation at the national level, the effective involvement of students in decision-making and policy formulation within HE agencies remains weak. Student associations are usually recognized by national HE agencies and ministries, but there is still an ambiguity as regards to their legal status and financing. This ambiguity has at least two implications. On one hand, student leaders use informal venues to interact with national HE authorities (Klemenčič et al., 2016). Informal negotiations may protect students' interests, as reported in South Africa (Magume and Luescher-Mamashela, 2015). However, informal arrangements often lead to student rallies and protests and manipulation of student leaders through corruption, exchange of favours and government political interference, as in case of Cameroon and Ethiopia (Ayele, 2016; Fongwa and Chifon, 2016).

On the other hand, the informal and ambiguous relationship between student associations and national authorities suggests the need to develop legislation and organizational structures that consider the interests of students in the decision-making and policy formulation in HE. African countries vary as regards to HE legislation and institutional acts and status regulating the involvement of students in national policy-making. Most countries seldom have national legislation or, when such legislation does exist, it rarely includes explicit statements about student relationship with national HE steering bodies (Klemenčič et al., 2016; Bailey, 2015).

Student representation in SSA is a widespread phenomenon at institutional governing bodies, rather than at the national level (Klemenčič et al., 2016). This is because students live their transient experience more intensely within the university and, therefore, are likely to be motivated to defend their interest at the level of university department governing bodies, rather than at the level of ministries and central agencies. In addition, in most cases, universities enjoy a certain degree of autonomy regarding the way they interact with students. In SSA, legislation on the extent of student involvement on institutional and sub-institutional levels of university governance varies from country to country (Bailey, 2015). In most African countries (e.g. Burundi, Cameroon, South Africa, Uganda, Kenya), university Acts and Status allow students to participate in university governing bodies. But in other countries, like Ethiopia, students' role is limited to commenting on cafeteria and clinical services (Ayele, 2016).

However, despite students having this formal right, their effective involvement and, most importantly, their power to influence decision-making through formal venues are often limited. In some cases, students' voice is not usually considered in institutional decision-making process; the only way for students to be heard is through protesting and revolting (Nigeria and Cameroon) (Oni and Adetero, 2015). In other cases (e.g. in Kenya, Cameroon, Nigeria), students' participation is constrained through corrupting or exerting political influence over student leaders (Mulinge and Arasa, 2017; Fongwa and Chifon, 2016; Oni and Adetoro, 2015). But there are also successful cases, such as some cases in South Africa in which students' participation has safeguarded students' interests (Magume and Luescher-Mamashela, 2015).

As a conclusion, student engagement in the governance of African HEIs varies from country to country and, sometimes, from institution to institution. This makes difficult to draw a conclusive taxonomy of common patterns and practices. However, a tentative hypothesis would be to state that, while most countries recognize in policies and legislation the relevance of student engagement, this recognition is hardly translated into effective practices of supporting and listening to students' voices in decision-making.

Students' engagement with learning in SSA

In SSA, a relevant issue deriving from this the expansion of HE is whether it has also resulted in improvements in the quality of HE. In this regard, two relevant questions are worth asking. First, to what extent do African university students engage with their own leaning? Second, by having more access to HE, are African students also learning, i.e., are they having access to relevant knowledge and skills? In this section, we will address these questions by summarizing findings from selected relevant literature.

In South Africa, relevant studies have been carried out about the degree of engagement of students, and its impact on academic success. For example, the Council on Higher Education has commissioned a study on student engagement to understand what students do while at university and how this might impact their success in South Africa (Strydom et al., 2010). A team of researchers, coordinated by J.F. Strydom, undertook the assignment in 2009, through administering the South African Survey of Student Engagement (SASSE) to over 13,600 undergraduate students at seven South African universities (Strydom and Mentz, 2010). Overall, findings from this survey suggest that South African HEIs provide a sound academically supportive environment, but students are less engaged in learning activities and devote less time to academically relevant activities. Results on *academic challenge* indicate that, while almost 82% of the surveyed students acknowledge that their institutions place emphasis on spending time studying, only 1 in 4 students devotes more than 20 hours to studies per week and less than 10% spend the recommended amount of time, i.e. 25–30 hours per week. Results on *active and collaborative learning* show that, despite the fact that about 60% of students often discuss ideas from their classes with others outside of class, about 60% of first-year students have never made a presentation in any of their classes, and more than 60% of senior students have never participated in a community-based project as part of a regular course. Results on *student–staff ratio* show that three-quarters of students report to have discussed marks and assignments with academic staff, but 44% have never discussed their career plans with lecturers or counsellors. Results on *enriching educational experience* reveal that about 80% of students have used electronic media as a pedagogic tool, but only 42% had serious conversations with students from different racial and ethnic groups and about 70% have spent no time in co-curricular activities. Results on *supportive campus environment* show that three-quarters of students described their relationships with other students as positive and 71% received the support they needed on campus to success academically, but only 38% of students described their relationships with administrative staff as positive. Overall, among the five benchmarks, academic challenge and supportive campus have higher scores (about 50 out of maximum 100) than active and collaborative learning, student–staff ratio interaction and enriching educational experience (mean score less than 40) (Strydom and Mentz, 2010). These findings suggest that, in South Africa, wider access to HE, particularly by historically disadvantaged racial/social groups (i.e., Black, Asian, Coloured), does not necessarily imply wider access to learning and knowledge.

Relevant literature produced similar findings in other African countries. Schendel (2015, 2016a, 2016b), for example, investigated the degree to which Rwandan university students are developing critical thinking during their time at university. The author surveyed 220 students enrolled in three prestigious universities in

Rwanda, and she found out that students are not substantially improving in their critical thinking (Schendel, 2015). Schendel (2016a) found out later that students graduating from the KIST Faculty of Architecture and Environmental Design were the exception to this situation, as they tended to exhibit deeper approaches to learning and stronger critical thinking skills than their counterparts. As in the case of South Africa, Schendel's (2016a, 2016b) findings suggest that the following factors are relevant in improving students' effective learning, namely department culture, students' exposure to learner-centred pedagogy, lecturers' personal experience with more active or collaborative teaching methods, lecturers' values and attitudes towards teaching, and faculty's supportive structures. A study on the Ghanaian situation enlarges the scope of relevant factors, to encompass factors related to family, particularly family expectation, financial and social support, as well as the strategies used to monitor students' academic performance (Asare et al., 2017).

One of the relevant factors affecting students' engagement with their learning is the enlargement and social diversification of classes as a result of rapid expansion of HE. The *Higher Education* journal has dedicated a special issue (Vol. 67, Issue 6) to the challenge of teaching, learning and acquiring/producing knowledge in large and demographically diverse classes, with particular reference to SSA. In their introduction, the guest editors begin by situating the emergency of large classes within a context of massification and democratization of HE. Then, editors emphasize the opportunities (e.g. more social justice and social and economic benefits) and challenges (threat to quality; development of new methodologies) associated with large classes (Hornsby and Osman, 2014).

The two conceptual articles of the issue diverge as regards to challenges and opportunities associated with massification and large classes. In the first article, Allais (2014) argues that the expansion of HE through large classes is self-defeating because large classes make difficult for students to acquire knowledge through face-to-face student-teacher interaction, which she considers to be the most relevant pedagogic method. In addition, the promise of promoting economic growth and jobs through expansion of knowledge is unrealistic because mass HE undermines knowledge acquisition and it is unable to solve all socio-economic problems, since the demand for (knowledge) workers also depends on the dynamics of external labour market (e.g. speed and limits in job creation). In the second article, Arvanitakis (2014) challenges Allais's position, by claiming that massification is rather an opportunity for widening access to HE of historically denied social groups; massification will not undermine the quality of knowledge, if suitable pedagogical practices are adopted. The special issue then includes some papers which, based on African context, suggest innovative pedagogical strategies to assure quality and acquisition knowledge in large and demographically diverse classes. These strategies include usage of technology, such as mobile technology and SMSing (Foley and Masingila, 2014) or blended and open online learning (Shrivastava and Shrivastava, 2014).

To conclude, this literature seems to suggest that most African students are not substantially engaging with academically-relevant activities while at university, either because they do not devote adequate time and effort to these activities, or simply because they are exposed to inadequate teaching and learning methods.

Student engagement in Mozambican higher education - a case study

Activism, protest and institutional governance

In Mozambique, since the establishment of the first higher education institution in 1962, there has been a scarce account of student involvement in university governance and in the lives of university in general students. This section sheds light on the place of students in Mozambican HE governance, their forms of participation and expression. This is done mainly through review of the legislation and policy in HE. The main objective is to examine the role played by students in governing bodies HE at national and institutional level. This section is divided into three main parts. The first part addresses student activist in the early days of university, which also coincided with the late days of the colonial regime in Mozambique (1964–1975). The second part covers the period from 1975 to the fall of the socialist experiment in 1986. While 1975 is the year of the proclamation of the independence, 1986 is the year of the death of Samora Machel, the first president of independent Mozambique, which also symbolizes the end of almost 10 years of post-colonial socialist experiment in Mozambique (Langa, 2006; Mário et al., 2003). The last period starts in 1990 with the enactment of the country's second Constitution to date. This is also a period of institutionalized political freedoms, establishment of multiparty democratic society and liberalization of the economy towards a more market orientation.

The early days of university student activism (1962/4–1975)

In 2016, a book was published which documents the early days of the history of one of the first student societies in Mozambique, the *Associação Académica de Moçambique* (AAM). The book recounts almost 10 years of student activism during the period of war for independence and the downfall of colonial rule (1964–1975), which also coincided with the first decade of the newly established University of Lourenço Marques (ULM). The association of students of the University General Studies of Mozambique (EGUM), the prior name of ULM, was established around 1963/64, while the EGUM was established in August 1962 (Langa, Cumaio and Rafael, 2014). The AAM worked within the university grassroots in various areas including: social, sporting, pedagogic and cultural activities.

AAM was often targeted by repression of the colonial authorities through censorship and prohibition of student publications, compulsory incorporation of its leaders in the colonial army, closure of the Association's premises, interrogations by the Portuguese Secret Police Forces (PIDE/DGS), disciplinary proceedings, threats to students and university assistants (Pereira and Gonzalez, 2016).

According to Pereira and Gonzalez, (2016) the AMM started its activism by claiming the university's autonomy, freedom of expression and information for its students and a quality teaching that is oriented towards the Mozambican reality. The authors recount that many young people repressed by the academic, government, police and military authorities of Portuguese colonial-fascism quickly turned from rebels to democrats, to patriots, and to courageous fighters of the cause of Mozambican independence.

The overwhelming majority of students and members of AAM were white, some mixed-race, and an insignificant number of black students. The demographic of the AAM resembled that of the ULM at the time, where native black students were also underrepresented (Langa, 2006; Mário et al., 2003, Beverwijk, 2005). Student engagement was mainly characterized by protests against the fascist regimes and by demand for improvement of teaching and learning conditions.

Student engagement during the socialist experiment (1977–86/1990)

In 1977, two years after Mozambique independence, the Front for the Liberation of Mozambique (FRELIMO) metamorphosed into a single party and self-proclaimed the sole and legitimate representative of the people of Mozambique while adopting Marxism-Leninism as the ideology of the State. In 1976 ULM had been renamed after Eduardo Mondlane honouring the first president of the FRELIMO who died in 1969 during the struggle for independence. Mondlane himself had been a very active student activist and leader. Mondlane was involved in the creation of the *Núcleo des Estudantes Africanos Secundários de Moçambique (NESAM)*, a student association linked to the *Centro Associativo dos Negros de Moçambique* (Mondlane, 1969).

Mondlane did not live long enough to see the impendence of Mozambique. He was murdered in February 1969. The newly independent country saw the birth of the Mozambique National Resistance RENAMO, and the escalation of a civil war against FRELIMO's government which lasted 16 years. The civil war arguably against FRELIMO's adoption of Marxist-Leninist ideology ended in 1992 with the signing of a peace agreement in Rome, Italy, between RENAMO and FRELIMO 's government. Not much has been written and said about student engagement and activism. This is probably because the country was embroiled and ravaged by 16 years of civil war in which many youths were involved.

By 1990 the country had two more higher education institutions, the Higher Pedagogic institute (later renamed Pedagogical University), and the Higher Institute for International Relations (ISRI) (Mário et al., 2003). No major student activism is reported during this second period. The revolutionary forces had taken into their realm to define the vision and mission of the higher education institutions and the roles students should play in it. A number of legislative decrees were enacted which illustrate a centralized governance. For instance, Decree No. 19/76 of 18 May regulated the provision of services to the Republic Popular of Mozambique by university students and graduates.

A number of governmental and law-making procedures were taken to ensure the students complied with the revolutionary nature of the new State. Students could not choose careers, since these were allocated according to perceived abilities and the State needs and priorities. In the political discourse of Mozambique, there is a generation ("The 8th March Generation") whose professional careers were determined by the State, without their voices being heard (cf. Langa, Cumaio and Rafael, 2014, p. 33). Education in general and university education in particular had a major role in the fabric of the post-colonial society and the "New Man" (Mazula, 1995; Cabaço, 2007).

In Machel´s Mozambique, the affirmation of the "New Man" implied a change of mentality of Men formed by the colonial apparatus (Mazula, 1995: 179). To this end, the "New Man" would receive an education or vocational training within the framework of a pre-established economic, political and cultural ideal. In other words, there was not room for the student voice, since the State knew better what the best was for every student. Student engagement was mainly characterized by cultural manifestation in national events, joining the youth organization, and also actively participating in university recession fieldwork activities once, and if, deployed to the communities.

With hindsight, the role of the thousands of students who ended up in careers they had never planned (e.g., teachers, nurses, soldiers and so forth) is presented as one of the necessary sacrifices that had to be done for the country. Most of the legislation on this period refers to the students' obligations to society, more than their rights to participate in the governing structures of higher education (Langa, Cumaio and Rafael, 2014).

Student engagement in a democratic constellation: 1990–onwards

Winds of change

The enactment of the second Constitution in 1990 inaugurates a new legislative framework, which aims at promoting the rule of law, democracy and participatory governance model. In this new dispensation the student voice became more noticeable and at times was perceived as inconvenient.

The first student protest

In 1990, the country experienced one of the most significant event involving university students as a preamble to the new democratic dispensation. Narciso Matos, a Mozambican who earned his doctorate in East German in Chemistry, also one of the very few black Mozambican students who had studied at the ULM, had just become the first black Rector of UEM. An uproar led by students caught the attention of major actors in society. The student protest led to the Head of State, the then President Joaquim Chissano, to come to campus to, together with the Rector, listen to students' grievances. Eusebio Maceta, the President of the

University's student association, took the stage and delivered a compelling speech describing what they considered to be an ostentatious wealth and well-being of the country's leaders in contrast with the poverty of the students and the people as a whole (Mário et al., 2003).

According to Mário et al. (2003) although this strike does not feature in the official annals of UEM, they interviewed those who considered the protest to be a crucial moment in marking the transition to democracy. University students inaugurated the new democratic rights and brought to the government what they saw as glitches of HE. The government did in fact take the strike seriously and adopted measures to increase support to the university. But more importantly, the frank confrontation between the students and the authorities signalled the emergence of the freedom of expression that had been seriously curtailed throughout the colonial period and the post-independence war. It is significant that this signal came from the UEM. It is also significant that shortly afterwards the university took important steps to diagnose its ills and to prepare a strategic plan for their resolution, even though there was no direct relationship between the strikes and the planning process.

Institutionalisation of student governance

Although student activism had a long tradition in Mozambique, student representation in HE governance bodies was almost absent. As indicated in the previous sections, students associations were regarded as a space for cultural entertainment. The 1990 protest was a wakeup call for the power that students might exhibit when united for a cause. From being mere spectators and voiceless actors within the governance of HEIs, students gradually paved the way to become acknowledged and earn space as major actors in the legislation and governance structures at both national and institutional level.

The place of students at national level governance bodies

In Mozambique, there are three major HE councils, the National Council on Higher Education (CNES), the Council on Higher Education (CES) and the National Council on Quality Assurance (CNAQ) (Langa, 2014a). These councils were created to bring the government and all HEIs together at the national level in a collaborative effort to shape the mechanisms supporting policy implementation in the sector. The CNES is the consultative body for the Council of Ministers as well as a broader forum for overseeing the implementation and integration of planning processes between the higher education, science and technology sectors. The CNES evaluates policy implementation progress, and examines new policies and proposals before they reach the Council of Ministers for approval and law-making (Langa, 2014a). The CNES comprises representatives from various sections of government, the CES, research institutes and HEIs, business associations and civil society. While students found their place in most governance to be crucial, more specifically consultative forums, which advise government on HE issues, there has not been studies on the real impact of their presence in such forums. Their presence could be more decorative, than actually as key actors influencing policy.

The place of students at national level governance bodies

An overview of most HEIs statutes shows that student representatives are included in their governance bodies (Langa, Cumaio and Rafael, 2014). University councils are the highest body in which students can be represented and make their voices heard. The other forms of student participation and engagement are through their own established societies. There is a dearth of studies describing the lives of these student associations. Occasionally, there are reports in the press about student initiatives, some supported by the government. For instance, one such initiative is the student recess in the district. The initiative is organised by the Association of Final Year University Students (AEFUM) a non-profit organization that brings together some 5000 members, including finalists and graduates of all HEIs.

> As a Government, I would like to commend the work that the Association of Final [Year] University Students of Mozambique (AEFUM) has been developing since the year 2006, greatly contributing to the socio-professional insertion of finalist students and recent graduates, as well as to increase the quantity and quality of existing human resources in the districts, administrative posts and localities of the country. (Jorge Nhambiu, Minister of Science Technology, Higher Education and Professional Training)[1]

While the courteous relationship between government (officials) and student organisations can be regarded as desirable, the cordial nature of the rapport may also represent a certain level of student capture into the promises of a better future.

Student engagement with the quality assurance system in Mozambique: the case of Eduardo Mondlane University

As elsewhere in Africa (Materu, 2007), Mozambique established its QA system during the 2000s (Zavale et al., 2015). Since the mid-1990s, Mozambican HE has experienced transformations that are similar to those that occurred in other international and African HE systems: rapid expansion and diversification, growth of private HEIs, funding constraints and demands for accountability (Langa, 2014b). From 1975 to 1994, Mozambique had only 3 HEIs, with less than 4,000 students. From 1995 to 2014, the number of HEIs reached 46 (18 public and 28 private) (MINED, 2014), and the number of students increased to 130,000 (UNESCO Institute for Statistics, 2015). The QA system was established to cope with these changes, as well as to drive HEIs to meet regional and international standards (Langa, 2014b). In 2007, the Council of Ministers approved the National System of Evaluation, Accreditation and Quality Assurance of Higher Education

(SINAQES). SINAQES sets up rules for the QA system and establishes an agency for implementing those rules – the National Council for Quality Evaluation (CNAQ) (Zavale et al., 2015).

Before the establishment of an Internal Quality Assurance (IQA) system, quality concerns at UEM were handled by academic councils and ad-hoc commissions. However, since quality concerns were not their unique functions, they used unsystematic mechanisms which hardly involved the use of specific quality standards. In 2012, UEM's University Council approved, for the first time, the IQA system, as well as the establishment of a QA office to coordinate the implementation of the system. UEM's IQA is ascribed the overall function of developing and promoting a culture of continuing search for quality (UEM, 2012; Zavale et al., 2015). As in most QA systems (Westerheijden et al., 2007), UEM's IQA was created to promote both improvement and accountability of the institution. However, as an internal mechanism, the main strategies developed to attain the IQA's objectives are concerned with improvement rather than accountability. These strategies include systematic and regular self-assessment at institutional and programme levels, the analysis of reports and results, the drafting and implementation of improvements plans, and the establishment of a structural organisation to coordinate the self-assessment, analyse results and implement improvement plans (UEM, 2012: 12; Zavale et al., 2015).

Students are engaged in the newly established UEM's IQA through three venues. *Firstly*, they are involved in the sub-commissions for self-assessment of programmes. From 2013 up to 2017, about 40 % of the 85 total undergraduate programmes and about 20% of the 60 total graduate programmes were self-assessed (UEM, 2017). For each self-assessed programme, a sub-commission was created, composed of representatives of lecturers, academic managers, administrative staff, including students. The role of student representatives is, at least in principle, to safeguard students' interests in the process. *Secondly*, students serve as informants both for self-assessment and external evaluation. During the self-assessment process, students are administered questionnaires to find out their level of satisfaction regarding several issues of programme delivery (Zavale et al., 2015; UEM, 2017). The voice of students is also taken into consideration when academic programmes are submitted to external evaluation in view of obtaining accreditation. From 2016 up to 2018, the national agency for quality assurance has sent at least 15 external evaluation sub-commissions to assess several UEM programmes. Listening to students, both through interviews and group discussions, was one of the mechanisms used by these external sub-commissions to validate self-assessment reports, determine the level of quality of UEM programmes and advise the agency regarding accreditation. *Thirdly*, students' engagement in QA occurs through being involved or considered when developing improvement plans (Zavale et al., 2015).

There are at least two remaining challenges to fully engage students in the UEM's IQA. The first challenge regards the power of students to influence decision-making. Students are often involved, but they are not so powerful or do not possess instruments enabling them to make their voices heard. Lecturers and academic managers continue to hold the largest share of power as regards to what to do or not with data collected through evaluations. The second challenge regards the likelihood of students participating in the forum where discussions and decisions on QA are held. In most managing boards, both at university and faculty levels, students do not have representatives. For example, at university level, most issues are regularly discussed at the council of deans and directors, but students are not represented in these forums. Students are only represented in University Council, which is the main decision-making forum of the university. However, the university council meets ordinarily only three times a year, while other forums are more regular. In addition, students' weight is not so significant if one takes into account that there is only 1 representative of students among the 24 members of the university council (http://www.uem.mz/index.php/membros-do-conselho-u niversitario, consulted in July 2018), representing managers, lecturers, external stakeholders (government, civil society, companies, etc.), administrative staff and so on. This situation is replicated at the faculty level. Only 1 student represents the voice of students in the faculty council – the main decision board – which is composed of about 20 members representing academic managers, lecturers, administrative staff and external stakeholders. The faculty management council, which meets regularly and whenever there is a necessity, is composed of representatives of managers, but students are not represented. The scientific council, which is responsible for scientific issues of the faculty, does not have students' representative. The pedagogical council is composed of about 25 members (dean, deputy-deans, heads of department, lecturers), but only 2 representatives of students (see, for example, the *regulamento interno* of the faculty of education, http://www.faced.uem.mz/index.php/regulamentos).

These challenges suggest that, although students are not completely ignored within the UEM's IQA, reforms at regulations, policy and practical levels are needed to enable their full engagement and participation in the decision-making process about the quality of the education provided by the institution.

Mozambican students' engagement with their learning: some trends

To the best of our knowledge, a systematic survey on students' engagement has not yet been conducted in Mozambique. There is a dearth of studies on how Mozambican students engage with their learning and knowledge. Our objective in this section is to discuss some data and findings, albeit partial, on the degree of engagement of Mozambican students with their learning and knowledge.

Malombe (2017), a former Master student from the Faculty of Education-UEM, studied the influence of academic and social adjustment to HE on academic achievement. Based on questionnaire administered to 65 first-year students enrolled in 2015 at Higher Institute of Arts and Culture (ISARC), Malombe (2017) found that academic and social adjustment matters to academic achievement. While both social and academic adjustment are relevant, Malombe's (2017) findings reveal that academic adjustment is more relevant to academic achievement than social adjustment.

Chiruru (2017), another former Master student from the Faculty of Education-UEM, examined the effect of employment on academic achievement of 75 students attending day and night-shift BA programmes in Sociology and in History and Public Management in 2015 at Pedagogical University, the second oldest university in Mozambique. Based on data collected through a questionnaire, Chiruru (2017) concluded that, in general, student employment had no significant negative effects on academic achievement. Both Malombe's (2017) and Chiruru's (2017) findings suggest that external factors may have less impact on Mozambican students' engagement with their learning and knowledge than academic factors. This hypothesis is backed by a study on determinants of graduation rates, which concluded that the graduation rates at UEM are mostly affected by academic aspects of students and institution (Zavale et al., 2017).

However, both Malombe (2017) and Chiruru (2017) did not focus on pedagogical practices occurring within HEIs that might affect students' learning. Covele's (2017) case study seems to provide insights on such practices. Covele (2017), also a former Master student from the Faculty of Education-UEM, studied the research-teaching nexus, i.e., the linkages between teaching and research in two undergraduate programmes at UEM: BA in Environmental Education at the Faculty of Education and BSc in Civil Engineering at the Faculty of Engineering. Covele (2017) carried out documentary analysis, conducted classroom observations and administered questionnaires, and conducted interviews, to students and lecturers, in order to examine the curriculum designs and teaching practices used to link teaching and research in these programmes. Covele's (2017) findings reveal that the integration of research and teaching in these programmes is very low. In other words, both programmes predominantly use a research-led curriculum (learning about others' research, lectures and traditional written tests), associated with lecturer-focused method, in which lecturers are "knowledge transmitters" and students "passive recipient of knowledge". Other practices, particularly those leading to students' active and critical engagement with research, are hardly used. The hypothesis that teaching methods used at UEM may not be adequate to positively impact students' active learning is consistent with data produced by the UEM's QA Office. In 2014, the QA Office surveyed about 289 graduates from 13 academic programmes from several UEM colleges on different aspects of their perception and experience at university. The survey's findings reveal that about 90% of graduates consider teaching methods at UEM theoretical and only about 30% indicate professional internships and dramatization as the methods used (Zavale et al., 2015). The UEM's QA Office also surveyed about 1816 students from 17 academic programmes representing 15 of the total 17 UEM colleges on different aspects of their perception and experience at university. The survey's findings reveal that about, while most students (about 80%) are satisfied with the content of the curriculum, less than 50% are satisfied with the quality of lecturers, students' assessment process, including timely feedback, and lecturers' availability to students (UEM, 2014).

These findings are in line with Schendel's (2015) claim that students in some Rwandan universities are not substantially improving in their critical thinking during their time at university.

In conclusion, the degree of engagement of Mozambican students with their own learning is still an under-researched terrain. The scant available literature seems to suggest two trends or insights. Firstly, that external factors impact less on Mozambican students' engagement than academic factors. Secondly, that universities seem to be using teaching methods that are inadequate to impact students' active learning. Thirdly, at least by 2014, the structure of HE and the labour market enabled graduates to easily obtain jobs and employers assessed positively the knowledge and skills of UEM's graduates, but caution is needed given the methodological bias of the survey to graduates and employers.

Conclusions

In this chapter, we examined students' engagement in African HE. Two conclusions can be drawn from our literature review. Firstly, it is difficult to draw a conclusive taxonomy of common patterns and practices of student engagement in governance of African because of variation across countries. However, a tentative trait suggests that, while most countries recognize in policies, and sometimes in legislation, the relevance of student engagement, this recognition is not always translated into effective practices of supporting and listening to students' voices in decision-making and policy-formulation. Secondly, most African students are not substantially engaging with academically-relevant activities while at university and that HE policies should shift from only expanding HE to enabling access of students to relevant knowledge and skills. Mozambique is still an under-researched terrain as regards to students' engagement, but available literature and findings seems to be consistent with the general African trends.

Note

1 http://www.portaldogoverno.gov.mz/por/Imprensa/Noticias/Governo-reitera-apoio-a o-programa-ferias-desenvolvendo-o-distrito

References

Allais, S. (2014). A critical perspective on large class teaching: the political economy of massification and the sociology of knowledge. *Higher Education*, 67(6), 721–734.

Ansah, F. (2016). Conceptualising external and internal quality assurance in higher education: a pragmatist perspective. *International Journal of African Higher Education*, 2(1), 136–152.

Arvanitakis, J. (2014). Massification and the large lecture theatre: from panic to excitement. *Higher Education*, 67(6), 735–745.

Asare, S., Nicholson, H. and Stein, S. (2017). You can't ignore us: what role does family play in student engagement and alienation in a Ghanaian university? *Journal of Higher Education Policy and Management*, 39(6), 593–606.

Astin, A.W. (1984) Student involvement: a developmental theory for higher education. *Journal of College Student Development*, 25, 297–308.

Ayele, B. W. (2016). Student participation in the governance of Ethiopian higher education institutions: the case of Addis Ababa University. In: Luescher-Mamashela, T. M.et al. (eds.) *Student Politics in Africa: Representation and Activism*. Cape Town: African Minds, pp. 129–161.

Bailey, T. (2015) The roles of national councils and commissions in African higher education system governance. In: Cloete, N., Maassen, P. and Bailey, T. (eds) *Knowledge Production and Contradictory Functions in African Higher Education* (AHED Series Vol. 1). Cape Town: African Minds, pp. 171–202.

Bennell, P. (1996). Rates of return to education: does the conventional pattern prevail in Sub-Saharan Africa? *World Development*, 24(1), 183–199.

Beverwijk, J. M. R. (2005). *The Genesis of a System: A Coalition Formation in Mozambican Higher Education, 1993–2003*. Enschede: CHEPS/University of Twente.

Bianchini, P. (2016). The three ages of student politics in Francophone Africa: learning from the cases of Senegal and Burkina Faso. In: Luescher-Mamashela, T. M.et al. (eds.) *Student Politics in Africa: Representation and Activism*. Cape Town: African Minds, pp. 85–108

Bloom, D., Canning, D., Chan, K. and Luca, D. (2014). Higher education and economic growth in Africa. *International Journal of African Higher Education*, 1(1): 23–57.

Cabaço, J. L. (2007). *O. Moçambique: Identidades, Colonialismo e Libertação*. Sao Paulo: USP.

Chiruru, F. (2017). *Effects of Student Employment on Academic Success/Failure: A Study Conducted with 2015 Third Year Sociology and Political History and Public Management students at the Pedagogical University-Maputo*, MA Dissertation. Maputo: Universidade Eduardo Mondlane.

Cloete, N., Maassen, P. and Bailey, T. (eds.) (2015). *Knowledge Production and Contradictory Functions in African Higher Education*. Cape Town: African Minds. African Minds Higher Education Dynamics Series Vol. 1.

Covele, V. J. (2017). *Teaching Nexus in Mozambican Higher Education Curricula. The Case Study of Eduardo Mondlane University*, Master's Dissertation. Maputo: Universidade Eduardo Mondlane.

Hornsby, D. J. and Osman, R. (2014). Massification in higher education: large classes and student learning. *Higher Education*, 67(6), 711–719.

Foley, A. R. and Masingila, J. O. (2014). Building capacity: challenges and opportunities in large class pedagogy (LCP) in Sub-Saharan Africa. *Higher Education*, 67(6), 797–808.

Fongwa, S. N. and Chifon, G. N. (2016). Revisiting student participation in higher education governance at the University of Buea, Cameroon: 2004–2013. In: Luescher-Mamashela, T. M.et al. (eds.) *Student Politics in Africa: Representation and Activism*. Cape Town: African Minds, pp. 109–128.

Klemenčič, M., Luescher-Mamashela, T. M. and Jowi, J. O. (2015). Editorial: student power in Africa. *Journal of Student Affairs in Africa*, 3(1), vii–xiv.

Klemenčič, M., Luescher-Mamashela, T. M. and Magume, T. (2016). Student organising in African higher education: polity, politics and policies. In: Luescher-Mamashela, T. M.et al. (eds.) *Student Politics in Africa: Representation and Activism*. Cape Town: African Minds, pp. 9–26.

Kuh, G. D. (2003) What we are learning about student engagement from the NSSE. *Change*, 35(2), 24–35.

Kuh, G. D., Kinzie, J., Schuh, J. H. and Whitt, E. J. (2005) *Student Success in College: Creating Conditions that Matter*. San Francisco: Josey-Bass.

Langa, P. V. (2006). *The Constitution of the Field of Higher Education Institutions in Mozambique*, MA dissertation. Cape Towan: University of Cape Town.

Langa, P.V. (2014a). Alguns desafios do ensino superior em Moçambique: do conhecimento experiencial à necessidade de produção de conhecimento científico. In De Brito, L., Castel-Branco, C.N., Chichava, S. and Francisco, A. (eds.). *Desafios para Moçambique 2014*. Maputo: IESE, pp. 365–395.

Langa, P.V. (2014b) *The Roles and Functions of Higher Education Councils and Commissions in Africa: A Case Study of the Mozambique's CNAQ*. Cape Town: CHET.

Langa, P.V.Cumaio, G. and Rafael, D. P. (2014). *Cinquenta anos de Legislação e Políticas Públicas do Ensino Superior em Moçambique*. Cape Town: African Minds.

Luescher-Mamashela, T. M. (2005). *Student Governance in Africa: Thematic Summary of Key Literature, Prepared for the Center for Higher Education Transformation*. Wynberg (South Africa): Centre for Higher Education Transformation (CHET).

Luescher-Mamashela, T. and Magume, T. (2014). Student representation and multiparty politics in African higher education. *Studies in Higher Education*, 39(3), 500–515.

Luescher-Mamashela, T. M., Klemencic, M. and Jowi, J. O. (2016). *Student Politics in Africa: Representation and Activism* (Vol. 2). Cape Town: African Minds.

Malombe, R. (2017). *The Influence of Academic and Social Adjustment to Higher Education on Academic Achievement: A Study Conducted with First-Year University Students of Cultural Studies and Management*, MA Dissertation. Maputo: Universidade Eduardo Mondlane.

Mário, M., Fry, P., Levey, L. A. and Chilundo, A. (2003). *Higher Education in Mozambique*. Oxford: James Curry.

Materu, P. (2007) *Higher Education Quality Assurance in Sub-Saharan Africa: Status, Challenges, Opportunities and Promising Practices*. Washington DC: World Bank.

Mazula, B. (1995). *Educação, Cultura e Ideologia em Moçambique-1975–1985: Em busca de fundamentos filosófico-antropológicos*. Santa Maria da Feira: Edições Afrontamento.

Magume, T. and Luescher-Mamashela, T. M. (2015). The politics of student housing: student activism and representation in the determination of the user-price of a public–private partnership residence on a public university campus in South Africa. *Journal of Student Affairs in Africa*, 3(1), 1–17.

MINED (Ministério da Educação) (2014) *Dados Estatísticos sobre o Ensino Superior em Moçmbique 2012*. Maputo: MINED.

Mohamedbhai, G. (2014). Massification in higher education institutions in Africa: causes, consequences and responses. *International Journal of African Higher Education*, 1(1): 60–83.

Mondlane, E. (1969). The struggle for Mozambique. Chapter 5. *Resistance – The Search for a National Movement*. London: Zed Press.

Mulinge, M. M. and Arasa, J. N. (2017). *The Status of Student Involvement in University Governance in Kenya: The Case of Public and Private Universities*. Dakar: CODESRIA.

Oanda, I. (2016). The evolving nature of student participation in university governance in Africa: An overview of policies, trends and emerging issues. In: Luescher-Mamashela, T. M.et al. (eds.) *Student Politics in Africa: Representation and Activism*. Cape Town: African Minds, pp. 61–84.

Odhiambo, G. O. (2014) Quality assurance for public higher education: context, strategies and challenges in Kenya. *Higher Education Research & Development*, 33(5), 978–991.

Ogachi, O. (2009). Internationalization vs regionalization of higher education in East Africa and the challenges of quality assurance and knowledge production. *Higher Education Policy*, 22(3), 331–347.

Oni, A. A. and Adetoro, J. A. (2015). The effectiveness of student involvement in decision-making and university leadership: a comparative analysis of 12 universities in South-West Nigeria. *Journal of Student Affairs in Africa*, 3(1), 65–81.

Pascarella, E .T. and Terenzini, P .T. (2005) *How College Affects Students: A Third Decade of Research* (Vol. 2). San Francisco: Jossey-Bass.

Pereira, C. L. and Gonzalez, L. (2016). *História da AAM: Associação Académica de Moçambique (1964–1975)*. 1st edn. Vila Nova de Gaia: Calendário de Letras.

Schendel, R. (2015). Critical thinking at Rwanda's public universities: emerging evidence of a crucial development priority. *International Journal of Educational Development*, 42, 96–105.

Schendel, R. (2016a). Adapting, not adopting: barriers affecting teaching for critical thinking at two Rwandan universities. *Comparative Education Review*, 60(3), 549–570.

Schendel, R. (2016b). Constructing departmental culture to support student development: evidence from a case study in Rwanda. *Higher Education*, 72(4), 487–504.

Schendel, R. and McCowan, T. (2016). Expanding higher education systems in low-and middle-income countries: the challenges of equity and quality. *Higher Education*, 72(4), 407–411.

Shrivastava, M. and Shrivastava, S. (2014). Political economy of higher education: comparing South Africa to trends in the world. *Higher Education*, 67(6), 809–822.

Strydom, F., Kuh, G. and Mentz, M. (2010). Enhancing success in South Africa's higher education: Measuring student engagement. *Acta Academica*, 42(1), 259–278.

Strydom, J. F., and Mentz, M. (2010). *Focusing the Student Experience on Success through Student Engagement*. Pretoria: Council on Higher Education.

UEM (2012) *Sistema de Garantia de Qualidade Académica da UEM (SISQUAL)*. Maputo: UEM.

UEM (2014). *Relatório Global de Auto-avaliação dos Cursos*. Maputo: UEM. Available at: http://gqa.uem.mz/images/pdf_files/relatorioglobal2014.pdf (accessed 27 May 2015).

UEM (2017) *Sistema de Garantia de Qualidade Académica da UEM (SISQUAL): Estado de Implementação. Relatório 2012–2016*. Maputo: UEM.

UNESCO. (2015). *UNESCO's Scientific Report towards Horizon 2030*. Paris: UNESCO.

UNESCO Institute for Statistics (2015). *UNESCO Data-tables*. Available at: http://data.uis.unesco.org/ (accessed 23 September 2016).

Westerheijden, D. F., Stensaker, B. and Rosa, M. J. (Eds.) (2007). *Quality Assurance in Higher Education: Trends in Regulation, Translation and Transformation* (Vol. 20). Dordrecht: Springer Science & Business Media.

World Bank (2009). *Accelerating Catch-up: Tertiary Education for Growth in Sub-Saharan Africa*. Washington, DC: World Bank.

World Bank (2010). *Financing Higher Education in Africa*. Washington, DC: World Bank.

Zavale, N.C. (2017). Expansion versus contribution of higher education in Africa: university-industry linkages in Mozambique from firms' perspective. *Science and Public Policy*, 1–17 (Oxford University Press), First Online paper: doi:10.1093/scipol/scx089

Zavale, N. C., Santos, L. and Dias, M. da C. (2015). Main features and challenges of implementing an internal quality assurance in African higher education institution: the case of the Eduardo Mondlane University, in Mozambique. *International Journal of African Higher Education*, 2(1): 101–134.

Zavale, N. C., Santos, L. A., Manuel, L., Maria da Conceição, L. D., Khan, M. A., Tostão, E. and Mondjana, A. M. (2017). Decision-making in African universities demands rigorous data: Evidence from graduation rates at Eduardo Mondlane University in Mozambique. *International Journal of Educational Development*, 52, 122–134.

Zeleza, P.T. (2016). *The Transformation of Global Higher Education, 1945–2015*. New York: Palgrave-MacMillan.

9

STUDENT ENGAGEMENT IN QUALITY ASSURANCE OF HIGHER EDUCATION IN KAZAKHSTAN

Ambiguous forms and invisible procedures

Kuanysh Tastanbekova

UNIVERSITY OF TSUKUBA

Introduction

The Republic of Kazakhstan appeared on the international arena as an independent state at the end of 1991, following the collapse of the Soviet Union of which it was a member for more than seven decades. A public education system with universal access to free education at all levels was established during these years and was common for all fifteen Soviet socialist republics. A top-down command administration centralised this system across all spheres: planning, governance, financing, curriculum design and implementation control, quality assurance and evaluation. Specifically, higher education was featured by:

> a centrally planned organization and financing, subordination to multiple sectoral ministries, a national curriculum, a vocational orientation based on the combination of strong basic education and narrow specialized job–related training, a nomenclature of types of higher education institutions, tuition-free study places and guaranteed employment upon graduation combined with mandatory job placement. (Smolentseva et al., 2018: 1)

Shifting from a centralised planned economy to a liberal market economy, ideological changes and integration into international education standards have led to significant transformations in Kazakhstani higher education. Meanwhile, education quality has been addressed as an essential issue of education reform only from the second decade after independence and was driven by complex internal and external factors.

This chapter provides an overview of higher education reforms in post-independence Kazakhstan to highlight the stages of the system's transformation from a Soviet system to a new one. It outlines significant elements of the quality assurance system focusing on the influence of the Bologna Process. Applying the three-level framework of Healey et al. (2010), which is adopted by this book, this chapter observes only two levels of student engagement in quality assurance: macro- and meso-level engagement. The macro level takes the form of the participation of selected students in the process of university accreditation. The meso level represents student participation in questionnaires related to a particular teacher and subject's quality conducted by a university for internal quality monitoring and assessment. Examples of student engagement at the micro level regarding the organisation of self-learning and peer-learning processes might exist, although no evidence was found among the materials provided on university websites or in related scholarly works. This might mean the absence of systematic approach to this level.

This chapter argues that student engagement in quality assurance of higher education in Kazakhstan was driven by the implementation of the Bologna Process framework and is still in its formation. This process is challenged by Soviet legacies of formalisation and bureaucratic practices which leads to ambiguous forms and invisible procedures.

Reform of higher education: marketisation and the Bologna Process

As mentioned earlier, the education system in general and higher education, in particular, was established and developed during the Soviet period. Froumin and Kouzminov (2018: 46) argue that the Soviet system of higher education was:

> an element of a grand social engineering project—a master plan for a system where higher education institutions (HEIs) were specialized parts of state-controlled machine for manpower production, for the production of a 'new man' and for reshaping the social and ethnic structure of the country.

Hence, the development of higher education in the former Soviet ethnic republics contained four major functions: economic development, ethnic, cultural development and the Russification and equalisation of access (ibid., 66).

Upon gaining independence, higher education in Kazakhstan was represented by 55 HEIs with 287,400 students enrolled. Most of HEIs were either regional institutes or specialised institutes that were subordinate to the Ministry of Education (currently the Ministry of Education and Science [MoES] but, at that time, the Ministry of Higher and Secondary Special Education) or other Ministries such as the Ministry of Health Care, Ministry of Transport, Ministry of Internal Affairs and others. Regional institutes were established to meet the basic needs of the region, for instance, teacher training (pedagogical) institutes existed in each regional centre. Whereas sector specific specialised institutes (e.g., oil and gas, engineering) were concentrated in the former capital (then Alma-Ata, after independence, renamed to Almaty) (Ahn et al., 2018: 201–202).

Political, economic and social transformations happening in Kazakhstan after independence led to large-scale reforms that significantly reshaped the higher education landscape. They are the marketisation of higher education (introduction of non-government sector and privatisation of public HEIs) and the implementation of the Bologna Process framework.

Marketisation

The collapse of the Soviet Union was followed by the breaking up of the severely centralised planned economy. Each newly independent republic, including Kazakhstan, has faced economic decline leading to a deterioration of various indicators. According to World Bank (WB) data, GDP has dropped by 39% in the period from 1991 to 1996 (cited in Ahn et al., 2018: 203). In 1993 four-digit inflation worsened the budget deficit (Akanov and Suzhikova, 1998: 236; cited in Azimbayeva, 2017: 9). Government expenditure on education in general and higher education notably decreased. The share of higher education expenditure in GDP dropped from 0.3% in 1991 to 0.04% in 1992 (Azimbayeva, 2017: 9). Although containing dispersed data, Figure 9.1 shows that government expenditure on education has not changed significantly since its drop in the early years of independence. Funding shortfalls, lack of experience, an urgent need to recover the economy and solve social issues were addressed by international development assistance. Assistance from the WB, Asian Development Bank (ADB), International Monetary Fund (IMF) and international NGO (e.g., Open Society Institute/Soros Foundation), as well as from donor countries, was expected to contribute to a

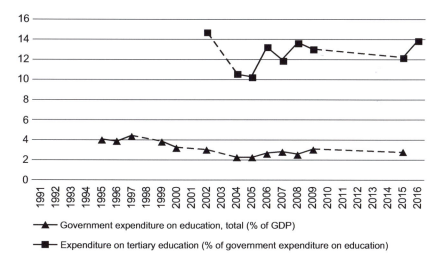

FIGURE 9.1 Expenditure on education in Kazakhstan (1991–2016)
Data on government expenditure on education as % of GDP for years 1991–1994, 1998, 2001, 2003, 2010–2014, and data on expenditure on tertiary education as % of government expenditure on education for years 1991–2002, 2004, 2010–2014 are not available.
Source: This figure was created by the author based on the World Bank databank 'World Development Indicators'.

solution of these problems on the one hand, and the modernisation of national education systems to meet international standards on the other. Specifically, in the area of education, large-scale financial and consulting assistance was received from ADB (Asanova, 2006). Recommendations were based on the neoliberal principles of market economy and they stressed the decentralisation and liberalisation of education as the most important issues. Silova and Steiner-Khamsi (2008) framed these reforms into 'post-socialist education reforms package' and characterised them as a trend of 'policy borrowing and lending' practice that has circulated across many developing countries.

The transition from a planned economy to a market economy required a reduction of state ownership. In 1993, the 'Law on Higher Education' outlined market principles and permitted the establishment and operation of the private sector in higher education. Since then, the number of private HEIs has risen rapidly. In a short period, 32 private HEIs were opened. By 1996–1997 the share of public HEIs to private was 43.2% to 56.8% (Ahn et al. 2018: 206). According to data available from the website of the Committee of Statistics, the overall number of HEIs increased to its maximum of 181 in the 2003–2004 academic year where 58.6% of students were enrolled in 130 private and 41.0% of students in 51 public HEIs. The total gross enrolment in higher education increased from 38.8% in 1990 to 57% in 2006 and decreased to 46.8% in 2016 (WB data). Figure 9.2 shows the growth in the number of HEIs and enrolled students until 2004–2005. Increased accountability can explain the decrease in both numbers from MoES (optimisation of the number of HEIs due to tightening of regulations for private HEIs and the merger of regional HEIs) and a demographic decrease (Ahn et al., 2018: 206).

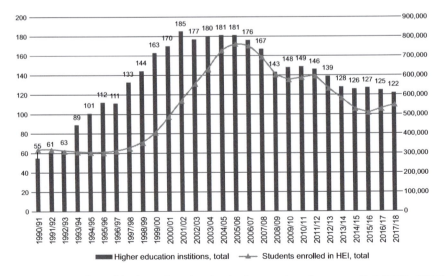

FIGURE 9.2 Number of higher education institutions and students enrolled (1991–2017)
Source: This figure was created by the author based on the Ministry of National Economy Committee on Statistics

The 'Law on Education' of 1999 introduced two-channel financing for public HEIs—state funding and student tuition fees. State funding follows students that received grants (full scholarship) based on their performance at an admission test (unified national test). In 2017, 40–50% of the revenue of public HEIs was generated from paid educational services (European Commission, 2017: 4).

Furthermore, the 'Law on the List of Republican State Enterprises and Institutions to be privatised in 2000–2001' allowed for the privatisation of public HEIs. In short order, 12 public HEIs were corporatised in joint-stock companies (Kazakhstani government shared ownership with private individual/s and corporations). This led to the further marketisation of higher education and diversification of the higher education landscape (Ahn et al., 2018: 208).

As of 2016–2017 the academic year for higher education was represented by 125 HEIs: 9 national (7 universities, 1 Academy of choreography, 1 Academy of art, all public), 31 public (mostly regional), 13 non-civil (e.g. military, internal affairs, diplomacy academies), 16 corporatised, 54 private, 1 international and 1 AOE (Autonomous Organisation of Education Nazarbayev University).

Implementation of the Bologna Process framework

Another factor of higher education reform was the integration into the European Higher Education Area through the implementation of the Bologna Process framework. Isolated from international education trends and the labour market during the Soviet period, the Kazakhstan government intended to 'facilitate increased student and faculty mobility in and out of Kazakhstan, as well as the greater degree of recognition and alignment with international education structures' (Ahn et al., 2018: 212). On 12 March 2010, at the EHEA ministerial conference in Vienna, Kazakhstan became the first Central Asian country to join EHEA by signing the 'Lisbon Convention on the Recognition of Qualifications concerning Higher Education in the European Region'. Joining the Bologna Process of higher education has been transformed in following ways:

1. a three-degree cycle (bachelor four years, master two years, doctoral three years) was implemented;
2. a European Credit Transfer System (ECTS) was introduced in HEIs;
3. students and faculty mobility was ensured by allocating state funding to HEIs;
4. an internal and external quality assurance system was established.

Notwithstanding that system has been reconstructed with significant financial and human sources invested, the Bologna Process still inspires many controversies. Some scholars argue that joining the Bologna Process was politically and economically driven project for both Kazakhstan and the European Union (Tomusk, 2011; Jones, 2011, Soltys, 2014). Others claim that those who criticise the government for being interested in the Bologna Process politically and economically misinterpreted the reform due to an oversimplified view of the country's reconstruction process

(Tampayeva, 2015: 77). Still others argue that Kazakhstan's higher education practices are far from the Bologna Process requirements because 'rather than understanding the philosophy of the integration process' action lines and principles, higher education institutions behave in a way that aims at pleasing international accreditation authorities by basing themselves on control'. Thus, 'novelties included in Kazakhstan's higher education ... have become mere formalities without practical functions' (Yergebekov and Temirbekova, 2012: 1477). Another argument is represented by those who, while admitting significant accomplishments in reforms, argue that the reasons for the slow implementation of the Bologna Process are 'rooted in the incompleteness of basic administrative reforms' (Monobayeva and Howard, 2015: 159–160).

Nevertheless, it is evident that marketisation and implementation of the Bologna Process framework required the development of a quality assurance system which will now be discussed.

The higher education quality assurance system: from state control to the competitive environment

Quality assurance for higher education has developed in two stages (Kalanova, 2016; Kerimkulova and Kuzhabekova, 2017).

The first stage covers the period from 1999 to 2009. The 'Law on Education' of 1999 and the later law of 2007 legalised such procedures as licensing, attestation and accreditation. It was a period of highly centralised top–down quality control. The strategic document, the 'State Programme of Education Development for 2005–2010' ('SPED 2005–2010') set up three dimensions of the education quality assurance—development of a national system of quality assessment, implementation of institutional evaluation and accreditation, and implementation of the system of quality management. Infrastructure and the mechanism for the development of a quality assurance framework were concentrated in government agencies subordinated to MoES. They are the Accreditation Council (AC, established in 2001), National Accreditation Center (NAC, established in 2005), Committee for Control in Education and Science (CCES) and the Committee for Supervision and Attestation (CSA) (both established in 2007). All of these bodies are unified in a National System of Education Quality Assessment (NSEQA, established in 2004) for the realisation of external evaluation (licensing, attestation, accreditation, certification, rating, the unified national testing and comprehensive testing of applicants and the intermediate state control). The first state accreditation of HEIs was carried out in 2001 by the Accreditation Council within one week for 59 (47 public and 12 private) out of 182 HEIs. It was based solely on quantitative data and was highly criticised by private HEIs and the public. Following this criticism, state accreditation of HEIs was suspended and, in response to that, NAC was established for developing standards and procedures of institutional accreditation (Kalanova, 2016: 15).

As for the latter two bodies, CCES and SCA, they have delegated quality control mechanisms through licensing (CCES) and state attestation (SCA). Licensing was an obligatory procedure for HEI to check its adequacy to meet the minimum requirements (e.g., faculty-student ration, facilities, libraries, etc.) imposed by the government for delivering particular study programmes. State attestation procedure followed licensing and was carried out every five years to assess the adequacy of the realisation of state compulsory education standards for the level, content, quality and qualifications requirements reported for the licensing. Attestation presented a comprehensive assessment of inputs, outputs and mechanical procedures of education process (Kerimkulova and Kuzhabekova, 2017: 93).

The second stage of the development of quality assurance covers the period from 2010 to 2016. In March 2010, Kazakhstan was accepted to EHEA and joined the Bologna Process. In December 2010, the 'State Programme of Education Development for 2011–2020' (SPED 2011–2020) was adopted, where integration into EAHEA was declared as a strategic goal of higher education policy. To achieve this goal one of the tasks was the implementation of independent accreditation of HEIs by national and international agencies. It was declared that all accreditation agencies would be registered in the European Register of Quality Assurance in higher education (ERQA), and it was planned that, by 2020, 14% of all HEIs would get international accreditation, and national agencies would accredit 65%. In October 2011, the 'Law on Education' of 2007 was amended to emphasise the importance of accreditation quality assurance, and to move its realisation from government bodies to independent agencies, accreditation was stated to be voluntary based, and HEIs were free to choose an agency to conduct it. The adoption of SPED 2011–2020 and the amendment to the 'Law on Education' served as a renewal of the legal framework of education reforms and have sped them up. At the end of 2011, the National Register of Accreditation Agencies was established and followed by the creation of the Republican Accreditation Board in May 2012. All of these actions were taken upon consultation with the representatives of EQAR (Kalanova, 2016: 16). The number of registered accreditation agencies has increased from six in 2012 to 14 in 2017. They are the:

1. Independent Kazakh Agency for Quality Assurance in Education (IQAA, Kazakhstan)
2. Independent Agency for Accreditation and Rating (IAAR, Kazakhstan)
3. Eurasian Center for Accreditation and Quality Assurance in Higher Education and Healthcare (ECAQA, Kazakhstan)
4. Independent Accreditation and Education Quality Assessment Agency (ARQA, Kazakhstan)
5. Kazakh Society of Engineering Education (KazSEE, Kazakhstan)
6. Accreditation Board for Engineering and Technology (ABET, USA)
7. Accreditation Council for Business Schools and Programmes (ACBSP, USA)
8. Accreditation, Certification and Quality Assurance Institute (AQCUIN, Germany)

9. Accreditation Agency Specialised in Accrediting Degree Programmes in Engineering (ASIIN, Germany)
10. Foundation for International Business Administration Accreditation (FIBAA, Germany)
11. Agency for Quality Assurance and Accreditation Austria (AQ, Austria)
12. Institute of Marine Engineering, Science and Technology (IMarEST, UK)
13. Middle States Association of Colleges and Schools—Commissions on Elementary and Secondary Schools (MSA-CESS, USA)
14. Music Quality Enhancement (MusiQUE, Belgium).

To enhance HEIs' motivation to gain accreditation, MoES exempted obligatory state attestation for those HEIs which have undergone accreditation by 2015 and provided them state funding for undergraduate and postgraduate courses (Assylbekova and Kalanova, 2015: 296). Eventually, as it was planned in the new 'State Programme of Education Development for 2016–2019' (SPED 2016–2019), state attestation was entirely replaced by accreditation in 2017. According to the 'National report on the state and development of educational system in the Republic of Kazakhstan. Years of Independence', as of the end of 2016, 96 out of 125 HEIs, and 2,852 undergraduate and postgraduate programmes have been accredited by national and international agencies (IAC, 2017).

In summary, quality assurance systems in Kazakhstan have departed from the Soviet legacy of highly centralised government control to be carried out in the independent competitive environment. However, the impact of accreditation is rather unclear. Kerimkulova and Kuzhabekova (2017: 97) argue as follows: 'It is possible that Kazakhstani HEIs, being used to centralised regulations, take a formalisation and superficial approach to accreditation. A lack of understanding of standards, content, and procedures of accreditation can be observed at the school and department levels.'

OECD experts also find limitations in the current system stressing that the

> legacy of centralized control hampers progress of independent external quality assurance. And as far as MoES remains the authority which stands behind accreditation decisions and the consequences of these decisions … internal institutional quality assurance and improvement mechanisms, as well as broader accreditation system, still appear to be underdeveloped. (OECD, 2017: 23)

The presence of a significant number of institutions and programmes that have been accredited mostly by two national agencies in relatively short time 'raises concern about the thoroughness of the process, given the limited number of faculty in Kazakhstan who have the expertise needed to serve on review panels' (OECD, 2017: 23).

Furthermore, it should not be left unnoticed that state control over education quality remains in the form of licensing, control over educational organisations' compliance with the legislation, state attestation for specialised HEIs (e.g. military) and the external assessment of student learning outcomes (such as unified national tests as competition for enrolment in HEIs, and external tests of academic achievements conducted to evaluate student performance and efficiency in the educational process). The latter practice of external assessment was criticised by OECD and WB experts in their reviews of higher education in Kazakhstan in 2007 as an inadequate and inefficient way that 'push[es] students and institutions to become more concerned about the test than about their wider learning' (OECD/WB, 2007: 119). In 2007, it was recommended to 'move towards quality assurance arrangements that make it safe to allow HEIs to develop and set their final tests (and interim tests if necessary) to test the mastery of their curricula (OECD/WB, 2007: 120). However, the over-emphasis on testing, as well as HEIs' limited autonomy, remains (OECD, 2017: 84).

Student engagement in quality assurance: ambiguous forms, invisible procedures

Student engagement in quality assurance is a crucial component of the Bologna Process. The EHEA ministerial Prague Communiqué of 2001 recognised students as 'competent, active and constructive partners in the establishment of EHEA', and declared that students 'should participate in and influence the organisation and content of education at universities and other higher education institutions'. The Berlin Communiqué of 2003 confirmed the expansion of student roles in higher education governance. The first European Standards and Guidelines for Quality Assurance in the EHEA (ESG) were developed in 2005, for students to begin participating in the evaluation of educational programmes through external audits and accreditation councils. The Yerevan Communiqué of 2015 reconfirmed students as stakeholders to be involved in the process of quality assurance. The ESG states that students are responsible for the quality of higher education on the equal basis with HEIs and its employees (Standard 1.1). Students should participate as experts in the development of accreditation methodology and peer-review of both internal and external quality assurance of HEIs and educational programmes (Standard 1.7, 1.9, 2.3). Furthermore, accreditation agencies are required to ensure that experts are carefully selected, have appropriate skills and are competent in performing their tasks, supported by appropriate training and/or briefing (Standard 2.4).

Since Kazakhstan has joined the EHEA and implemented the Bologna Process framework, accreditation agencies that are registered in the National Register and conduct audit and accreditation of Kazakhstani HEIs and educational programmes, as well as HEIs, must follow the ESG requirements mentioned above. Student engagement in quality assurance at the macro level will be discussed further using the example of student participation in accreditation conducted by external bodies and, at the meso level, using the example of participation in the questionnaires conducted by HEIs for self-evaluation and quality monitoring.

Macro level

One of the leading national accreditation agencies, IQAA, has accredited the most HEIs (61) and educational programmes (1,210) as of 2016 (Kalanova, 2016: 17). By IQAA regulations, the accreditation council making a final decision on accreditation includes student representatives in expert groups who conduct the external assessment. Information provided on the IQAA website (www.iqaa.kz) states that candidates for student representation that are provided by HEIs should correspond to the following requirements:

- to be a current senior student of bachelor course, master student or doctoral student;
- to have experience in representing student issues at the faculty level, university or a country;
- to have some experience in the field of quality assurance or active participation in the life of his/her HEI;
- to have analytical skills and be able to analyse, organise and synthesise information;
- to have good writing skills and be able to write a report; to be able to use computers and information technologies;
- to have good communication skills to interact in the course of external visits (review) with other experts and representatives of HEI;
- to know the programme, which is to be evaluated;
- to be accountable to the public and university undergoing institutional and programme accreditation, and to the agency;
- to have a complete understanding of the trends in the development of the educational system: the Bologna Process, the credit system of study, modular education, and others.

IQAA conducts regular training workshops for all experts (including students), provides videos and interactive materials and actively utilises social networks (official pages on Facebook, Twitter and YouTube) for students to demonstrate different stages of conducting accreditation and enhance the understanding of the role of students in education quality assurance.

IQAA has made a case study analysis of expert student experiences who have participated in their accreditation procedures (Assylbekova and Kalanova, 2015). According to their findings, although the practice of student involvement in accreditation processes do not differ from international analogues, there are issues to be solved. In particular, one case study revealed that 81.2% of respondents (student–experts and student board members) are not provided with full and effective guidance on accreditation procedures. The main difficulties faced by student-experts are a 'lack of information and instructions' (25%) and a 'lack of necessary knowledge and skills of the students to participate in accreditation' (37.5%) (Assylbekova and Kalanova, 2015: 298). Simultaneously, authors stress that respondents 'believe that the participation of students in accreditation as experts and board members is useful in enriching their life and professional experiences' (ibid., 299).

The study does not discuss factors that might cause insufficiency in the accreditation preparation process. However, bearing in mind that a large number of HEIs and programmes have been rapidly accredited in the period from 2012–2016, leading accreditation agencies lacked time for preparation and highly qualified personnel for conducting accreditation, this making the procedures mere formalities (OECD, 2017: 23).

Meso level

As mentioned, HEIs of EHEA must include students in quality assessment procedures. Almost all HEIs in Kazakhstan have a structural allowance for units in charge of quality control. These units carry out procedures of licensing and accreditation, develop mechanisms for the monitoring of academic achievements and internal quality assurance and conduct student surveys on the quality of the teaching process (Kerimkulova and Kuzhabekova, 2017: 101–102).

For this chapter, I accessed websites of 62 universities out of 122. Although many universities claim that they conduct questionnaires, only a few publish the content of questionnaires and their results. Questionnaire samples from three universities, two national (one classic and one teacher training) and one regional public, were received by the author through personal contacts. The questionnaires are titled 'Teacher with student's eyes'. A brief analysis of the sample questionnaires reveals similarities in questions. Questions can be divided into two parts: questions related to the teacher's personal and professional skills, and questions related to the content of the course. Two national universities use unipolar and bipolar Likert scale questionnaires. The regional public university uses dichotomous questions. Two national universities conduct questionnaires online. Students must register on the website, pick a subject, check the related information (e.g., study year, term, teacher's name) and answer a questionnaire. The regional public university conducts a paper-based questionnaire. All questionnaires are anonymous.

According to the introductory parts of questionnaires, their purpose is to monitor and assess teaching quality and to help the teacher to renew course content and improve her/his teaching and assessment methods. However, informal conversations with three teachers at two national universities reveal that teachers do not have access to online questionnaires. They are only provided with reports on some points they received according to a questionnaire's results. Teachers use these points to include in their applications for research funds or to participate in the contest 'Best teacher of the HEI' which is rewarded by funding for research and professional development from foreign universities. In other words, these points serve as incentives for competition between teachers. One teacher mentioned that questionnaires are not always anonymous. In particular, informants of paper-based questionnaires can be identified when they submit the sheets to the unit in charge of the survey. According to this teacher, insufficient mechanisms of anonymity can lead to severe consequences for students.

A limited number of sample questionnaires and a lack of in-depth content analysis alongside an absence of results makes it difficult to generalise, but these three cases confirm the argument presented by Kerimkulova and Kuzhabekova (2017: 105). More specifically, Kazakhstani HEIs are used for 'compliance mentality' caused by a centralised approach to quality assurance. Thus 'HEIs were not used to look critically at the results of their performance, and therefore the process of self-assessment was focused on finding some flaws in work and hiding them, rather than considering them critically with further improvement in mind'.

Conclusion

It should be admitted that, given it went through tectonic transformations after a systemic collapse, Kazakhstan's achievements in the reformation of higher education are significant. However, they should not be overpraised, and it should not be overestimated that these reforms mostly mean structural changes. An understanding of their idiosyncratic meaning, as well as readiness and willingness to accept the changes, are still forthcoming. Student engagement in quality assurance in higher education can serve as an example of this problem. Ambiguous forms and invisible procedures of student engagement in quality assurance are coming, as Ahn et al. (2018: 221) argue, from the 'lack of substantive stakeholder involvement in higher education process' which leads to the 'lack of incentive to supporting reform implementation process meaningfully, as evidenced by the disengagement from the reform process of both external stakeholders (business and civil society organisations) and internal stakeholders (faculty, lower- to mid-level administrators and students)'. Moreover, as with most basic and readily achievable measures, student engagement in quality assurance should be transparent and efficient, starting the real involvement of stakeholders in the reformation process.

References

Ahn, E.S., Dixon, J., Chekmareva, L. (2018) 'Looking at Kazakhstan's higher education landscape: from transition to transformation between 1920 and 2015', Huisman, J., Smolentseva, A., Froumin, I. (Eds.), *25 Years of Transformation of Higher Education Systems in Post-Soviet Countries: Reform and Continuity*, Palgrave Studies in Global Higher Education, Cham: Palgrave Macmillan, 199–227.

Akanov, A., Suzhikova, B. (1998) 'Kazakhstan', Brooks, D., Thant, M. (Eds.) *Social Sector Issues in Transitional Economies of Asia*, New York: Oxford University Press, 235–236.

Asanova, J. (2006) 'Emerging regions, persisting rhetoric of educational aid: impact of the Asian Development Bank on educational policy making in Kazakhstan', *International Journal of Educational Development*, 26, 655–666, doi:10.1016/j.ijedudev.2006.03.003.

Assylbekova, A., Kalanova. Sh. (2015) 'Students' participation in accreditation: the experience of the Republic of Kazakhstan', *Asian Social Science*, 11(6), 294–300, doi:10.5539/ass.v11n6p294.

Azimbayeva, G. (2017) 'Comparing post-Soviet changes in higher education governance in Kazakhstan, Russia, and Uzbekistan', *Cogent Education*, 4, 1399968, doi:10.1080/233186X.2017.1399968.

European Commission Erasmus Plus (2017) *Overview of the Higher Education System. Kazakhstan*, doi:10.2797.985596.

Froumin, I., Kouzminov, Y. (2018) 'Common legacy: evolution of the institutional landscape of Soviet higher education', Huisman, J., Smolentseva, A., Froumin, I. (Eds.), *25 Years of Transformation of Higher Education Systems in Post-Soviet Countries: Reform and Continuity*, Palgrave Studies in Global Higher Education, Cham: Palgrave Macmillan, 45–72.

Healey, M., Mason O'Connor, K., Broadfoot, P. (2010) 'Reflections on engaging students in the process and product of strategy for learning, teaching and assessment: an institutional case study', *International Journal for Academic Development* 15(1), 19–32, doi:10.1080/13601440903529877.

Information Analytical Center (2017) *National Report on State and Development of Educational System in the Republic of Kazakhstan. Years of Independence*, http://iac.kz/sites/default/files/nacdok-2017_ot_kgk_final_09.08.2017_10.00-ilovepdf-compressed.pdf (accessed on 1 March 2018).

Jones, P.D. (2011) 'Education as foreign policy', Silova, I. (Ed.) *Globalization on the Margins: Education and Postsocialist Transformations in Central Asia*, Charlotte: Information Age Publishing, Inc., 63–93.

Kalanova, Sh. (2016) *Thematic Analysis. Higher Education and Quality Assurance of Higher Education in the Republic of Kazakhstan*, Independent Kazakh Agency for Quality Assurance in Education, https://iqaa.kz/images/doc/thematic_analisys_03.pdf (accessed on 1 March 2018).

Kerimkulova, S., Kuzhabekova, A. (2017) 'Quality assurance in higher education of Kazakhstan: a review of the system and issues', Shah, M., Do, Q. (Eds.) *The Rise of Quality Assurance in Asian Higher Education*, Oxford: Chandos Publishing, 87–108.

Ministry of Education and Science of the Republic of Kazakhstan Information Analytical Center (2017) *National Report on Status and Development of Education in the Republic of Kazakhstan*, http://iac.kz/sites/default/files/nacdok-2017_ot_kgk_final_09.08.2017_10.00-ilovepdf-compressed.pdf (accessed on 1 March 2018).

Monobayeva, A., Howard, C. (2015) 'Are post-Soviet republics ready for the new public management? The case of educational modernization in Kazakhstan', *International Journal of Public Sector Management* 28(2), 150–164, doi:10.1108/IJPSM-08-2014-0102.

OECD (2017) *Higher Education in Kazakhstan 2017*, Reviews of National Policies for Education, Paris: OECD Publishing, doi:10.1787/9789264268531-en.

OECD/The World Bank (2007) *Reviews of National Policies for Education: Higher Education in Kazakhstan 2007*, Reviews of National Policies for Education, Paris: OECD Publishing, doi:10.1787/9789264033177-en.

Silova, I., Steiner-Khamsi, G. (Eds.) (2008) *How NGOs React: Globalization and Education Reform in the Caucasus, Central Asia and Mongolia*, Bloomfield: Kumarian Press, Inc.

SmolentsevaA., Huisman, J., Froumin, I. (2018) 'Transformation of higher education institutional landscape in post-Soviet countries: from Soviet model to where?', Huisman, J., Smolentseva, A., Froumin, I. (Eds.), *25 Years of Transformation of Higher Education Systems in Post-Soviet Countries: Reform and Continuity*, Palgrave Studies in Global Higher Education, Cham: Palgrave Macmillan, 1–43.

Soltys, D. (2014) 'Similarities, divergence, and incapacity in the Bologna Process reform implementation by the former-socialist countries: the self-defeat of the state regulations', *Comparative Education*, doi:10.1080/03050068.2014.957908.

Tampayeva, G. (2013) 'Importing education: Europeanization and the Bologna Process in Europe's backyard – The case of Kazakhstan', *European Educational Research Journal* 14(1), 74–85, doi:10.1177/1474904114565154.

Tomusk, V. (2011) 'The geography and geometry of the Bologna Process', Silova, I. (Ed.) *Globalization on the Margins: Education and Postsocialist Transformations in Central Asia*, Charlotte: Information Age Publishing, Inc., 41–62.

Yergebekov, M., Temirbekova, Zh. (2012) 'The Bologna Process and problems in higher education system of Kazakhstan', *Procedia – Social and Behavioural Sciences*, 47, 1473–1478, doi:10.1016/j.sbspro.2012.06.845.

Law on Higher Education of the Republic of Kazakhstan1993 (Adopted 10. 04. 1993, repealed 07. 06. 1999) https://online.zakon.kz/document/?doc_id=1001895#pos=0;0 (in Russian, accessed 2 March 2018)

Legislation

Law on Education of the Republic of Kazakhstan1999 (Adopted 07. 06. 1999, repealed 27. 07. 2007) https://online.zakon.kz/document/?doc_id=1013384 (in Russian, accessed 2 March 2018)

Law on Education of the Republic of Kazakhstan2007 (Adopted 27. 07. 2007, as amended and restated 28. 12. 2017) https://online.zakon.kz/document/?doc_id=30118747#pos=101;-70 (in Russian, accessed 2 March 2018)

State Programme on Education Development2005–2010 (Adopted 11. 10. 2004, repealed 07. 12. 2010) http://online.zakon.kz/Document/?doc_id=1050925 (in Russian, accessed 2 March 2018)

State Programme on Education Development2011–2020 (Adopted 07. 12. 2010, repealed 01. 03. 2016) https://online.zakon.kz/document/?doc_id=30906915#pos=0;168 (in Russian, accessed 2 March 2018)

State Programme on Education Development2016–2019 (Adopted 01. 03. 2016) https://online.zakon.kz/document/?doc_id=32372771 (in Russian, accessed 2 March 2018)

Legislation related to Bologna Process framework

EHEA (1997) *Lisbon Convention on the Recognition of Qualifications concerning Higher Education in the European Region Legislation related to Bologna Process and EHEA*http://media.ehea.info/file/Lisbon_Recognition_Convention/04/5/Lisbon_Recognition_Convention_579045.pdf (Accessed 1 May 2018)

EHEA Ministerial Conference Bologna (1999) *Bologna Declaration*, http://media.ehea.info/file/Ministerial_conferences/02/8/1999_Bologna_Declaration_English_553028.pdf (Accessed 1 May 2018)

EHEA Ministerial Conference Prague (2001) *Prague Communique*, http://media.ehea.info/file/2001_Prague/44/2/2001_Prague_Communique_English_553442.pdf (Accessed 1 May 2018)

EHEA Ministerial Conference Berlin (2003) *Berlin Communique*, http://media.ehea.info/file/2003_Berlin/28/4/2003_Berlin_Communique_English_577284.pdf (Accessed 1 May 2018)

EHEA Ministerial Conference Budapest-Vienna (2010) *Budapest-Vienna Declaration*, http://media.ehea.info/file/2010_Budapest_Vienna/64/0/Budapest-Vienna_Declaration_598640.pdf (Accessed 1 May 2018)

EHEA Ministerial Conference Yerevan (2015) *Yerevan Communique*, http://media.ehea.info/file/2015_Yerevan/70/7/YerevanCommuniqueFinal_613707.pdf (Accessed 1 May 2018)

EQUIP, Standards and Guidelines for Quality Assurance in the European Higher Education Area (ESG). (2015). Brussels, Belgium. http://www.enqa.eu/wp-content/uploads/2015/11/ESG_2015.pdf (Accessed 1 May 2018)

Online resources

Ministry of National Economy of the Republic of Kazakhstan Committee on Statistics https://stat.gov.kz
Independent Kazakh Agency for Quality Assurance in Education https://iqaa.kz
European Higher Education Area and Bologna Process http://www.ehea.info/
World Bank Open Data https://data.worldbank.org

10

STUDENT ENGAGEMENT IN CHINESE HIGHER EDUCATION INSTITUTIONS FOR THE IMPROVEMENT OF EDUCATIONAL QUALITY

Tong Yang

SOUTHEAST UNIVERSITY

Introduction

The modern Chinese higher education system consists of nine years of compulsory education, three years of high-school education, and higher education. Compulsory education comprises six years of elementary education and three years of primary education. Higher education comprises three types of universities: "full time ordinary university" for high school graduates, "adult education university," which provides continuing education for adults, and "military university", which aims to cultivate qualified people relating to military affairs. "Full time ordinary university" can be further categorized into three stages: four or five years of undergraduate education (bachelor degree), two or three years of specialized or vocational education (associate degree), and graduate education (three years of master degree and three years of doctorate degree).

According to the "Higher Education Law of People's Republic of China", the Ministry of Education (hereinafter referred to as "MOE") has the final authority over the establishment of higher education institutions. The MOE establishes basic orientation, policies, and standards for education, supervising general education in China. The organizations that are authorized to supervise higher education institutions are divided into three administrative levels: 1) central government level, such as the MOE and other central agencies; 2) local level, which includes education committees or agencies of provinces, autonomous regions or cities, and districts; and 3) non-government level. Higher education institutions (hereinafter referred to as "HEIs"), managed by the central government and local government levels, are national or public universities. On the other hand, HEIs managed by non-government agencies are private universities. According to the Education Statistics Yearbook of China,[1] in 2016, there were 4,486 HEIs in China, of which 2,925 were national or public universities, accounting for 65.2% of the total number of HEIs. The number of private universities was 1,561 in 2016, accounting for 34.8% of all HEIs.[2] Thus, in China's higher education, central and local governments are highly influential and HEIs are mainly constituted of national or public universities.

Since 1990, China's economic system has undergone a transformation from a planned economy to a market economy. As tuition fees became the most important resources of universities, the role and the voices of students are more prioritized by universities to satisfy students' needs about learning and career development. At the same time, higher education in China went from a system aimed at the elite to one in which education was a goal for the masses.[3] After the quantitative expansion of higher education, the policy gradually focused on improving the quality of higher education. Particularly, HEIs belonging to the "985 project" (hereinafter referred to as "985 institutions"), "211 project" (hereinafter referred to as "211 institutions") receive intensive investment in education from the government and most of them are national or public universities. The "211 project" was implemented by the MOE in 1995 for building 100 major HEIs in China for the 21st century. The MOE issued "Education Promotion Action Plan for the 21st Century" and decided to implement the "985 project" in 1999. This project has aimed to establish a group of world-class universities and high-level research-oriented universities by giving priority financial support to these universities; 985 institutions were recognized as the most excellent universities in China.

Since the 2000s, the government has given more emphasis on improving the quality of education. It is necessary to explore a standard for measuring the elusive qualities, which includes not only the learning outcomes but also learning experiences and processes. Influenced by the Cooperative Institute Research Program with America, 27 universities participated in the NSSE Survey (National Survey of Student Engagement) in 2009, and three universities became members of the SERU (Student Experience in the Research University) in 2011. In 2015, the "Double First Class University Plan (Double Top University Plan)"[4] was implemented to develop a group of elite universities and disciplines into world-class level by giving financial support on a disciplinary basis. The "985 project" and "211 project" are taken into consideration as a whole of the "Double First Class University Plan", in order to simplify the evaluation work of universities. This plan has given further balance to investments in higher education by supporting both individual university departments and elite universities at hard (infrastructure) and soft sides (cultures and ideologies).

In the past 10 years, there has been an increasing transferring trend of assessing the learning process and experiences in universities to make them reflect appropriately on the measurement of educational quality of higher education. In July 2010, the government published the key policy "The Outline of National Long-term Education Reform and Development from 2010 to 2020 (hereinafter referred to as "the Outline").[5] The Outline states detailed goals for all stages of education in the next decade. In 2011, the central government issued a follow-up action plan (hereinafter referred to as "the Action Plan"), stipulating details about the implementations. These two policies received public concern for quality assessment features prominently in new policies in response to a suffocating environment of test score-equivalent-quality and outcome-centered assessment (Ross, Cen & Zhou, 2011, p.25). In 2016, the State Council of the People's Republic of China issued "The 13th Five-Year Plan of National Education Development".[6] According to this policy, the total number of students in HEIs was estimated to reach 38.5 million in 2020. Higher education enrollment will also reach 50% in the same year. With the scale expansion and the quality problem that this entails, the improvement of educational quality was once again confirmed as the policy theme. The cultivation of students' qualities, especially their morality, is the fundamental task of 2016 to 2020.

The macro-level

The Outline, the Higher Education Law of People's Republic of China, the Regulations on Student of Higher Education Institutions, and other laws published by the government provide the basic legal foundation for student engagement in university management (Cai & Fu, 2016, p.34).

The Outline stipulated that "it is necessary to expand the autonomy of HEIs, build a modern higher education system with Chinese characteristics, and improve the governance structure of universities." In addition, it states that "it is necessary to explore effective ways for professor committees to administer the university, strengthen the features of teaching staff and student committees, and give the mass and other organizations more chances to participate in university management." In 2014, at the National Education Work Conference, the theme and key goal of education reform and development was confirmed as the need "to deepen comprehensive education reform and accelerate the advancement of education governance system and governance capacity" (Feng & Ding, 2017, p.37).

Article 11 of the Higher Education Law stipulated that "higher education institutions should be society-oriented, operate according to the law, and enforce democratic forms of management" (Chen & Zhang, 2012,, p.12). This article ensures the rights of HEIs to conduct their management with less control from central and local governments. Besides, the MOE clearly stated the rights relating to the engagement of students in university management in Chapter 4, Article 50, of the Regulations on Student Management of HEIs in 2017. It stipulated that "universities should encourage students to criticize and advise their work, and support students to engage in their democratic management" (Luo & Wu, 2014, p.74). It may be noted that despite the fact that the definition and scope of students' rights of participating in university management have not been clearly stated in these polices and laws, the government has realized that more autonomy should be given to HEIs and that the roles of teachers and students in participating in the decision-making process should also be emphasized.

Apart from these policies and laws, several universities also assume their leading roles to ensure that their students' benefits are reflected in the universities' decision-making processes. For example, East China Normal University started to implement the student representation system in 2004, so that students can speak freely about major issues of the university, such as scholarship assessment (Kang & Guo, 2007, p.21). The president of Nankai University presented the following proposition at the university student congress in 2012: "The university board should set fixed seats for student representatives. (From this year), two students will join the university councils: the president of the undergraduate student council and the president of the graduate student council of our university." In addition, another 16 students joined the Complaint Handing Committee, the Traffic Management Committee, and the Dietary Work Committee. The president of Nankai University also said that he hopes that "students can take on involvement in university management as a learning process, a social experience, a growing experience, and a preparation for a future career" (Li, 2013, p.68).

According to several studies about the situation of student engagement in university management (Hu, 2010; Qi, 2012; Ren & Zhao, 2008), the common trend is that HEIs agree with student engagement in university management and most students also show great interest in participating in the process. However, the actual rate of student engagement is remarkably low in these universities. Fang, Qian, and Wu (2017) indicate that students are only able to engage in daily campus management decisions, such as teaching methods, accommodation, and traffic alternatives to the university, not being able to give an opinion on vital issues related to them, such as policy making, construction, renovation of infrastructure, and public facilities. Thus, student engagement in university management in China is still in a hard process to be implemented.

The reasons why student engagement in university management is difficult are discussed in existing studies and can be summarized as follows:

1. Universities do not have democratic management concepts as well as trust and attention to students. They are inclined to think that students are immature and have no professional vision. They also think that, as students are just temporary passengers at the university, they cannot provide long-term advice. Universities' offices and institutions also seem to have difficulty having equal dialogues with students (Kang & Guo, 2007).
2. There is a lack of guarantee and incentive system within universities for student engagement. On the one hand, there are no diverse channels for students to participate in university management. Two channels are regularly provided to students: the student congress, which can influence many students once every two years, and the small-scale forums, such as meetings with the university president and with directors of each functional office (for example, academic affairs and finance offices). The problem is that these forums are held randomly according to the willing of top management and at low frequency. On the other hand, universities lack an effective feedback and

supervision system to ensure that students' voices are effectively transmitted to the top management of the university (Fang, Qian, & Wu, 2017).

3. Students feel that they lack related knowledge, capacity, and confidence to engage in university management (Ren & Zhao, 2008).
4. There are not clear rules and regulations on the issues in which students should be involved, the limit of students' rights, and how universities ensure students participation rights. (Fang, Qian, & Wu, 2017; Qian, 2015).

Therefore, while there is an increasing encouragement to promote students' participation in university management in policies and national laws, there are still difficulties in actual implementation due to the reasons coming mainly from universities. Most universities still consider that teachers should be in a leading position on students. Most of them have not issued their own regulations on how students should engage in the decision-making process and the limits of their rights. The channels provided by universities for student engagement are also not flexible and multiple enough.

The meso-level

The Outline reiterated the significance of quality evaluation as a complex process demanding diverse assessment approaches that involve multiple stakeholders (Ross, Cen, & Zhou, 2011, p.26).

> We will improve teaching evaluation. We will set up scientific and diverse benchmarks for such evaluation, according to teaching goals and concepts on talents or professionals. Teaching quality shall be evaluated with the participation of the government, schools, parents, and communities. We will keep records of students and improve the assessment of the overall quality. Diverse evaluation approaches that help promote student development shall be explored to encourage students to be optimistic and independent and become useful persons. [Translation referred to Ross, Cen & Zhou, 2011, p.26]

In addition, the Outline stated the following: "We will improve the quality of students. We will deepen the education reform, fully mobilize the enthusiasm and initiative of students' leaning, and motivate students to study assiduously." It affirms that the learning enthusiasm, the learning initiative, and the efforts from universities to motivate students to study hard have important influences on improving educational quality. It also affirms that the government has started to approach the educational quality by increasing the participation of diverse groups, including students, which were absent in the past, and also by increasing student engagement in the learning process.

Until now, several big-scale surveys on student engagement have been implemented and their results have been empirically described and utilized by universities to improve their educational quality. The most representative ones are

"The National Survey on Student Engagement (NSSE-China)", the "Student Experience in the Research University (SERU)", and the "Beijing College Student Survey conducted by Beijing University". The former two came from the USA, so the analysis was more focused on a comparison with the participating universities in American and European countries. The last one was made by Beijing University by mainly referring to the instruments in the USA but also adding the benchmarks reflecting Chinese characteristics.

Created on account of the chance to collaborate with Tsinghua University, the NSSE instrument was introduced in China and translated into the Chinese context by a group of doctoral students (Ross, Cen, & Zhou, 2011, p.28). The first survey was conducted in 2009 and 27 universities from different provinces voluntarily joined the survey. According to the Survey 2009 report from Tsinghua University (Shi et al., 2011), students' learning experiences in Chinese universities are not very satisfactory and especially present differences when compared to American universities in the benchmarks of "student-teacher interaction", "active collaborative learning", and "level of academic challenge". In addition, American research universities prioritize the achievement of high-level cognitive goals, such as comprehensive capacity, judgment capacity, and application capacity. However, Chinese universities emphasize more the cultivation of lower-level cognitive goals, including analysis capacity and memory capacity. Furthermore, there are also differences in student engagement among different types of Chinese universities. Students in the 985 institutions group are found to have more academic-oriented engagement, while the students in the 211 institutions group have more social-oriented engagement. Students in other local universities are more likely to engage in learning connected to their future careers.

In 2011, Nanjing University, Hunan University, and Xi'an Jiao Tong University attended the SERU survey and utilized the benchmarks to measure the capacities and learning experiences of their undergraduate students. According to the report of Lv and Zhang (2015) based on SERU data, similarly to the results of NEES-China, in the classroom, Chinese students seem to be more conservative in academic discussion. They present less interactions with teachers and less engagement in critical thinking and reasoning thinking in comparison with students in American and European universities. Besides, Chinese students tend to spend more time in classroom study but less time in extra-curricular learning, which is the inverse of American and European students. Chinese students are also revealed to have lower satisfaction degrees in both academic and social learning experiences than students from American universities (Lv & Gong, 2016). However, Lv and Zhang (2015) also indicate that these characteristics of student engagement are influenced by the culture of their countries, as cluster analysis showed that the students from China and Korea shared more common traits of learning engagement.

The Beijing College Student Survey was conducted by the College of Education of Beijing University. It was conducted every year from 2010 and covered the most important HEIs in Beijing.[7] According to the time allocation of students in "after class self-learning," "campus social activities," "physical fitness," "part-time jobs," and "entertainment," Li (2017, p.35) divided students into four types: A. academic type (spend 47.3% of their spare time in self-learning), B. practical type (spend 29.8% of spare time in social activities in campus, 26.3% in entertainment), C. work type (spend 25.3% of their spare time in part-time jobs outside of campus, 20.5% in entertainment), D. entertainment type (spend 54.9% of their spare time in entertainment). She found that in the 985 institutions group, the distribution of each student type was A>C>B>D; in the 211 institutions group, it was C>B>A>D. In local universities and independent colleges,[8] the rate was C>B>D>A; In vocational colleges, it was C>B, D>A (Figure 10.1). It can be concluded from Li's research that as most of the 985 institutions group is composed of research-oriented universities, their students tend to engage more in academic studies, while students in the 211 institutions group are more likely to engage more in experiences connected to career and society. Local universities and independent colleges share similar trends and both have high rates of work type and practical type, but only very few have academic type. Nearly 60% students in vocational colleges are C type, which replies that one of the apparent characteristics of vocational colleges is the non-academic cultivation of students. The worrying phenomenon is that, in all these HEIs, entertainment type of students accounts for over than 15% (Li, 2017, p. 41). That means that there is still a big amount of students in China who do not in both their learning and campus lives. This needs attention from universities.

From these three surveys, it is possible to infer that undergraduate education in China still has gaps compared to the USA and other developed countries. In order to improve educational quality, it is crucial to enhance student engagement in and out of the classroom by transforming their learning ways. However, it will be less successful merely to emulate other Western countries. To change Chinese students from introverted and conservative to more active and creative learners, we also need to consider the unique characteristics of Chinese students and the Chinese educational environment. This means that Chinese students are not regularly

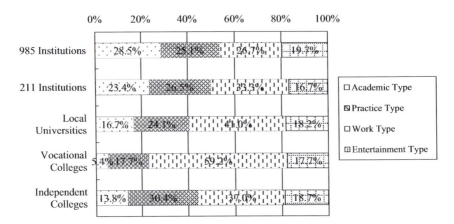

FIGURE 10.1 Distribution of different types of students in HEIs
Source: Li (2017).

encouraged to speak in classes and may lack initiative in active learning. In order to improve the educational quality by encouraging student engagement, changing the concepts of learning and teaching and being more open to other countries' educational ideas are considered important measures.

The micro-level

As student engagement begins to connect with the improvement of educational quality, most universities gradually turn their attention from the learning outcomes to how to improve student engagement in their own learning and that of other students, in and outside the campus. To improve student engagement, both universities and students need to make efforts and realize their deficiencies. Particularly, universities need to know the main factors that influence students' engagement so that they can better visualize and propose targeted solutions.

The factors that affect student engagement and are mainly discussed in current research can be divided into two categories. The first category is composed by demographic variables and includes gender, birth place (urban or rural areas), types of high schools, socio-economic statuses, and grades, among other factors. One of the interesting findings is that the majority of female students engage more in learning than male students (Xiang & Zhang, 2016; Qu 2017; Yang & Zhang, 2016; Liao, 2011). For example, female students were found to be more active in collaborative learning and more likely to participate in class discussions, as well as to prepare the lessons more carefully. Another finding about Chinese students is that being born in urban or rural areas apparently influences factors related to student engagement, such as level of academic challenge, participation rate of active and collaborative learning, richness of educational experiences, and the performance of the former being better than that of the latter (Yang & Zhang, 2016, p.54). Li, Hu, and Lei (2015) also found that students from urban areas engage more in their lessons and social activities. However, Xiang and Zhang (2016) found that there was no apparent difference of engagement between students born in urban or rural areas, but the gap existed between students who are only children and those who are not. Non-only children tend to work harder in their lessons and extra-curricular learning than students who do not have siblings (Xiang & Zhang, 2016, p.48). The reasons are not clear but in China, students born in rural areas are regularly not only children and usually have less social resources regarding economics and culture. Thus, they may tend to study harder than urban students.

The second category is composed by the factors that were identified based on students' reports about their learning and life at university and can be divided into two groups (Zhang, Hu, & McNamara, 2015, p.111). The first group is personal factors such as motivation and goals, recognition about the major, academic expectations. The second group is named as external factors. It contains contextual factors such as students' friendship and family, and institutional factors mainly include course design, teachers and facilities. Based on other surveys of Chinese university students, it was found that among the personal factors, motivation and goals are the key factors that affect student engagement (Sun, 2017; Xu & Xu, 2015;

Wang, Guo, & Liu, 2014; Yang & Zhang, 2016). Students who are more interested in their majors or feel that their studies are meaningful are inclined to have a high degree of engagement (Yang & Zhang, 2016, p.58). Among all of the external factors, Zhu (2010) states that students' interaction with teachers has the most apparent impact upon their engagement. However, peer support also plays an important role. As mentioned in the empirical study of Jia, Wang, Chen and Wang (2014, p.79), college students tend not to be proactive in group work if the evaluation or task assignment from the teacher is not reasonable enough (for example, doing more or doing less being the same), or if other students in the same group perform negatively.

Therefore, based on these findings, what Chinese universities should do to improve student engagement is to give more support to male students and students who come from rural areas, pushing students who are only children to participate more in their studies. More research should be done to further understand why there are differences among these students and what kind of support they exactly need from universities. Second, in order to keep students' high motivation and provide them with more precise information to help them choose their majors, it is necessary to provide transparent and detailed information about the university and its programs, teaching resources, and services by updating campus websites, distributing pamphlets, and holding more public seminars. Universities should also understand students' expectations about majors and careers to improve their curriculum and campus environments. Third, to improve the interactions between teacher and student, teachers may need to improve their methods and contents in order to encourage creative thinking and collaborative learning. They need to be more proactive in interacting with the students so as to get more students to engage in class discussions.

Conclusion

The analysis of all the developments in student engagement at the macro, meso, and micro-levels reveals that, over the past 10 years, most Chinese universities have approached the issue of educational quality not only by upgrading students' learning outcomes, but also by improving student engagement. The role of student engagement is closely connected to the promotion of educational quality, as the Outline has been stipulated in the context of the expansion of higher education. To be specific, universities make their efforts by improving students' learning experiences at the micro-level and by participating in big-scale student engagement surveys to do self-promotion at the meso-level.

At both the meso and micro-levels, more detailed research regarding the factors affecting student engagement should be done in future. Besides, there are apparent differences among the 985 institutions group, the 211 institutions group, and other universities. More universities are expected to participate voluntarily in large-scale surveys, so that they can accurately know their education positions in relation to all HEIs in China, grasp the unique characteristics of their students, and promote more targeted reforms.

There is also an increasing encouragement to promote students' participation in university management at the macro-level. Although the related polices or laws have not been issued to ensure the students' rights on university management, several universities have implemented their own regulations to involve student representatives in the decision-making process, especially in the daily issues related to the benefits for students. However, only a few students can participate in this process and the channels that lead to management are not always open to all of the students. Therefore, there is still a long way to go in engaging students at the macro-level. It is a challenge for administrators to be more open-minded to students' voices and build a mutually beneficial relationship with them.

Notes

1 The Website of Ministry of Education of the People's Republic of China, "Educational Statistics Yearbooks of China 2016": www.moe.gov.cn/s78/A03/moe_560/jytjsj_2016/2016_qg/2017/5/16
2 In 2016, the number of higher education institutions is 4486, among them there are 1561 private universities. Private universities here include undergraduate program universities, independent colleges, vocational universities, adult education universities and other higher education institutions.
3 According to the "Education Statistics Yearbook of China", in 1998, the number of enrolled undergraduate students at higher education institutions was about one million and this number doubled in 2000. In 2002, the number of enrolled undergraduate students was 3.2 million and in 2010, it was 6.6 million.
4 The "double first class university plan" is a measure with the aim of developing a group of elite Chinese universities and individual university departments into the world-class level. The full list of the universities and disciplines that are selected into this plan was published in September 2017, which includes 36 Class A universities and 6 Class B universities, 465 first class disciplines. The majority of Class A universities are those that were selected into the "985 project".
5 Website of The Central People's Government of the People's Republic of China: www.gov.cn/jrzg/2010-07/29/content_1667143.htm   (2010/7/29   updated,   2018/5/30 referred)
6 Website of Ministry of Education of the People's Republic of China: www.moe.gov.cn/jyb_xxgk/moe_1777/moe_1778/201701/t20170119_295319.html (2017/1/10 updated, 2018/6/10 referred).
7 88 HEIs in Beijing participated in the survey in 2010 and 53 HEIs participated in the survey in 2015.
8 Independent college here is the English translation of "Du Li Xue Yuan". It is one of the HEIs in China. According to the Regulations for the Establishment and Management of Independent Colleges promulgated by the MOE in 2008, it refers to the HEIs that provide undergraduate education in cooperation with non-government agencies such as social organization and individuals, by receiving financial funds from these organizations.

References

Cai, W. B. and Fu, J., (2016). Xuesheng canyu daxue guanli de zhidu luoji he moshi xuanze [Student participation in university management: institutional logics and model selection], *Fudan Education Forum*, 14, 4, 30–35.
Chen, D. X. and Zhang, Y. Y., (2012). Xiandai daxue gongtong zhili zhong xuesheng canyu de yanjiu shuping [A review of studies on student engagement in the management of modern university], *Education and Vocation*, 738, 12–14.

Fang, X., Qian, Y. F. and Wu, C., (2017). Daxuesheng canyu xiandai daxue guanli de shi-jian tanjiu [Undergraduate students' engagement in the practice of the management of modern university], *The Party Building and Ideological Education in Schools*, 557, 46–48.

Feng, Z. Y. and Ding, S. Q. (2017). Xuesheng canyu daxue zhilii: xingdong beijing yu xianshi zhixiang [Student engagement in university management: background and orientation], *Jiangsu Higher Education*, 2017, 10, 36–39.

Hu, D. W. (2010). Fazhi shiye xia gaoxiao xuesheng canyu guanli de shizheng yanjiu [Empirical study of student engagement in university management from the perspective of law], *Journal of Sichuan University of Science & Engineering (Social Sciences Edition)*, 2010, 3, 41–45.

Jia, Y. Q., Wang, M., Chen, T. T. and Wang, D., (2015). Daxuesheng hezuo xuexi canyu chengdu diaocha yanjiu [An investigation on cooperative learning of undergraduate students], *Higher Education of Sciences*, Serial No. 122, 76–81.

Kang, C. P. and Guo, J., (2007). Woguo gaodeng xuexiao daxuesheng canyu xuexiao guanli de xianzhuang yu qushi [Current situation and trend of undergraduate students' engagement in the university management in China], *Modern Education Management*, 2007, 3, 21–24.

Li, C., Hu, L. and Lei, Z. X., (2015). Difang yuanxiao daxuesheng xuexi touru de yingxiang yinsu yanjiu [Research on the influential factors relating to student engagement in local universities], *Higher Education of Sciences*, Serial No. 124, 52–60.

Li, L. (2017). Gaoxiao xueye yingxiangli fugai de quntixing chayi: Jiyu 53 suo shoudu gaoxiao de shizheng yanjiu [Group differentiation of HEIs academic impact coverage: an empirical study on 53 Capital HEIs in China], *Shandong Higher Education*, General No. 40, 34–44.

Li, W. J. (2013). Daxuesheng ruhe canyu gaoxiao guanli [How undergraduate students engage in the university management], *Education and Vocation*, 2013, 4, 66–68.

Liao, Y. G. (2011). Daxuesheng xuexi touru wenjuan de bianzhi ji xianzhuang diaocha [Developing questionnaire of learning engagement for college students and surveying the current situation], *Journal of Jimei University*, 12, 2, 39–44.

Luo, Y. Y. and Wu, J. S., (2014). Chaoyue daxuesheng canyu guanli kunjing de zhihui jueze [Wise solutions to students: management dilemma in colleges and universities], *Education and Teaching Research*, 28, 3, 73–77.

Lv, L. H. (2016). Daxuesheng xuexi canyu de lilun yuanqi, gainian yanzhan ji celiang fangfa zhengyi [Theory of undergraduate student engagement: origin, expansion of concept and methodological discussion], *Exploring Education Development*, 2016, 21, 70–77.

Lv, L. H. and Gong, F., (2016). Zhongmei yanjiuxing daxue benkesheng xuexi jingli manyidu de bijiao yanjiu: jiyu SERU diaocha de shizheng fenxi [Comparing undergraduates' satisfaction with learning experiences between research universities in China and US: empirical analysis based on the SERU survey], *TsingHua Journal of Education*, 37, 2, 24–34.

Lv, L. H. and Zhang, H. X., (2015). Zhongguo yanjiuxing daxue benkesheng xuexi canyu de tezheng fenxi: jiyu 12 suo zhongwai yanjiuxing daxue diaocha ziliao de bijiao [The characteristics of undergraduates' learning engagement in Chinese research university: based on the comparison of 12 research universities in the world] *Educational Research*, General No. 428, 51–63.

Qi, X. M. (2012). Gaoxiao xuesheng canyu jiaoxue zhiliang pingjia de shizheng yanjiu: yi nanjing nongye daxue weili [Undergraduate students' engagement in teaching assessment: an case study of Nanjing Agricultural University], *Journal of Wuxi Institute of Commerce*, 12, 2, 72–75.

Qian, C. Y. (2015). Xuesheng canyuquan yu gaoxiao zhangcheng de duijie [The connection between the right of student engagement in university management and university regulations], *Jiao Shu Yu Ren-Gao Jiao Lun Tan*, 2015, 7, 18–19.

Qu, L. J. (2017). Yanjiuxing daxue benkesheng xuexi canyudu yanjiu: jiyu J daxue de gean fenxi [Undergraduates' learning engagement in research universities: analysis based on the case study of J university], *Survey of Education*, 6, 5, 4–7.

Ren, C. M. and Zhao, L.Y., (2008). Xuesheng canyu gaoxiao guanli de shizheng yanjiu: Dui wuhan 4 suo gaoxiao de diaocha [An empirical study of student engagement in university management: a survey of 4 universities in Wuhan province], *Modern Education Management*, 2008, 3, 40–43.

Ross, H., Cen, Y. H. and Zhou, Z. J., (2011). Assessing student engagement in China: responding to local and global discourse on raising educational quality, *Current Issues in Comparative Education*, 14, 1, 24–37.

Shi, J. H., Tu, D. B., Wang, S., Lv, Z.W., Xie, M. and Zhao, L., (2011). Jiyu xuexi guocheng de benke jiaoyu xueqing diaocha baogao 2009 [Annual report of the National College Education Survey 2009], *Tsinghua Journal of Education*, 32, 4, 9–23.

Sun, C. M. X. (2017). Difang Zonghexing daxue wenkesheng zhuanye rentong yu xuexi touru guanxi yanjiu: yi S daxue weili [Research on the relationship between professional identification and student engagement of students in liberal arts and social science disciplines in local comprehensive university: taking S university as an example], *University (Academic Version)*, 2017, 5, 65–68.

Wang, C. M., Guo, J. and Liu, J., (2014). Gaoxiao xuesheng xuexi canyu yingxiang yinsu de shizheng yanjiu [Empirical research on the factors affecting undergraduate students' engagement], *Helongjiang Researches on Higher Education*, Serial No. 239, 149–150.

Xiang, K. H. and Zhang, Y. D., (2016). Daxuesheng xuexi touru de xianzhuang diaocha yu duice fenxi : yi mousheng zhongdian gaoxiao weili [The current state survey of undergraduates' engagement in learning and the analysis on the countermeasure: the case study of one national university], *Journal of Wuhan Technical College of Communications*, 18, 4, 46–48, 63.

Xu, W. X. and Xu, X. L., (2015). Gaoxiao xuesheng xuexi canyudu yu xinli ziben guanxi: jiyu huazhong keji daxue de shizheng fenxi [Undergraduate student engagement and psychological capital: based on empirical analysis of the HUST], *Journal of Central China Normal University (Humanities and Social Sciences)*, 54, 6, 182–189.

Yang, L. J. and Zhang, W., (2016). Daxuesheng xuexi touru de yingxiang yinsu jiqi zuoyong jizhi [Undergraduate students' engagement: influencing factors and effect mechanism], *Higher Education Development and Evaluation*, 32, 6, 49–61.

Yu, L. Y. and Huang, S. P., (2017). Daxuesheng xuexi zhiliang baozhang tixi goujian lujing: jiyu xuesheng canyu de shijiao [A pathway for constructing a quality assurance system for undergraduate students' academic performance], *Journal of Ningbo University (Educational Science Edition)*, 39, 5, 72–75.

Zhang, Z., Hu, W. H. and McNamara, O., (2015). Undergraduate student engagement at a Chinese university: a case study, *Educational Assessment, Evaluation and Accountability*, 27, 2, 105–127.

Zhu, H. (2010). Gaoxiao xuesheng canyudu jiqi chengzhang de yingxiang jizhi: shinian shoudu daxuesheng fazhan shuju fenxi [The relationships between student engagement and undergraduate students' achievement: the analysis of 2010 annual data set of the Beijing College Student Survey], *TsingHua Journal of Education*, 31, 6, 35–43, 63.

11

STUDENT ENGAGEMENT FOR THE IMPROVEMENT OF TEACHING

The peculiar form of student faculty development in Japan

Masahiro Tanaka

UNIVERSITY OF TSUKUBA

Introduction

The term 'student engagement in quality assurance' is not widely known in Japan because the traditional role in managing quality assurance at the university level has always been the university's responsibility, specifically the teaching staff's, and not the students. Nevertheless, many universities have been administering teaching evaluation questionnaires and student surveys aiming to obtain students' views on improving their educational provision. In other words, students are, in fact, (directly or indirectly) contributing to the preservation and enhancement of the education quality in the university.

It appears that student engagement in quality assurance in Japan has developed in a unique manner; while the US/Australian model and the European model have been absorbed, a peculiar form of student faculty development (FD) has become widespread in Japan. This chapter, therefore, analyses the development of student engagement in quality assurance in Japan, focusing on student FD. The chapter adopts the three-level framework proposed by Healey et al. (2010) introduced at the beginning of this book and describes the historical development of each stage. Drawing from the findings from this analysis, the chapter examines the current situation and challenges of student engagement in education quality assurance in Japan.

Student engagement at the macro-level

In Japanese universities, the influence of student unions is weak; therefore, the demand for student representation or engagement at the macro-level of education governance is relatively scarce (i.e. student representatives participating as full members in important committees which decide on the university's strategic policies). However, there was a short period in the aftermath of the 1970s student revolts when many universities attempted to introduce student engagement at the macro-level.

Student revolts in Japan were triggered by student protests against unjustifiable and significant increases in tuition fees. This took place frequently after 1965. The revolts were centred on established and influential private universities, such as Keio and Waseda. It is important to note that the students' demands were not restricted to the reversal of the tuition fee increases but included as well demands relating to how the universities should be run: the improvement of education and the democratisation of university administration. This was important, because the idea that students might be able to reform the universities was spread across Japan. In fact, in the student revolts of around 1968, which were widespread across the country, 'the university itself became the object of students' struggle' (Osaki 1999: 240) because students rejected the conventional model used by universities at that time. The fact that students targeted the university itself in their struggle reflected their perception of the teaching staff's disinterest in their education; in other words, they 'demanded university teachers to be more student-oriented' (Amano 1997: 68).

The universities that experienced student revolts then initiated two major types of reform. One type of reform aimed to improve education by enhancing small-size seminar teaching and making curricula flexible. The other intended to empower students with the right to select Vice Chancellors and important section/ department heads of the university (Osaki 1999). For example, according to the 'Interim Report on the Selection of Vice Chancellors and Directors of Departments and Bureaus', published by the Reform Unit of the University of Tokyo in 1972, the 'Vice Chancellor is not only the head of the university who is ultimately responsible for the university as a whole but also the one who represents the university as a coherent body to the outside world. In this regard, the Vice Chancellor has to be trusted by the whole university community, including students and staff. Drawing from this understanding, it is desirable that those who constitute the university but are not members of the professorial committees (i.e. students) participate in the selection process of the Vice Chancellor in one way or another' (Reform Unit, the University of Tokyo 1972:1).

The idea that students should participate in the selection process of Vice Chancellors and Directors of various sections of the university was proposed in many national universities including the University of Tokyo from 1969 to 1972. A similar idea of reform was also suggested by influential private universities, such as Meiji University, Chuo University, Ritsumeikan University, and Kwansei Gakuin University. Additionally, the Science Council of Japan, which represents scientists and left-wing political parties, such as the Social Democratic Party of Japan and the Japanese Communist Party, issued statements supporting these reform plans. While the Japan Association of National Universities expressed its support, the Association of Private Universities in Japan, the Japan Association of Private Universities and Colleges, and the Japan Association of Private Junior Colleges expressed a negative view of these reforms. Furthermore, the Liberal Democratic Party of Japan, which was in power, did not approve of the reform plans (Osada 1973).

The decisive push towards the implementation of the reform plans came from the Ministry of Education, Science, and Culture (MEXT) and its advisory body, the Central Council for Education. Drawing from the trend in Western countries in which students were increasingly involved in university governance, the Central Council for Education presented its evaluation of the significance of and limits to student engagement in universities in Japan in its report 'On Policies to Respond to Current Challenges in University Education' (30 April 1969) as follows:

> In considering which areas are appropriate to take in students' wishes and views actively, the judgement criteria should be the degree to which students' knowledge, experience and the ability to take responsibility for each area can be reasonably expected to be in reference to the significance of student engagement. It is expected that student engagement would be effective in areas such as students' extra-curricular activities, wellbeing activities, the development and improvement of the learning environment and the improvement in the curriculum as well as teaching content and methods so long as the problem to be tackled is appropriate. However, it is inappropriate to invite student participation in areas including personnel administration of staff, student performance evaluation and university finance. It is also inappropriate to formalise student vote in the selection process of Vice Chancellors and Directors of Faculties.

Upon the adoption of the council's recommendations in the report, the MEXT proposed the 'Temporary measures on the administration of the university' bill to the Diet on 24 May 1969. The bill was steamrolled with a five-year limit on 3 August of the same year without passing through the proper debates at the *Kokkai* (Japan's National Diet).

Some organisations, such as the Japan Association of National Universities, were clearly opposed to the temporary measure bill in the beginning. Nonetheless, due to the culmination of most student revolts in 1971 and the cessation of student interest in university governance, an increasing number of universities (in particular, national universities) began accepting MEXT's guidance, which was based on the temporary measure bill. Therefore, while 'numerous reform plans' which aimed at the realisation of student engagement at the macro-level 'were drawn up, the majority of them were never implemented and remained something that were just "written" as plans' (Kitamura 2001: 56). As a result, with an exception of a very small number of private universities, such as Ritsumeikan University, student engagement at the macro-level in Japanese universities has yet to be realised.

The aforementioned bill was supposed to have expired after five years; the ideas expressed in its Article 3 Clause 3, which is almost identical to the recommendation by the Central Council for Education, are suggestive in the sense that it appears to have defined the ways in which student engagement in Japan has developed since then. In short, the idea that areas in which student engagement is appropriate in reference to students' knowledge, experience, and the ability to take responsibility is not found at the macro-level but at the micro-level or in some areas at the meso-level, such as the improvement of teaching methods.

The next section describes the development of student engagement at the micro-level (mainly in the form of peer support) in Japan.

Student engagement at the micro-level

Student engagement at the micro-level refers to the individual student's participation in various learning activities. The current section focuses on peer support in which students support other students' learning activities.

Peer support has rapidly spread across Japan since 2000, backgrounded by increasing academic, mental, and financial problems due to the extreme diversification of university students as a result of more than 50 per cent of the 18-year-old cohort entering universities. In other words, universities are now required to engage their students with various problems with systematic learning support. Below, we describe the current situation of learning support provided by universities, drawing from the findings of the survey on the implementation of student support that is conducted on a regular basis by the Japan Student Services Organization.

Figure 11.1 illustrates the present implementation of a student mutual support system, such as peer support, based on a survey performed by the Japan Student Services Organization with 777 universities in 2013 (number of responses: 739; response rate: 95.1%).

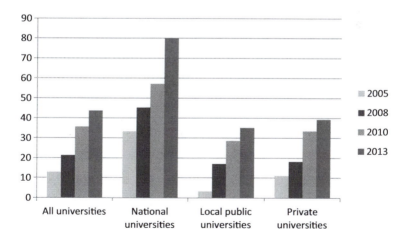

FIGURE 11.1 The implementation of student mutual support system such as peer support (by university type)

Source: Compiled by the author based on Japan Student Services Organization (2014: 25) and Japan Student Services Organization (2011: 75).

As Figure 1.11 shows, in 2013, 43.6 per cent of all institutions that comprised 80.0 per cent of national universities, 35.1 per cent of local public universities, and 39.3 per cent of private universities had support systems, such as peer support in place; it also shows that the type-specific and the overall implementation rates increased each time the survey was carried out.

Figure 11.2 shows findings from the 2013 survey on the areas of support in universities where peer support was implemented.

As shown in Figure 11.2, 40.0 per cent of universities implemented the peer support system in which 'learning support' by postgraduate students is given to undergraduate students. 'Curricular advice' with the second highest value (29.0 per cent) refers to a system in which older students counsel and dispense advice on appropriate module/course selection. It is interesting that 'facilitating bonding among students' has scored high at 28.3 per cent. In order to improve retention, universities are now helping students with building friendships in their private lives.

One of the examples of learning support comes from Tohoku University. It has a Learning Support Centre as an organisation that supports undergraduate students in their first and second years. The Centre provides four kinds of support: individual learning support (support in providing response to individual queries on the site), event-led learning support (support in providing learning opportunities such

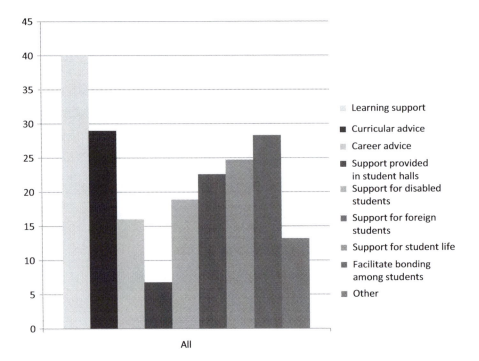

FIGURE 11.2 Areas of support in universities

Source: Compiled by the author based on Japan Student Services Organization (2014: 27).

as organising related events), support for independent learning, and class-linked learning support (support that is linked to particular classes). Students who provide learning support are called Student Learning Advisors (SLA), and a total of 48 registered SLAs are in operation as of the first semester in 2016 (16 in physics, 11 in mathematics, 5 in chemistry, 11 in English, and 5 in writing) (Tohoku University 2017).

As student engagement at the micro-level becomes institutionalised in universities in Japan, student engagement at the meso-level (i.e. direct or indirect contribution by students to quality assurance and improvement of university education) has also ensued. The next section, therefore, describes the development of student engagement at the meso-level, specifically focusing on student FD, which constitutes the main theme of the current volume.

Student engagement at the meso-level

The main factor that pushed universities in Japan to work towards the realisation of student engagement at the meso-level was the paradigm shift in education around 2000. The shift refers to the transition from university education that was centred on teaching staff (i.e. teaching staff teaching what they want to teach) to university education that is centred on students (i.e. teaching staff teaching what students should learn). As an example of this transition, in June 2000, the MEXT published a report entitled 'Enrichment of Student Life in Universities' (also known as the Hironaka Report), which suggested strategies to reshape universities in a more student-centred way. This report had garnered attention by advocating for strengthened student support, as well as the 'importance of appropriately reflecting the students' wishes and opinions in the management of the university' (MEXT 2000). To realise this vision, it proposed the following: 1. Conducting student surveys, 2. Hosting round-table discussions with students, and 3. Incorporating student engagement in various organisations within universities.

In the following statement, the report indicated and justified the reason behind the difficulty in implementing #3; however, it recommended that universities move forward with #1 and #2:

> In Europe and North America, university student representatives have traditionally been recognized as legitimate members of the university management and students are granted the right to participate in a wide range of activities within it. In Japan, however, the history of our education as well as the compatibility between such a system and the current decision-making process at universities needs to be taken into account before it can be adopted at the present time. It would therefore be advisable to be cautious when considering its introduction. Rather, it may be more effective to create opportunities for university students to express their wishes and opinions on topics on which it is appropriate for students to comment such as the course content/delivery method and student life, which would then be reflected as much as possible in the management of university. (MEXT 2000)

This suggestion is almost identical to what the aforementioned report, published in 1969 at the height of student revolts by the Central Council for Education, suggested. What was different this time around was that those who thought it was important to reflect students' wishes and views on teaching content and method were universities, not students.

Inspired by the Hironaka Report, in June 2001, Okayama University, a national institution, established the Student/Faculty FD Task Force, which includes students as official participating members. Initially, this task force was confined under the traditional faculty-only FD Advisory Committee; as such, the results of its discussions, albeit recognised as valuable, were subject to a re-evaluation process by the FD Advisory Committee. It then evolved into the Student/Faculty FD Committee during fiscal year 2004, equalising its role with the FD Advisory Committee (Amano 2012: 106). Creation of this committee can be considered to be an actualization of suggestion #3 in the Hironaka Report; however, it should also be noted that other national universities, including Kyoto University, Osaka University, and Nagasaki University, have attempted to create similar committees but without long-term sustainability (Kino 2012a).

Shortly after the aforementioned attempts at realising suggestion #3 from the Hironaka Report, the 'student FD' model (realisation attempt of suggestion #2), which centred on round-table discussions with students, became more widespread among private universities, including Ritsumeikan University (Kino 2012b: 7–9). According to Kino (2012b: 91–98), student FD includes the following initiatives: round-table discussions between students and faculty members (forums); course introductions presented by students; student proposals for course content improvement; student proposals for living and learning environment improvement; and public relations for student FD (including public advertisement to recruit student participants). A unique characteristic of the student FD is that its participants are publicly recruited student volunteers rather than official executive members of the university.

Some advantages of involving volunteer members include the following: 1. Participating students demonstrate a high level of awareness, 2. Student autonomy is respected, and 3. Existing committees comprising faculty members need not be reorganised. However, student volunteers do not have decision-making power (voting rights), and the organisation lacks longevity, as it may be based primarily on personal relationships. Furthermore, the student FD 'needs to be fun' (Ozaki 2012: 143), since the organisation must retain participating students through interest rather than by right or obligation. As a result, this type of initiative tends to be more student focused with activities, such as events and festivals. Given these drawbacks, the legitimacy of this type of organisation may ultimately be called into question.

For this reason, Oki's (2013) criticism categorizes the student FD model more as a type of PBL (project-based learning) or active-learning course, whose objective is to improve university education. Although he admits that the student FD may not be successful specifically as a faculty development activity, Umemura (2012: 193) contends that personal growth in the participating students, realised through experiences, such as event planning/hosting, has nonetheless been phenomenal; and he 'believe[s] that personal growth in each individual student will serve as an agent of change for the classes and, ultimately, the university'.

Other forms of student engagement at the meso-level aside from student FD includes class evaluation questionnaires, and student surveys, which have likewise spread rapidly from about 2000. While the class evaluation questionnaire is a tool to collect students' views on the classes they have taken, the student survey is a tool 'which captures each student's learning and life experiences comprehensively without being limited to the class situation' (Otawa 2016: 91). The student survey can be carried out at the institutional level (by specific department or university); it can also be conducted at the national level as a mass survey targeting all universities across the country (for instance, 'the national student survey' by the Centre for Research on University Management and Research, University of Tokyo). The research group led by Reiko Yamada has developed a Japanese version of a student survey called 'Japanese Cooperative Institutional Research Program (JCIRP)', drawing from a student survey used widely in the US, namely, the Cooperative Institutional Research Program (CIRP), (Yamada 2014, also see Yamada, Chapter 12, this volume). Based on the experience of using the findings from JCIRP, the Institutional Research (IR) consortium of universities was formed and implemented in various universities to conduct comparative analyses of universities. As of 2016, a total of 47 universities are members of the consortium.

The next section describes the case study of the University of Tsukuba that exemplifies student engagement at the meso-level.

Case study at the University of Tsukuba

The University of Tsukuba is divided into nine schools comprising 23 colleges; each student is affiliated with one of these colleges. These colleges are subdivided into classes, the basis for the entire student structure, with an assigned instructor for each. Each level of the structure has its own student organisation, with representatives from the lower-level organisations making up the members of higher-level organisations. Three levels of official student organisations exist:

- Class level: Class Meeting
- College/School level: Class Representatives' Meeting
- University-wide level: School and College Representatives' Meeting (usually known as *Zendaikai*)

An equivalent organisation of faculty members is established in tandem to correspond with each official student organisation on the school, college, and university-wide levels (School/College level: Class Coordinating Committee; University-wide level: Discussions with the vice president). These meetings serve as platforms for dialogue between the students and faculty members, as well as opportunities for the university to incorporate students' opinions in its decision-making processes.

During the Class Coordinating Committee meeting, which is held several times a year, members of the Class Representatives' Meeting would present student requests concerning improvement of educational facilities or course content directly to the faculty members of the relevant colleges, upon which the faculty would review and deliberate prior to approving any request. Coin lockers, for instance, were introduced as a result of this presentation. Furthermore, the Class Representatives' Meeting provides support for activities, such as the Freshmen Welcome Event and the University Information Session. The *Zendaikai* involves six committees (General Affairs, School Events, Educational Environment, Living Environment, Survey, and Public Relations). It is held several times a month to gather input from students, such as conducting a petition for a review of the university's semester system and presenting an official request to establish a system for a return of marked exams. This input is collectively presented during the meeting with the vice president, held approximately three times a year (Nagaki 2014).

However, a few issues in the present official student organisations remain unaddressed. First, some segments of the Class Meeting or Class Representatives' Meeting can be less active than others. When this occurs, discussion during the *Zendaikai* will no longer be based on collective consensus (Nagaki 2014). Second, the fact that students do not have voting rights is also problematic, although they are given the opportunity to exchange opinions with faculty members at meetings. Third, students' requests can occasionally be unrealistic, due in part to their lack of knowledge of the university's rules and regulations. Finally, the *Zendaikai* includes only undergraduate students; it excludes graduates.

Graduate students at the University of Tsukuba have created the unofficial Tsukuba Graduate Students' Network that comprises student-volunteers. Amongst other activities, it has hosted the 'Graduate Students Presentation Battle', aiming to improve students' presentation skills through competition in 'battles' to explain their research and communicate the appeal of their field to students from other fields of study. The organisation has also submitted a request to establish common courses for graduates to foster cross-field communication skills. Notably, a course entitled 'The Presentation: Acquiring Research Presentation Skills that Connect with Others' was created in 2012 in response to their request (Matsubara 2015).

Issues regarding the Tsukuba Graduate Students' Network are twofold: 1. The organisation is not officially recognised, and thus is not allocated any budget from the University, and 2. No established system exists for recruiting new members, which may affect the organisation's longevity. In addition, some of their requests, such as establishing a future-faculty preparation program (FFP), require very close collaboration with the university, which is difficult without an official line of communication.

The next section examines benefits that students who are involved in student engagement activities enjoy.

Does student engagement improve the quality of learning activities of the participating students?

An examination of the benefits accorded to students participating in student engagement activities is crucial to ascertain and predict the future development of student engagement. Since student engagement at the macro-level is yet to mature in Japan, this section focuses on student engagement at the micro- and meso-levels and examines possible benefits at both levels.

It is easy to imagine that there are benefits for both service providers (older students) and service users (younger students) participating in student engagement activities at the micro-level (for example, peer support). The peer supporter, who is the service provider, can enjoy some benefits in terms of learning – since when we teach, we also learn – in addition to the financial benefits of being paid. Nakajima and Kashima (2016: 109), who have analysed the outcomes of the writing support desk at their university, have commented on the development of tutors (peer supporters) as follows:

> Many postgraduate and research students who were involved in the running of the desk felt their own writing skills had improved through tutoring. Some tutors also felt that their own communication skills had improved through their efforts to understand the individual student's needs accurately and to give appropriate advice. In making efforts to provide some 'realisation' to students, the tutors themselves were learning even deeper by obtaining their own 'realisation'.

Furthermore, Nakajima and Kashima (2016) point out that because tutoring experience is seen as educational experience, students who seek a future post as a university teacher may derive benefit from it.

While the current chapter has not discussed this, the experience of supporting students with developmental difficulties, such as learning difficulties and autism, can be an excellent opportunity to learn how to provide appropriate support. In the words of Ito (2016: 159), who runs a support system mainly focusing on the psychological side, peer supporters:

> play an important role in a diverse range of capacities – as teachers, civil servants, clinical psychologists and parents – by interacting with people effectively and making the most of their highly developed communication skills and by being a good listener to others from time to time.

In a similar vein to the case of student engagement at the micro-level, there are many benefits for students involved with activities at the meso-level (predominantly in the form of student FD in Japan). Sato (2012: 49) argues that:

> when opposition or conflict (between students and teaching staff) emerges in the case of FD, we should not suspend the dialogue but turn the situation into

a learning opportunity for both to acquire new skills. (Because) students can acquire the ability to raise objection constructively as the student representative and to continue behaving as the representative vis-à-vis the problem they face.

Other notable views of the students who were involved in student FD are: 'I managed to form friendship' and 'I found where I stood' (Kino and Umemura 2013: 194–198). These feelings develop their self-appreciation and bring positive effects to their learning (Kino and Umemura 2013).

The author witnessed such positive effect during a research visit to Sapporo University (22 January 2015). There is a student FD organisation called 'Satsudai Okoshi Tai (The group to develop Sapporo University)'. A total of seven members agreed to take part in my research. Among them, there was an intriguing male student. While he dressed unconventionally, he looked to be a nice young man. However, other members told me that when he was in his first year, his hair was bleached and he looked menacing; no one would want to talk to him. This was because, according to the student, 'I did not have a place to be in the university and everything was boring'. In this case, discovering student FD might have been a turning point in his life.

Summary

In Japan, because student unions are weak, there has hardly been any movement by students to demand their right (or duty) for student engagement at the macro-level in the university since the end of the student revolts. However, cases in which students are invited into FD activities, which have been conventionally carried out by the teaching staff, have started to emerge. They constitute a form of student engagement at the meso-level, which is peculiar to Japan. Still, students are normally not given the autonomy and authority to realise their reform agenda by themselves. Therefore, it may well be the case that any information gathered through student FD is intended to reinforce information gathered through conventional student surveys from the university's perspective. We may need to ask students whether this is what they want.

With regard to the future direction of student engagement in Japan, the issue of accorded benefits and advantages to the participants is important. Here, 'participants' refer to the university, students, and society. If any of the three monopolises the benefits in student engagement, the system will be hollowed out. For example, the most important thing is for students to enjoy some benefits, but if the system becomes an avenue through which students' demands are unilaterally imposed on the university, the university may likely abolish such a system. It is also important that the society benefit from student engagement. In other words, if it is acknowledged that the skills acquired through student engagement are useful in society, the society will support the system. Therefore, the ideal situation for student engagement is Sanpo Yoshi, a Japanese old proverb meaning 'three yeses': supported by the seller (the university), the buyer (students), and the world (society).

Lastly, let me emphasise once again the importance of listening to students in terms of assuring the quality of university education. This is because when I attended the 'Student FD Summit, 2016 Summer' and was engaged in discussions about the educational system's need for reformative actions with students from various universities, I was surprised by their views. For example, one student said, 'I would like teachers to discuss among themselves what they teach since they tend to duplicate content in their lectures. Furthermore, sometimes, some teachers accuse us of not knowing what we have not learned.' I then checked the accreditation report of the student's university, which gave a high evaluation of the curriculum being systematically organised. Is this evaluation appropriate at all? Is this not just parroting what the university says? I would like to propose that students be engaged in external (and internal) quality assurance processes in order to secure the validity of such evaluations.

References

Amano, I. (1997) *Educational Reform for Universities.* Tokyo: Yushindo (in Japanese).

Amano, N. (2012) 'Student/Faculty FD Committee SweeT FooD,' in Kino, S. (ed.), *Changing Universities, Initiated by Students.* Kyoto: Nakanishiya, 105–126 (in Japanese).

Central Council for Education (1969) *On Policies to Respond to Current Challenges in University Education.* Tokyo:CCE(in Japanese).

Healey, M., Mason-O'Connor, K., and Broadfoot, P. (2010) 'Reflections on Engaging Student in the Process and Product of Strategy Development for Learning, Teaching, and Assessment: An institutional case study,' *International Journal for Academic Development,* 15(1), 19–32.

Ito, T. (2016) 'Peer Support Activity at Hakuoh University: Ten Years on', *Bulletin of Education Department of Hakuoh University,* 10(1), 143–161(in Japanese).

Japan Student Services Organization (2011) *The Survey on the Implementation of Student Support in Universities, Colleges and Specialised High Schools, 2010: Report on Aggregated Data (Simple Aggregation).* Tokyo:JSSO(in Japanese).

Japan Student Services Organization (2014) *The Survey on the Implementation of Student Mutual Support in Universities, 2013: Report on Aggregated Data (Simple Aggregation).* Tokyo: JSSO (in Japanese).

Kino, S. (2012a) 'Classes Created with Students, FD to be Pursued with Students', in Shimizu, R. and Hashimoto, M. (eds) *University Education Jointly Created by Students and Staff: New Ideas in FD and SD to Change the University.* Kyoto: Nakanishiya Shuppan, 136–151 (in Japanese).

Kino, S. (2012b) 'Student FD Summit', in Kino, S. (ed.), *Changing Universities, Initiated by Students.* Tokyo: Nakanishiya, 69–102 (in Japanese).

Kino, S.and Umemura, O.(eds.) (2013) *Student-Initiated Faculty Development.* Kyoto:Nakanishiya(in Japanese).

Kitamura, K. (2001) *Reform and Policies of Contemporary Universities: A Historical and Comparative Examination.* Tokyo: Tamagawa University Press (in Japanese).

Matsubara, Y. (2015) 'An Activity to Foster an Interdisciplinary Communication by Students and Its Limitations'. A presentation for the Faculty Development held on 18 Septemberat University of Tsukuba (in Japanese).

Ministry of Education, Science, and Culture (MEXT) (2000) *Enrichment of Student Life in Universities.* Tokyo: MEXT (in Japanese).

Nagaki, S. (2014) Initiatives at the University of Tsukuba, *Student Summit 2014 held on 8 March 2014 at* Tokyo University (in Japanese).

Nakajima, A. and Kashima, M. (2016) 'The Ideals and Practice of the Writing Support Desk at Ritsumeikan University: Reflections from the Tutors', *Ritsumeikan Kotokyoiku Kenkyu (Ritsumeikan Research into Higher Education)*, 16, 101–116 (in Japanese).

Oki, H. (2013) 'Concepts Relating to Student FD Activities: For Clearer Understanding of Student FD Staff', *Journal of Chubu University Education*, 13, 9–19 (in Japanese).

Osada, M. (1973) 'Some Considerations on the Reform of the Selection Process of the Vice Chancellor (President): Focusing on "Student Participation"', *Collection of Papers on Logistic Economics*, 8(2), 37–58 (in Japanese).

Osaki, H. (1999) *University Reform, 1945–1999.* Tokyo: Yuhikaku Sensho (in Japanese).

Otawa, N. (2016) 'How to Reflect the Student Survey on University Reform: Another "Student Survey and IR"', *Koto Kyoiku Kenkyu (Research into Higher Education)*, 19, 87–106 (in Japanese).

Ozaki, Y. (2012) 'Shagaku Fes' Steering Committee', in Kino, S. (ed.), *Changing Universities, Initiated by Students.* Kyoto: Nakanishiya, 127–146 (in Japanese).

Reform Unit, University of Tokyo (1972) *An Interim Report on the Appointment of President and Dean of Department.* Tokyo:University of Tokyo(in Japanese).

Sato, H. (2012) 'Significance and Challenges of Student Participation in Faculty Development', in Shimizu, R.and Hashimoto, M.(eds.) *University Education Jointly Created by Students and Staff: New Ideas in FD and SD to Change the University.* Kyoto:Nakanishiya, 40–50(in Japanese).

Tohoku University (2017) *About the Center for Learning Support,* http://sla.cls.ihe.tohoku.ac.jp/outline/(accessed25 July 2017) (in Japanese)

Umemura, O. (2012) 'Student FD Staff', in Kino, S. (ed.), *Changing Universities, Initiated by Students.* Kyoto: Nakanishiya, 167–194(in Japanese).

Yamada, R. (2014) *An International Comparative Study of University Students' Cognitive and Emotional Development through the Construction of Mass Continuous Data.* Kyoto: Kaken Research Report.

12

TRANSFORMATION TOWARD PRO-LEARNING OUTCOMES IN JAPANESE HIGHER EDUCATION INSTITUTIONS

The role and challenges of assessment for student engagement[1]

Reiko Yamada

DOSHISHA UNIVERSITY

Introduction

In recent years, the demonstration of learning outcomes as an ultimate goal of university education has been strongly emphasized in higher education policies, as well as demanded by society in general. Higher education institutions are facing this new reality. This perception is shared not only in higher education institutions but also in various academic disciplines in Japan. Higher education institutions have held countless discussions and taken several initiatives on measures to help students achieve the necessary learning outcomes and thus improve education. There is an increasing understanding that, in order to advance educational improvement, it would be highly useful to better assess the current state of students based on objective data on students' backgrounds in terms of learning and everyday behaviors during high school, as well as their academic progress and personal growth in the context of university life.

In such an environment, universities have frequently used direct assessments, represented by portfolios and rubrics, as well as indirect assessments such as self-reported student surveys (Yamada, 2014). Our research group had developed a Japanese version of standardized self-reported student surveys in order to assess students' engagement and learning outcomes. While there are many self-reported student surveys, such as NSSE and CIRP, which are used as comparative tools for assessing student engagement and experiences in the United States, there are few self-reported students' surveys in Japan to assess student engagement and learning outcomes as well as to reflect student voice to improve college education. Therefore, our project team started to develop a self-reported student survey to be used as a standard indirect assessment. In the next step, we tried to integrate the self-reported student survey for indirect assessment with the objective test for direct assessment in one form.

This chapter first describes the Japanese higher education policy, namely learning outcome-oriented policy, in recent years. Next, regarding this policy, I will show how we have developed a Japanese standard student self-reported survey and the integration of direct and indirect assessments.

Japanese higher education policy toward quality assurance and learning outcome-oriented reform

One of the major shifts in Japan's higher education policy, especially after 2005, was the quality assurance achievement—symbolized, for example, by emphasis on learning outcomes. The Report of the Central Council for Education (CCE) (2005), entitled *The Future of Japanese Higher Education,* declared that the 21st century is the age of a knowledge-based society, in which higher education becomes more important not only for the individual, but also for the nation. This implies that higher education institutions must cultivate intellectual elites and improve outcomes for the mass of students simultaneously. Thus, the Japanese government has invested more in the development of centers of excellence that undertake sophisticated research and educational programs to cultivate highly qualified students.

The 2008 Central Council for Education report pointed to the need for individual university institutions to enhance undergraduate education programs by serving as learning centers that carry out university educational missions and encourage student growth. The document includes recommendations for improving curricular programs and pedagogical methodologies, as well as promoting educational quality assurances. Additionally, the report proposes the new concept of "graduate attributes," which must be cultivated through individual fields of study as concrete guidelines on the common learning outcomes that are assessed throughout undergraduate education. The 2008 report defines "undergraduate education" as academic degree programs that require academic program–centered reforms that are based on the university's educational functions and also recognize the international trends existing among globalized societies. Herein, the urgent need is a curriculum that meets the standards required for the award of degrees by transcending the organizational boundaries of disciplines and departments.

Later, in 2012, the Central Council for Education announced the release of a report entitled *Transforming the quality of university education into the future: The role of university education in cultivating students who can learn lifelong and think proactively.* This report urges higher education institutions to achieve the qualitative transformation of undergraduate education. The report evaluates that most higher education institutions have promoted several university reforms, such as the introduction of first-year seminars, syllabi, and active learning styles over the last decade. After faculty development became compulsory, many faculties became more teaching-centered.

However, the report also suggests the concern that learning hours of non-class learning among Japanese students are relatively short compared to those of American students. At the same time, the report also observes differences in learning hours between different academic courses. Indeed, following the publication of this report, an intensive argument has emerged to discuss the meaning of student learning hours out of class. The report suggests that sufficient learning hours is the basis for establishing proactive student learning and urges higher education institutions to incorporate efforts to increase the learning hours of students out of class. The 2012 CCE Report is regarded as the turning point for the shift toward more outcome-oriented learning in Japanese higher education institutions. Since then, it is expected that quality assurance of education, in particular quality assurance of learning outcomes, will be developed in Japanese higher education institutions.

In 2016, three policies, including admission, curriculum, and diploma policies, were required to be open to the public in order to assure the quality of education. In particular, to consolidate the curriculum as well as diploma, policies are closely associated with securing learning outcomes. In the next section, I would like to show how we have developed a student self-reported survey system intended to track student learning, which leads to a quality assurance of education.

What the JCIRP research has aimed to achieve

In the move toward quality assurance in education, awareness about ensuring learning outcomes has been shared not only by higher education institutions but also by a large number of academic disciplines. Japanese higher education institutions have held countless discussions and taken several initiatives on measures to help students achieve the necessary learning outcomes and thus improve education. In fact, they have taken various initiatives in the first year of university education in Japan and have worked to advance faculty development. There is an increasing understanding that, in order to advance educational improvement, it would be highly effective to better assess the current state of students based on objective data on students' backgrounds in terms of learning and everyday behaviors during high school, as well as their academic progress and personal growth in the context of university life. However, in many cases, the assessments of the current state of students are still based on the relative experiences of faculty members.

While focusing its main attention on an empirical examination of "college impact," which is how undergraduate education leads to student growth and learning outcomes, our research group has developed and implemented a student survey as a method of assessing students' engagement and learning outcomes. The Japanese Cooperative Institutional Research Program (JCIRP) is a program consisting of the three student surveys: the Japanese Freshman Survey (JFS), the Japanese College Student Survey (JCSS), and the Japanese Junior College Student Survey (JJCSS). Their survey forms contain items on pre-enrollment student background, experience, satisfaction, acquired skills and abilities, lifestyle habits, self-assessment, values, and so on, in university or junior college, structured to enable understanding of students' overall image of the university or junior college, where the survey is conducted. In the case of participation in the JCIRP program, by returning the survey data to each of the participating universities and junior colleges, the participating institution is able to compare statistical data on the total body of students surveyed from other universities that participated in the same survey, as well as gain detailed data on the students in their particular university or junior college. As of October 2013, surveys had penetrated to the extent of becoming a standard survey with a cumulative total of about 140,000 respondents from 866 universities and junior colleges participating in the JFS, JCSS, or JJCSS. Therefore, it can be said that the so-called indirect assessment method has taken root as a result of this research.

In this chapter, we would like to show what we have tried to clarify, to what extent have we accomplished this and what were the issues in the ten years of accumulated research of this research group from 2004 to 2014.

The main purpose of this research has been to consistently demonstrate research on college impact in Japan through student surveys. The first stage of the research was conducted from 2004 to 2006. During this period, the research relied on the theory of involvement, which states that 1) student learning and development are proportional to the quantity and quality of student involvement and 2) educational policy and practice, and the involvement of the teachers with the students lead to student involvement. Additionally, the input–environment–output (I-E-O) model developed by Astin, who established the college impact theory, as well as Pascarella's growth model, were used to develop the JCSS, which is compatible with the College Student Survey (CSS) developed by the UCLA Higher Education Research Institute (HERI). JCSS was implemented for 5,400 students at 22 universities to examine the educational effect caused by the college impact in Japan. It has also became possible in Japan to examine the effectiveness of college environment (college impact), as well as the involvement of students and teachers in the affective and cognitive aspects of outcomes, which are found in the research achievements of Astin (1993) and others.

The second stage corresponds to the research conducted from 2007 and 2009. During this period, three research objectives were advanced: 1) comparison between US and South Korean students, 2) demonstration of the significance of a student survey that measures student growth, and 3) measurement of the effect of higher education institutes that support student growth. A Japanese Freshman Survey compatible with the HERI freshman survey (TFS) and a Japanese Junior College Student Survey (JJCSS) unique to Japan were developed. The JCSS was implemented for about 6,500 students at 16 universities in 2007, the JFS was implemented for about 20,000 students at 164 universities in 2008, and the JJCSS, which developed through this research following a request from the Japan Association for College Accreditation, was implemented for about 2,000 students at nine junior colleges in 2008. For the 2007 JCSS, an international Japan–US student comparison was conducted through coordination with the UCLA HERI research collaborators (CSS data disclosed). In 2009, the JCSS2009 was translated into Korean, thus gaining a toehold to the validation of college impact research in Korean universities through the implementation of the survey at Yonsei University.

The research accomplishments in this period were as follows. 1) In addition to direct assessments, such as course examinations and standardized examinations that measure student achievement, the relationship among different assessments was demonstrated by indicating the effect of indirect assessments that measure students' learning behavior and the process of their cognitive and affective growth, as well as the effect of student surveys as assessments of educational programs and institutions that support student growth. 2) From the Japan–US survey, while there were common points regarding learning behavior and experience, a disparity was confirmed in cognitive aspects in the self-assessment of captured achievements and lower frequency of learning experiences in the university education of Japanese students. 3) Through various analyses to make the enormous amount and complexity of the factor structure more visible, a foundation for the development of the JFS and JCSS was launched in standard surveys for indirect assessments.

The third stage comprises the research conducted from 2010 to 2014, when the research focused on solving remaining issues and pursued constructive achievements based on the knowledge gained in the first and second stages. In other words, 1) in the Japan–US comparative analysis of the 2007–2009 surveys, publicly released data was used for the US database and it was not possible to carry out analyses using strict statistical methods in the single database created by the combination of Japanese and US data. Thus, the third stage of the research purchased data from the US versions of the TFS or CSS data from HERI, combining them with data from the Japanese versions. Through the analysis of this new database, the commonalities and differences in the cognitive and affective growth processes were clarified more precisely, and the features and functions of the educational environment that promotes these processes were considered. Similarly, the Japan–South Korea data was also combined and studied. At that time, in parallel with the progress in theoretical research at the time of analysis and aiming for the effectiveness and stability of the large amount of survey data and to standardize the surveys, we began to work on the development of statistical methods that are advanced in terms of application to this research area, such as multilevel analysis, latent class analysis, and item response theory. The international comparative analysis permitted the validation of the universality of college impact research and the elucidation of the relationship between the environment and institutional features that bring the students' cognitive and affective growth and open the way to the possibility of institutional benchmarks for the formation of effective educational environments. 2) In order for JFS and JCSS to take root as highly stable and reliable standard surveys, standardization of items in different student surveys was carried out using the research team members' technical examination and development achievements. By publicly disclosing the results of the standardization of the items in the results database of this research, it was expected that each of the universities that have participated in the surveys would be able to check their own detailed analytical data.

Examining the trends of previous studies, both in Japan and overseas, while relying on outstanding research on college impact carried out in the US by Astin (1993), Pascarella and Terenzini (2005), and others, this research has the distinctive feature of having the standpoint of an "international comparison," which is lacking in the series of research studies that considered American students only as subjects. Preceding research on college impact in Japan has been broadened into the competency research by Ogata (2001), Yoshimoto (2004), and others. Large-scale student surveys have also been implemented with the aim of formulating a "grand design" for higher education, as performed by Kaneko's research group (2015). This research obtains a comprehension of the commonalities and differences in college impacts through empirical international comparative research, elucidating the relationship between educational institutions' environment and students' cognitive and affective growth processes. Through continuing surveys, this research also develops a standardized model for university student surveys that enables international comparisons. Furthermore, in constructing a survey database, it can be said that this research differs in purpose and anticipated outcomes from other Japanese research.

Achievements of the JCIRP research

The outcomes that have accrued as a result of this research in accordance with the plan can be summarized as follows. First, the KCSS (the Korean version of the university student survey) was implemented (with about 6,000 participants) in 2012, with mainly the collaborative Korean researchers, and the analysis was conducted by merging the Japanese and Korean data. As a result, it was discovered that students' autonomous activities, both within and outside the university, were associated with the learning outcomes in Korea, while in Japan teacher involvement with students affected learning outcomes, indicating differences in terms of college impact (Rhee 2013 and Yamada 2013). With the provision of the UCLA HERI data in 2013, an international comparative analysis involving three locations was made possible by combining data from Japan, the US, and Korea. In Japan, as of October 2013, JFS, JCSS, and JJCSS were in the process of permeating Japanese higher education as standard tests with, for example, a cumulative total of about 140,000 students at 866 participating universities and junior colleges. Moreover, in 2012, a trial implementation of a Chinese version of the CSS (translated from the Japanese version) was conducted in Shanghai International Studies University (SISU), which was later developed into the implementation of the Chinese version of the CSS centered on four-year university courses in Shanghai City, thereby creating the basis for the dissemination of a Japanese standard survey in Asia. The achievements in the Japanese research on college impact to date can be summarized in the theoretical model indicated in Figure 12.1.

The objectives and achievements of our research were indicated here mainly by demonstrating the effectiveness of research on college impact in Japan. In addition to the accumulation of achievements, we have concentrated our efforts on examining whether it is possible or not in Japan to verify the theory of college impact that has been developed in the US, and whether or not the college impact research that has been verified in Japan can also be applied to higher education in other Asian countries. Through comparative research involving Japan and Korea, we believe that this research has contributed to building a foundation that will lead to possibilities for the development of research on college impact in Asia.

Another research objective was to develop standardized student surveys that would enable the use of student surveys that measure students' learning outcome processes as indirect assessments. In this sense, by the JCIRP analysis of 140,000

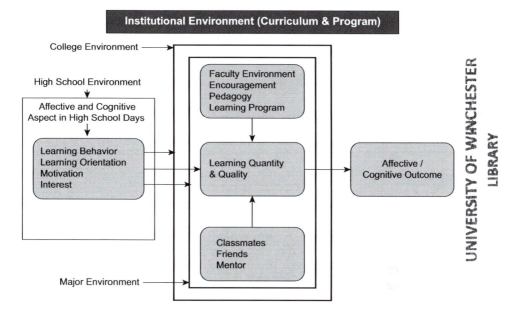

FIGURE 12.1 The relationship of precollege, college environment, and learning outcome

participating students and the expansion of the Japanese research on college impact, the foundation for a process assessment, i.e., an indirect assessment that looks at standard student growth and learning outcomes, has been laid, and this can be considered the achievements of this research to date.

Challenges faced by JCIRP

Direct assessment gauges students' direct learning outcomes through tests, essays, portfolios, graduation examinations and research papers, and standardized tests in both general and discipline-based education. On the other hand, indirect assessment gauges the learning process using student surveys about learning behaviors, experiences, self-perception, and satisfaction. These surveys are offered to students upon entering college, at the end of the first year, at the end of the senior year, and after graduation. When used in tandem, indirect and direct assessments complement each other. Instead of combing two assessments, it is more effective to improve the quality of teaching and learning. Since direct assessment appears to be more appropriate for assessing students' outcomes through paper and standardized tests, it cannot cover the learning process, motivation, and students' perception. There is a limitation to prove the relationship between students' learning outcomes and learning process. Conversely, indirect assessment is more appropriate to focus the learning process through the self-rated evaluation of affective aspects, such as motivation, expectation, satisfaction, and the side of engagement and involvement. Astin (1993) indicates that the relationships between student process measures and self-reported outcomes mirror the patterns shown in the relationships between the same student measures and directly assessed cognitive outcomes. Anaya's (1999) study also indicates that GPA, GRE scores, and student-reported growth are all valid measures of learning outcomes. By examining both direct and indirect assessment methods, Gonyea (2005) suggests that students' self-report data should be viewed as complementary to test performance data, although not substitutable.

Although indirect assessments, such as the NSSE and the Cooperative Institutional Research Program (CIRP), are being conducted by several universities in the United States, it cannot be ignored that the debate about the questionable nature of indirect assessments has become normalized. Among the various indirect measures available, much of the discussion focused on the NSSE due to its considerable influence. Porter (2012) questions the validity of the NSSE, criticizing that the participants' responses do not accurately reflect their engagement, and recommending that the NSSE and other indirect assessments should not be used alone but in combination with standardized multiple-choice tests, such as the Collegiate Assessment of Academic Proficiency (CAAP) or the Measure of Academic Proficiency and Progress (MAPP).[2] In fact, most universities that have introduced standardized tests, such as the newly-developed Collegiate Learning Assessment (CLA), to evaluate the outcomes of undergraduate education also use student surveys, such as the NSSE and CIRP, while positioning them as a way to assess the educational process. In other words, currently in the United States, there is a consensus that student surveys should be used in combination with direct assessments rather than as stand-alone measures (Gonyea, 2005). Among the various means of directly assessing learning outcomes, researchers and experts in the United States have been proactively engaged in the development of diverse, cutting-edge standardized tests. Most standardized tests in the United States were to assess learning outcomes for general education, writing ability, and critical thinking skills.

As explained above, direct and indirect assessments have both advantages and disadvantages. Thus, the integration of direct and indirect assessments is necessary to measure learning outcomes and student development. Unfortunately, although our JCIRP developed the college impact study by analyzing a cumulated large amount of survey data, we were unable to collect the direct assessment data and thus could not relate the direct and indirect assessment data for analysis. Our challenge is to integrate the direct and indirect assessment data and conduct a detailed analysis at a higher stage of college impact study hereafter.

Development process of a measure integrating direct and indirect assessments

The goal of this pilot research is to integrate or link direct and indirect assessments to core subjects, considering the results of previous studies (Figure 12.2).

According to previous research in the United States, we found that, while numerous standardized tests to measure learning outcomes of general education (core subjects) are conducted as direct assessments, standardized student self-evaluations, such as the NSSE and the CIRP, are being used as indirect assessments. In

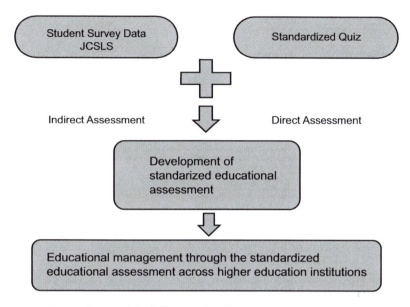

FIGURE 12.2 Integration model of direct and indirect assessments

recent years, a growing number of higher education institutions have introduced the VALUE rubric developed by the AAC&U. That said, even in the United States, few studies have attempted to measure learning outcomes using the NSSE or CIRP along with the VALUE rubric.[3]

Meanwhile, in Japan, the development of standardized tests to assess the learning outcomes of general education has had little research and little progress. It is in this context that we have endeavored to develop an objective test combined with students' self-evaluations to assess learning outcomes in Japanese general education. The first step entailed identifying the nature of learning outcomes for general education. To this end, we collected paper-based questionnaires focused on learning outcomes used in Japan and abroad, and formulated our own questionnaire with items related to relevant outcomes, which we tested in a pilot study at a university. The second step involved the development of a short, objective test to be combined with the abovementioned questionnaire, in order to develop a method for assessing learning outcomes that integrates direct and indirect assessments.

In general, the goal of general education is to provide students with a comprehensive education covering a diverse and wide range of topics. For this reason, in order to assess learning outcomes in general education areas, in addition to measuring achievement in individual courses, students need to be asked about their overall university experiences, as well as their perception regarding their own skills to accomplish what is expected at university. Thus, we carried out our investigation developing a method to indirectly assess learning outcomes and combining this indirect method with direct assessments as subthemes. Specifically in 2013, considering the accumulated experience with the Japanese College Student Survey (JCSS) (Yamada, 2014), we developed a questionnaire entitled the "Japanese College Student Learning Survey (JCSLS 2013)," comprising 92 questions in seven categories regarding students' experiences in various classes and with various teaching methods at the university, learning experiences, weekly time use, and self-evaluations of current competences in 19 skill areas compared to the time of entry into the university. We applied the questionnaire at a university between December 2013 and February 2014. Of the 295 respondents, 207 were first-year students. Based on our experiences with this trial survey, we considered two questions: (1) how can indirect assessments be used and (2) what kind of questionnaire should we develop in order to effectively link direct and indirect assessments? For example, in terms of students' self-evaluations on growth in various areas, the proportions of positive responses (skill has improved substantially + skill has improved) varied widely depending on the skill area: "knowledge in academic disciplines" (81.0%), "liberal arts knowledge" (73.0%), "problem analysis and solving skills" (61.4%), "leadership skills" (30.6%), "ability to work with people from different cultures" (31.8%), and "preparedness to find employment after graduation" (31.9%). Further, considering the students' classroom experiences since entering university, students who had classes in which "the students presented their own ideas or research" had a higher self-perception of growth in these areas.

We identified three potentials and two limitations of indirect assessments based on the results of the pilot study and in terms of the research questions. One of the potentials is to position indirect assessments as a comprehensive evaluation of the educational processes, learning environment, and educational programs offered in terms of (subjective) achievement of multiple educational objectives. The second potential is to use indirect assessments to analyze and examine the relationship among different items to verify and ultimately improve the effectiveness of university education. The third potential is to use indirect assessments to visualize students' classroom experiences and abilities (subjective) by identifying "student groups" and their characteristics based on various survey items. The limitations include, first, the fact that, given the aggregate nature of indirect assessments, it is not possible to see the relationship between individual students and individual educational activities; second, given that the data are based on the self-evaluations of the respondents, it is necessary to verify the reliability and the validity of this data.

Considering these potentials and limitations of indirect assessments, we endeavored to develop rubric-type questions to refine the questionnaire's effectiveness to measure students' level of skills acquisition and quiz-type questions to directly test students' skills. Specifically, we (1) used concrete numbers and terminology in questions for indirect assessment and (2) developed a measure to make explicit the relationship between the data from the short, objective quiz-type questions for direct assessment and indicators from the questions for indirect assessment contained in the same questionnaire. The result of these efforts is the Japanese College Student Learning Survey 2015 (JCSLSs). Indirect assessment comprised 101 questions divided into 14 categories, along with five questions regarding the respondent's attributes. Examples of the categories include students' self-evaluations regarding learning outcomes, learning behaviors including time spent studying, and rubric-type questions to be linked to the results of the quiz-type questions.

The short objective test for direct measures comprised 12 questions, consisting of six questions in English including five questions to assess reading comprehension and one question to assess knowledge of current affairs, as well as three questions in Japanese to assess students' ability on logical thinking and reading comprehension, and three math and sciences questions to assess students' ability on logical thinking.

The questionnaire consisted of seven A4-sized pages, with an estimated response time of 20 to 30 minutes and a maximum allowable response time of 30 minutes. Thanks to the cooperation of numerous national and private universities, we were able to assemble approximately 500 students to participate in the survey.

The indirect measures included in the student survey consisted of questions about the students' self-evaluations, for example, their ability to write and speak persuasively, analytical thinking skills, mathematical reasoning skills, and cooperativeness, with four possible responses, including "extremely confident," "very confident," "not very confident," and "not at all confident." Thus, we proposed to link the indirect assessments, including these new categories, to the actual content of subject courses (i.e. direct assessment).

Insight gained from integration of direct and indirect assessment

We have carried out the pilot study and we are now in a deep analysis process. Thus, instead of presenting the result of analysis, we would like to show that the tentative results of the questionnaire survey combining direct and indirect assessments developed by our team yielded the following three insights: (1) students' confidence level in their English proficiency has been correlated to some degree with the number of correct answers in the English questions of the objective test; (2) students' perceptions of their ability or inability are largely accurate; (3) students' study hours spent in or out of class were not correlated with the results of the general-content short objective test. The survey results are meaningful since they provide evidence to respond to criticism regarding the significance of indirect assessments.

As evidenced by Porter's skepticism regarding the efficacy of indirect assessments (2012), there is substantial debate on the reliability and validity of indirect assessments. Similarly, in Japan, skepticism is frequently expressed in relation to the validity of students' subjective self-evaluations. That said, in this research, we have observed a certain correlation between indirect and direct assessments, i.e., between students' self-evaluations on their acquisition of knowledge and skills and objective measures of learning outcomes. In this sense, our results are in agreement with those of Pascarella and Terenzini (2005), who argue that the results of students' self-evaluations of their own learning outcomes, which constitute indirect assessments, are consistent with the results of direct assessments. We tried to integrate direct and indirect assessments in one form. However, this is the pilot study and there is a limitation at this point to suggesting some recommendation. Thus, further research must be conducted in order to obtain stable results, as well as to test reliability and validity. Nevertheless, we have developed a standardized self-reported student survey and are now at the stage of developing direct and indirect assessment on a single form. We expect that many Japanese universities will participate in these programs in order to promote the learning outcome assessment movement in Japan.

Notes

1 This chapter adds to and is revised from my chapter "Measuring Learning Outcomes on General and Liberal Arts Education Integration of Direct and Indirect Assessment", in *Student Learning: Assessment, Perceptions and Strategies* (Ed. Dale Bowen), Nova Publishers, 2016.
2 MAPP has changed its name to ETS Proficiency Profile.
3 It refers the keynote speech of Dr. Caryn Musil of AAC&U at the 2013 Research Project Conference of Japan Association of College and University Education.

References

Anaya, G. (1999). "College impact on student learning: Comparing the use of self-reported gains, standardized test scores, and college grades", *Research in Higher Education*, 40 (5), 499–526.

Astin, A. W. (1993). *What Matters in College?: Four Critical Years Revisited*. San Francisco, CA: Jossey-Bass.

Gonyea, R. M. (2005). "Self-reported data in institutional research: Review and recommendations", *New Directions for Institutional Research, Survey Research Emerging Issues*, 127, 73–89.

Kaneko, M. (2015). "Empirical research in university education: Achievements and challenges" (paper presented at the 2015 Annual Conference of the Japanese Association of Higher Education Research).

Ogata, N. (2001)."How competency changes undergraduate education?", *Japanese Journal of Higher Education Research*, 4, 71–91 (in Japanese).

Pascarella, E. T., Terenzini, P. T. (2005). *How College Affects Students*. San Francisco, CA: Jossey-Bass.

Porter, S. R. (2012). "Learning gains across academic majors: A comparison of actual versus self-reported gains" (paper presented at the meeting of the Association for Institutional Research, New Orleans, LA).

Rhee, B. S. (2013). "Gains in learning outcomes of Korean and Japanese college students: Factors affecting the development of generic skills in undergraduate students" (paper presented at AIR2013, Long Beach).

The Central Council for Education (2005), *Report, The Future of Japanese Higher Education*. Tokyo: MEXT.

The Central Council for Education (2008), *Report, Building Undergraduate Education*. Tokyo: MEXT.

The Central Council for Education (2012). *Report, Qualitative Transformation of University Education for Building a New Future: Universities for Promoting Lifelong Learning and Nurturing Independent Thinking*. Tokyo: MEXT.

Yamada, R. (2013). "Assessing and improving undergraduate education in Japan: University students' involvement in learning based on the data of Japanese college students" (paper presented at 2013 KEDI (Korea Educational Development Institute), Higher Education Policy Forum).

Yamada, R. (Ed.) (2014). *Measuring Quality of Undergraduate Education in Japan: Comparative Perspective of Quality Assurance*. Singapore: Springer.

Yoshimoto, K. (2004). *Comparative Study of Competency of Higher Education between Japan and Europe, Report of Science Research Fund* (in Japanese). Accessed on January 10, 2018 from https://kaken.nii.ac.jp/ja/report/KAKENHI-PROJECT-14310128/ 143101282004kenkyu_seika_hokoku_gaiyo/

13

THE FUTURE OF STUDENT ENGAGEMENT

Masahiro Tanaka, Ryan Naylor, Jani Ursin and Nelson Casimiro Zavale

UNIVERSITY OF TSUKUBA, LA TROBE UNIVERSITY, UNIVERSITY OF JYVÄSKYLÄ AND EDUARDO MONDLANE UNIVERSITY

The future of student engagement

Student-engagement activities vary from country to country, but will this diversity continue to progress in the foreseeable future, or will student engagement ultimately converge on a single model? Finding the answer to this question is very important for those currently involved in student engagement as well as for those who will become involved in the future. Given that student engagement may converge on a single model, the process will be more efficient if the reform which paves the way for that model is first implemented. However, answering that question will not be easy and viewing student engagement from a singular model has been criticised as a reductionist 'one fits all' approach (Zepke 2015). First, we should determine why student engagement has developed differently in each country (to identify the factors that have determined the direction of development in each case). Second, we should forecast the kinds of changes that will be brought about by these factors in each country in the future.

In Chapters 2 through 12 of this volume, the process of the development of student engagement in ten countries across five continents is carefully depicted. Please note: in Chapter 1, it was proposed that to determine the main axis of this analysis, student engagement should be examined on three levels, in accordance with the classifications provided by Healey et al. (2010: 22):

- Micro: engagement in their own learning and that of other students
- Meso: engagement in the quality assurance and enhancement processes
- Macro: engagement in strategy development

Each country differs in the extent to which it develops student engagement at each level. Such discrepancies can be viewed as dependent on who introduced and developed student engagement in each country and for what purpose. In other words, the objective of student engagement can be assumed to be an important factor in determining its direction.

Another potentially important factor is whether the universities who are involved view their students as disciples, customers, or partners. Even in instances in which student engagement is motivated by the same objective, the method and content of student engagement can be expected to differ significantly, depending on whether the students are viewed as disciples who are obliged to follow the instructions (guidance) of the teaching staff, as customers who should be offered a service commensurate with tuition fees paid, or as partners obliged to cooperate in educational improvement. In Chapter 1, the way students are viewed in each country surveyed is represented within a triangular model. The model is reproduced in Figure 13.1. The arrows in the model show the way the positions of each country are moving (the way the view of students is changing). In addition, the model implies that the countries are now converging on *positions that are not at any of the three peaks of the triangle.*

When this study was being developed, the assumption was that the development of student engagement was likely a linear process. In other words, we considered the Northern European model as the 'most developed' (in that, students were viewed as partners, and students and teaching staff both did their best in their own domains to improve education), and we believed that other countries would, in due time, come to view students not as disciples but as customers, and then as partners; we expected that the nature of student engagement would eventually resemble the Northern European model. However, as this study progressed, we realised that the supposition that development would follow this linear path in all countries was probably erroneous. This is because, although there are movements which indicate changes in the way students are viewed, in countries where the idea that students are disciples or customers is entrenched, to construct a new kind of student engagement in which students are viewed as partners, these movements do not necessarily completely repudiate the existing kind of student engagement.

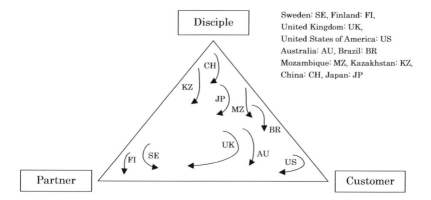

FIGURE 13.1 Views of students and positioning of responsibility for student engagement

For example, Australia is experiencing a problem with its quantitative method for listening to student voices (indirect student engagement), in that the response rate is continually falling (see Chapter 6). Despite this, there is a relative absence of widespread, radical discussion in favour of alternatives, such as methods in which students' voices are heard directly through, for example, a presence at relevant meetings (direct student engagement). However, existing systems are sometimes completely repudiated, and an attempt is made to switch to a new system. A good example of this type of country is Kazakhstan. There, as a result of external pressure imposed by the Bologna Process, the decision has been made to replace the student-engagement style of the Soviet era with a new style of student engagement (see Chapter 9). Another good example is Mozambique, as in many African countries and particularly those that shifted from the Socialist experiment into free-market principles, the student-engagement style has evolved from the traditional public discourse of viewing students as disciple into viewing them as partners and, more recently, as customers (see Chapter 8; see also Klemenčič et al. 2016).

In countries subject to this type of influence, external pressure, such as that from the Bologna Process, can be a significant element that forcibly changes how students are viewed. Similarly, demands for improvements revealed by analysis of existing systems serve as internal pressure and become an important element in re-examining how students are viewed. Changes in the environment surrounding a university (for instance, a rapid rise in the university entrance rate, public funds reduction and tuition fee increases, or intensification of international competition) can also be important elements in altering how students are regarded. Thus, we would now like to discuss the kinds of actual reforms that these elements will gradually bring about, based on the outcomes of the analysis of each country in this volume.

Drivers of change

Whether a country views its students as disciples, customers, or partners is affected by its history and culture. However, in all countries, how students are viewed is gradually changing. What role have the elements above played in these changes?

External pressure

The energy to reform student engagement sometimes comes from outside of the universities. In this chapter, we refer to this energy as 'external pressure' (e.g. Baron & Corbin 2012). Amongst the organisations spearheading this external pressure, we may find government agencies, government-related agencies, and international organisations. In cases where government agencies intervene in student-engagement reforms, we commonly see laws enacted identifying student engagement on the macro level as a student right. Such laws exist not only in Northern Europe, but also in Kazakhstan and China, and are a strong impetus for considering students as partners.

External pressure from government agencies can be seen in meso-level student-engagement reforms. For example, in the United Kingdom, the third-party assessment body, Quality Assurance Agency for Higher Education (QAA), includes amongst its assessment items whether all students are partners who engage in work to ensure educational quality (see Chapter 4). Such an item gives rise to a situation in which students must be seen as partners.

As an example of external pressure from an international organisation, UNESCO has made the following recommendation: 'National and institutional decision-makers should place students and their needs at the centre of their concerns, and should consider them as major partners and responsible stakeholders in the renewal of higher education' (UNESCO 1998: Article 10, c). For those planning and implementing reforms that cause students to be seen as partners, such a recommendation from a highly influential international organisation becomes a 'rallying banner' that legitimises those reforms.

As seen above, student-engagement reforms driven by external pressure have more coercive force than internal pressure and environmental changes, which are discussed below. However, since these reforms are imposed from the outside, these systems are easy to reduce to mere formalities, lacking any real substance. This reduction to a formality suggests that, at the same time, the traditional way of viewing students has not substantially changed.

Internal pressure

The energy to reform student engagement sometimes comes from inside the universities. In this chapter, we refer to this energy as 'internal pressure' (e.g. Kahu & Nelson 2017). We suspect that the content and methods of the reforms differ depending on whether the internal pressure is led by students, teachers, or university executives. This is because student leadership necessitates a different approach from that of teachers or executives, depending on whether they have the power to realise their own reform proposals.

If student representatives on university councils and other boards have voting and speaking rights, those student representatives need to establish a system for collecting the reform suggestions of the student body as a whole and turning them into reform proposals. The analyses from various countries in this volume suggest that strengthening the management of the student council is an important part of this process. Moreover, if there is a system for hearing student voices by way of student surveys or other similar means, students may use that system to exert influence. If there is no system by which the university hears the students' opinions, there is a risk of student dissatisfaction exploding into riots, similar to events which transpired in the late 1960s.

If the reforms are teacher-led, it will be necessary for teachers themselves to find a basis by which to legitimise them. One way to do this is to refer to successful examples of other universities or other countries. Reforms modelled after other countries' institutions or principles are discussed in this volume in some detail. For example, the methods of student surveys developed in the United States (National Survey of Student Engagement: NSSE, Cooperative Institutional Research

Program: CIRP) have been exported to Australia, China, and Japan by researchers from those countries, and are being promulgated as AUSSE in Australia (see Chapter 6), NSSE-China in China (see Chapter 10), and JCIRP in Japan (see Chapter 12).

The importation of student survey methods from the US suggests that the idea of students as customers could also have been imported. Yet, it is very likely that the researchers who imported the US models did not spread this idea, either consciously or unconsciously, or that this idea was rejected during the 'indigenisation' (Schriewer 2000) process, which happens before the imported model takes root as a domestic institution. In fact, despite the rapid spread of student surveys, which were modelled after those of the US, in China and Japan, there is little to suggest that students are seen as customers.

If the reforms are led by university executives, they are likely not active reforms, and are instead passive reforms driven by (the aforementioned) 'external pressure'. Alternatively, they happen in response to 'environmental changes', as discussed below.

Environmental changes

The energy driving the reform of student engagement sometimes comes from changes to the environment surrounding the universities (e.g. a higher rate of university enrolment, higher tuition fees). In this chapter, we refer to this energy as 'environmental changes'. For example, according to Trow (1973), a higher rate of university enrolment causes changes to university aims, functions, and structures at three stages: 'elite' (rate of less than 15%), 'mass' (between 15% and less than 50%), and 'universal' (50% or higher). All ten countries discussed in this volume have experienced rapid increases in enrolment rates, and many have already reached the universal stage. As these countries are characterised by striking student diversification, this has made it more difficult for students to understand and share perceptions with each other. As a result, doubts are being raised about student representatives' 'representativeness', and whether they truly represent the students. These doubts are present even in Finland (see Chapter 3).

Doubts about representativeness grow stronger when student councils, the bodies that elect student representatives, disintegrate. In Sweden, for example, it is no longer mandatory to join the student council, and its power has clearly become weaker (see Chapter 2). As such, we foresee that we will soon have to rethink student engagement, based on the idea that students are partners. In other words, we are seeing indications that in the current era of universal university attendance, the Northern European model is no longer the ultimate form of student engagement.

Introducing or raising university tuition fees becomes a powerful impetus for the idea of students as customers. For example, since introducing tuition fees in 1998, the United Kingdom has repeatedly raised its fees and has been forced to make diligent efforts to increase student 'customer satisfaction' (see Chapter 4). Similarly, numerous private universities in the United States, Brazil, Mozambique, Kazakhstan, China, and

Japan depend on tuition fees for their operating funds, and as competition over students (for survival) is fierce between the private universities, they work to increase student satisfaction by providing impeccable 'customer service'. It is only natural that student engagement, based on the assumption that students are customers, will develop further in these countries.

The competition for students between universities also concerns national universities, except for those in some European countries. Additionally, the popularisation of international university rankings is spurring on a ferocious rat race for increasing one's assessment points by even a little, which also involves the world's renowned research universities. Since student satisfaction and foreign student ratios are included in the assessment, universities are concerned with creating an environment that can attract customers, beautifying the campuses, building new dormitories for foreign students, and opening offshore offices for overseas entrance exams. This is true for renowned universities around the world, not only famous American universities. This environmental change in the form of intensifying international competition is laying the groundwork, especially for elite universities, to accept the idea of students as customers.

Conclusion

On the basis of a comparative study of cases from the ten countries across five continents, as well as the discussion in this chapter, we can conclude the following with regard to the future of student engagement.

Due to external pressure, macro-level student engagement in most universities in the world must reform in the direction of viewing students as partners. The reason is that the argument for seeing students as partners on par with teachers, rather than as disciples or customers, garners much popular support by virtue of being 'politically beautiful words'. International organisations in particular have no need to consider one country's cultural and historical background, and so are more prone to using such beautiful words. Yet, if environmental changes cast further doubt on student representativeness, it is very likely that people will call for some change to the conventional approach to macro-level student engagement in which students are viewed as partners.

Due to external pressure and environmental changes, meso-level student engagement is likely to move in the direction of viewing students as both customers and partners. This is because while we see more opportunities for students to engage in quality-assurance activities, it is also probable that the results of student surveys will become increasingly important as evidence of quality assurance. That is, while students are partners who engage in quality assurance in collaboration with teachers, they are also customers who gauge the outcomes of educational activities. Yet, will students become dissatisfied if they are conveniently treated as partners on some occasions and as customers on others? This is a concern.

Mainly due to internal pressure, micro-level student engagement should preferably be realised by positioning students to be seen as partners; even though the universities and the teachers implement peer support or other systems, such initiatives cannot succeed unless the students take a leading role. Yet, with the environmental change of higher tuition fees, fee-paying students may feel reluctant to take care of their classmates for meagre pay (or on a volunteer basis). If the strength of this reluctance increases, the universities will have to hire (non-student) specialists to provide learning support.

As an aside, it may be natural for approaches to student engagement to differ in a single country according to whether universities are elite, mass, or universal. This is because student engagement that views students as disciples may be the most suitable for an elite postgraduate university in which research students are taught in the tutorial style. As such, those tasked with creating and reforming systems for student engagement should perhaps consider the general trends in their country. They should promote system design and reform only after gaining a precise grasp of the role that their university is expected to play and the characteristics of their students.

The aim of student engagement is to improve the learning outcomes of the engaged students. We do not think many would object to this in any country. Yet, precisely because of the appeal and necessity of this objective, all countries and universities will devise different answers to the question of how to engage students. As such, we hope that those involved in planning and implementing student engagement consider the three factors of external pressure, internal pressure, and environmental changes; these should be used to develop clear and appropriate measures on each of the macro, meso, and micro levels with regard to whether students are viewed as disciples, customers, or partners.

References

Baron, B. and Corbin, L. (2012) "Student Engagement: Rhetoric and Reality", *Higher Education Research & Development*, 31(6), 759–772.

Healey, M., Mason-O'Connor, K. and Broadfoot, P. (2010) "Reflections on Engaging Student in the Process and Product of Strategy Development for Learning, Teaching, and Assessment: An institutional case study," *International Journal for Academic Development*, 15 (1), 19–32.

Kahu, E.R. and Nelson, K. (2017) "Student Engagement in the Educational Interface: Understanding the Mechanisms of Student Success", *Higher Education Research & Development*, 37(1), 58–71.

Klemenčič, M., Luescher-Mamashela, T. M. and Mugume, T. (2016) "Student Organising in African Higher Education: Polity, Politics and Policies", in Luescher-Mamashela, T. M.et al. (eds.) *Student Politics in Africa: Representation and Activism*, Cape Town: African Minds, pp. 9–26.

Schriewer, J. (2000) "World System and Interrelationship Networks: The Internationalization of Education and the Role of Comparative Inquiry", in Popkewitz, T. S. (ed.) *Educational Knowledge: Changing Relationships between the State, Civil Society, and the Educational Community*, Fourth Edition, Albany, New York: State University of New York Press, 305–343.

Trow, M. (1973) *Problems in the Transition from Elite to Mass Higher Education*, Berkeley, CA: Carnegie Commission on Higher Education.

UNESCO (1998) *World Declaration on Higher Education for the Twenty-first Century: Vision and Action and Framework for Priority Action for Change and Development in Higher Education*, adopted by the World Conference on Higher Education Higher Education in the Twenty-First Century: Vision and Action (9 October 1998), Paris: UNESCO.

Zepke, N. (2015) "What Future for Student Engagement in Neoliberal Times?" *Higher Education*, 69(4), 693–704.

INDEX

academic role 62, 69
accreditation 5, 25, 51, 59, 76, 81, 101–2, 110, 114–9, 147, 152
active learning 46, 48–51, 54, 104–5, 131, 142, 150
Africa 90–105, 164
Astin, Alexander 2, 152–3, 155
attestation 114–6
Australia 1, 3, 7, 57–69, 136, 163–4, 166

Beijing College Student Survey 129
belonging 31, 40–2, 49, 59, 65–7
Bologna Process 4, 11, 109–11, 113–5, 117–8, 164
Brazil 1, 3, 7, 73–86, 163, 166
Bryson, Colin 6, 43

Central Asia 113
Central Council for Education in Japan 138, 142, 150
Centralisation 109, 111,114, 116, 120
China 1, 3, 7, 124–33, 164, 166
co-creation 42–3
collective(s) 4, 37, 54, 76–8, 82, 84–6, 144
competition 18, 47, 53, 117, 119, 144, 164, 167, international competition 164, 167
consumer 3, 35–6, 54, 62–3, see customer
Cooperative Institutional Research Program (CIRP) 143, 151, 156
Counterpublics 78, 83, 86
curriculum design 9–10, 40, 42, 104, 109
customer 3, 31, 35, 39, 46, 53–4, 62, 163–4, 166–8, see consumer

direct assessment 149–50, 152, 155–9, see indirect assessment
disciple 3, 85, 163–4, 167–8

educational enhancement 1, 4–6, 9, 37, 46, 50, 61, 85, 136, 150
equity 46, 48
evaluation 1, 4–6, 9–10, 12–3, 18, 25–6, 40, 42, 51, 58, 74–8, 81, 85, 101–3, 109, 114, 117, 125, 128, 132, 136, 138, 142–3, 147, 155–9; course evaluation 9, 12, 18, 143; evaluation survey 58; self-evaluation 13, 76, 117, 156–9

Finland 1, 3, 7, 24–32, 163, 166
Fiori, Ernani Maria 75

Healey, Mick 4, 10, 58, 61, 77, 85, 110, 136, 162
high-impact practices (HIPs) 46–9, 54
Hironaka Report 141–2

Independent Kazakh Agency for Quality Assurance in Education (IQAA) 115, 118
indirect assessment 149–50, 152–60 see direct assessment
integration model 157

Japan 1, 3, 7, 60, 136–47, 149–60, 163, 166–7
Japanese Cooperative Institutional Research Program (JCIRP) 143, 151–6, 166

Kazakhstan 1, 3, 7, 109–20, 163–4, 166
Kuh, George 2, 6, 47, 49, 51, 90

Latin American model 75
learning community 40–2
learning outcome(s) 2, 5–7, 11, 51, 117, 125, 131–2, 149–60, 168
learning process 10, 12–3, 29, 74, 110, 125, 127–8, 155

mindset 21, 49
marketisation 110–4
Ministry of Education 76–7, 110, 124, 138, 141
Mozambique 1, 3, 7, 90–105, 163–4, 166

National Survey of Student Engagement (NSSE) 2, 5, 41, 47, 51, 125, 129, 149, 156–7, 165–6; NSSE-China 129, 166

partner 1, 3–4, 9–10, 17–8, 20–1, 35–43, 46, 49–55, 59–60, 65, 69, 84–6, 117, 163–8
peer support 5, 30, 42–3, 132, 139–40, 145, 168
policy 17, 26, 31, 52–3, 60–2, 73, 77, 80–1, 84, 86, 91, 93–4, 97, 100–1, 103, 105, 112, 115, 125–7, 150, 152; higher education policy 91, 97, 115, 150
political pressure 82

quality assurance 4–5, 10–6, 18, 26, 35–41, 43, 46, 51–2, 54, 58–64, 68, 73–4, 76, 80–1, 91, 100–4, 109–10, 113–20, 136, 141, 147, 150–1, 162, 165, 167
Quality Assurance Agency for Higher Education (QAA) 36–7, 39, 165

sociopolitical context 74, 78, 81, 84
student activism 73, 75, 77, 82, 84, 86, 97–8, 100
student engagement, definition 2–7; development 17, 19, 136, 139, 141, 145, 162–3; objective 1, 4–6, 163; responsibility 2–4, 12, 16–7, 20, 50, 54, 138–9, 163
Student Experience in the Research University (SERU) 125, 129
student experience survey 61, 68
student Faculty Development (student FD) 136, 141–3, 145–7
student–faculty partnership 4, 9–10, 17–8, 20–1, 37–43, 46, 49–51, 54–5, 59, 84
student feedback survey 60–3
student representative 1, 10, 12–4, 17–8, 25–7, 30–1, 39, 58–60, 63, 66, 68, 74–5, 77, 80–1, 85–6, 93, 101–3, 118, 127, 133, 136, 141, 143–4, 146, 165–7
student revolts 137–8, 142, 146
student satisfaction 24, 41, 54, 61, 67, 167
student success 65
student survey 1, 6, 38, 41, 47, 58, 119, 129, 136, 141, 143, 146, 149, 151–7, 159–60, 165–7
student union 9, 12–4, 25, 27, 77, 136, 146
Sub-Saharan Africa 90
Sweden 1, 3, 7, 9–22, 163, 166

triangular model 3, 163
tuition fee 3, 24, 35, 113, 125, 137, 163–4, 166–8

United Kingdom (UK) 1, 3, 7, 35–43, 163–4, 166
United Nations Educational, Scientific and Cultural Organization (UNESCO) 90, 165
United States of America (USA) 1–3, 7, 46–55, 149, 156–7, 163, 165–6
university management 21, 26, 126–8, 132–3, 141, 143
university ranking 15, 61, 167
University of Tsukuba 143–4

Vieira Pinto, Álvaro 75

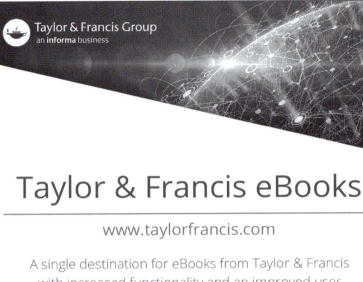

Printed in Great Britain
by Amazon